WOMEN IN DEVELOPING COUNTRIES

Selected Titles in ABC-CLIO's
CONTEMPORARY WORLD ISSUES
Series

Animal Rights, Clifford J. Sherry
Autism Spectrum Disorders, Raphael Bernier and Jennifer Gerdts
Climate Change, David L. Downie, Kate Brash, and Catherine Vaughan
DNA Technology, David E. Newton
Domestic Violence, Margi Laird McCue
Education in Crisis, Judith A. Gouwens
Environmental Justice, David E. Newton
Gay and Lesbian Rights, David E. Newton
Genocide, Howard Ball
Global Organized Crime, Mitchel P. Roth
Global Refugee Crisis, Mark Gibney
Identity Theft, Sandra K. Hoffman and Tracy G. McGinley
Lobbying in America, Ronald J. Hrebenar and Bryson B. Morgan
Modern Piracy, David F. Marley
Modern Sports Ethics, Angela Lumpkin
Obesity, Judith Stern and Alexandra Kazaks
Same-Sex Marriage, David E. Newton
Sentencing, Dean John Champion
Sexual Crime, Caryn E. Neumann
Sexual Health, David E. Newton
Substance Abuse, David E. Newton
U.S. Border Security, Judith A. Warner
U.S. Space Policy, Peter L. Hays, Ph.D.
U.S. Trade Issues, Alfred E. Eckes, Jr.
Women in Combat, Rosemarie Skaine

For a complete list of titles in this series, please visit **www.abc-clio.com**.

Books in the Contemporary World Issues series address vital issues in today's society, such as genetic engineering, pollution, and biodiversity. Written by professional writers, scholars, and nonacademic experts, these books are authoritative, clearly written, up-to-date, and objective. They provide a good starting point for research by high school and college students, scholars, and general readers as well as by legislators, businesspeople, activists, and others.

Each book, carefully organized and easy to use, contains an overview of the subject, a detailed chronology, biographical sketches, facts and data and/or documents and other primary-source material, a directory of organizations and agencies, annotated lists of print and nonprint resources, and an index.

Readers of books in the Contemporary World Issues series will find the information they need to have a better understanding of the social, political, environmental, and economic issues facing the world today.

WOMEN IN DEVELOPING COUNTRIES

A Reference Handbook

Karen L. Kinnear

CONTEMPORARY WORLD ISSUES

Santa Barbara, California • Denver, Colorado • Oxford, England

Library of Congress Cataloging-in-Publication Data

Kinnear, Karen L.
Women in developing countries : a reference handbook / Karen L. Kinnear.
p. cm. — (Contemporary world issues)
Includes bibliographical references and index.
ISBN 978–1–59884–425–2 (hard copy : alk. paper) —
ISBN 978–1–59884–426–9 (ebook)
1. Women—Developing countries. 2. Women—Developing countries—Social conditions. 3. Women's rights—Developing countries.
I. Title.
HQ1870.9.K577 2011
305.409172′4—dc22 2011013356

ISBN: 978–1–59884–425–2
EISBN: 978–1–59884–426–9

15 14 13 12 11 1 2 3 4 5

This book is also available on the World Wide Web as an eBook.
Visit www.abc-clio.com for details.

ABC-CLIO, LLC
130 Cremona Drive, P.O. Box 1911
Santa Barbara, California 93116-1911

This book is printed on acid-free paper ∞

Manufactured in the United States of America

To Evelyn—world traveler, constant inspiration, and dear friend

Contents

Preface

The purpose of this book is to provide a survey of the literature and other resources on the topic of women in developing countries and to provide sources for further research. The vast range of literature and resources available offers many opportunities to learn more about these women's lives, including the challenges many of them face on a daily basis. A tremendous amount of growth in knowledge and research has occurred in this field in recent years and this volume reviews current knowledge and resources in order to help the reader understand the evolving issues surrounding this important and timely topic.

While some progress has been made in alleviating the many problems faced by women in developing countries, there is still much room for improvement. International law and many national laws prohibit various forms of discrimination against women, but in reality discrimination and abuse still exist.

This book, like other books in the Contemporary World Issues series, provides a balanced survey of the resources available and a guide to further research on the topic of women in developing countries. Chapter 1 provides background and historical information. Chapter 2 discusses important issues and controversies in the area of women and development. Issues that are of concern to the United States are examined in Chapter 3. Chapter 4 provides a chronology of significant events in the recent history of women in developing countries. Chapter 5 offers biographical sketches of women who have played or are playing key roles in transforming developing societies and cultures. Chapter 6 provides statistical and other data and information and includes summaries of the key UN conventions designed to provide women with rights equal to men. Chapter 7 contains a directory of representative private and public organizations, associations, and government agencies involved in working with women in developing countries in a variety of areas, including education, health, family planning, and development. Chapter 8 annotates books and other materials that focus on women in developing countries.

List of Developing Countries

Africa

Angola
Benin
Botswana
Burkina Faso
Burundi
Cameroon
Central African Republic
Chad
Comoros
Congo, Democratic Republic of
Congo, Republic of
Cote d'Ivoire
Djibouti
Equatorial Guinea
Eritrea
Ethiopia
Gabon
Gambia
Ghana
Guinea
Guinea-Bissau
Kenya
Lesotho
Liberia
Madagascar
Malawi
Mali
Mauritania
Mauritius
Mozambique
Namibia
Niger
Nigeria
Rwanda
Sao Tome and Principe
Senegal
Seychelles
Sierra Leone
Somalia
South Africa
Sudan
Swaziland
Tanzania
Togo
Uganda
Zambia
Zimbabwe

East Asia and the Pacific

Brunei Darussalam
Burma
Cambodia
China
Fiji
Indonesia
Kiribati
Korea, Democratic People's Republic of
Korea, Republic of
Laos
Malaysia
Marshall Islands
Micronesia, Federated States of
Mongolia
Nauru
Palau
Papua New Guinea
Philippines
Samoa
Singapore
Solomon Islands
Thailand
Timor-Leste
Tonga
Tuvalu
Vanuatu
Vietnam

South and Central Asia

Afghanistan
Bangladesh
Bhutan
India
Maldives
Nepal
Pakistan
Sri Lanka

Near East and North Africa

Algeria
Bahrain
Egypt
Iran
Iraq
Jordan
Kuwait
Lebanon
Libya
Morocco
Oman
Qatar
Saudi Arabia
Syria
Tunisia
United Arab Emirates
Yemen

Latin America and the Caribbean

Antigua and Barbuda
Argentina
Barbados
Belize
Bolivia
Brazil
Chile
Colombia
Costa Rica
Dominica
Dominican Republic
Ecuador
El Salvador
Grenada
Guatemala
Guyana
Haiti
Honduras
Jamaica
Mexico
Nicaragua
Panama
Paraguay
Peru
Saint Kitts and Nevis
Saint Lucia
Saint Vincent and the Grenadines
Suriname
Trinidad and Tobago
Uruguay
Venezuela

1

Background and History

This chapter provides an overview of women in developing countries—their status, the conditions under which they live, and many of the social, political, and economic forces that affect them. But first, we need to define what we mean by the term *developing countries* and several other key concepts used throughout this book.

In previous decades, the commonly used term was *Third World* countries, rather than developing countries. *Third World* is still used today, but fewer people, organizations, and governments are using this term because of political and economic changes in the world, as well as the negative connotation of the term to many people. The term generally means less developed countries, or countries with relatively low per capita incomes, short life expectancies, and high rates of illiteracy.

First World countries are industrialized, democratic countries, such as the United States, Canada, many European countries, Australia, New Zealand, Japan, and other countries that are not considered communist. *Second World* countries refers to countries that were part of the communist bloc, including Poland, Hungary, Romania, Bulgaria, the former Soviet Union, China, and Cuba. Today, the line between Second and Third World countries has blurred, and together, many of these countries are considered emerging or developing countries (see the front of the book for a list of developing countries).

The term *developing countries* describes countries in which the majority of people earn less income and have less access to basic public services than those living in industrialized countries. Other characteristics of developing countries include a population primarily located in rural areas, an agriculturally based economy, and low levels of education, health, transportation, infrastructure, and potable water. Historically, many developing countries were once colonies of European countries.

Developing countries are also referred to as the *Global South,* based on the geographical location of most developing countries—the majority of countries south of the equator are classified as developing countries. *Global North* refers to the more industrialized, developed countries. The usage of the term *Global South* is becoming more widespread than many other terms, in part because it is not perceived as an emotionally loaded, demeaning term; it is seen as less divisive than the contrast between developed versus developing countries, industrialized versus nonindustrialized countries, or rich versus poor countries.

Basic Concepts Important to the Study of Women in Developing Countries

In order to understand the study of women in developing countries, an understanding of several basic sociological terms is helpful. These concepts include sex roles, gender roles, social stratification, patriarchy, and cultural relativism.

Sex Roles versus Gender Roles

Sex roles are behaviors that are determined by the biological differences between women and men, such as pregnancy, lactation, erection, and ejaculation. Gender roles, on the other hand, are behaviors that are determined by the social and cultural context in which people live and how they define femininity and masculinity. Societies organize themselves based on these definitions; they rank women's and men's roles according to their importance to the society as a whole. Gender roles are one of the basic sources of division and definition in a particular society. They determine who is considered a citizen, who is allowed to vote, who is allowed to own land, and who is granted other rights. Gender defines men and women according to the social relationship between them. Approaches to development in terms of gender are concerned with the ways that such relationships are socially constructed.

Societies use gender as a primary means of determining the division of labor and the provision of rights and responsibilities for citizens. Gender roles may vary across cultures, although there are many similarities; most often women are assigned roles in domestic and family areas while men are expected to participate primarily in public and political areas. Women's status within each country is determined by institutional factors such as family, politics, religion, and economic systems within the culture, as well as by the level of power, prestige, and control over property that they have. The power women wield and their influence over others may change as they age, with added prestige provided to elderly women in some cultures. Women's roles and positions also vary by the socio-economic class within cultures and countries; women in the upper classes of all countries enjoy many advantages that women in lower classes within those same countries are denied.

Women have both reproductive and productive roles in most societies. Their reproductive role includes biological reproduction (bearing children, rearing children, and maintaining the household) and social reproduction (maintaining the status quo in their society). Productive work includes all activities that generate income or have some sort of exchange value. Women's reproductive role is often undervalued; most societies do not see reproductive work as productive, that is, as having any economic value—even though if a woman gives birth to a male child, that child is expected to provide value to the family. As a result, the value of women to a society is considered to be less than that of men because value is most frequently measured in terms of economic value.

Even when women participate in income-generating activities, men often control the financial part of the enterprise. For example, while on a trip to Kenya, I visited a Maasai village; the men came out to greet us, invited us into their community, and explained their way of life to us. Then we were escorted to an area just outside the central community circle where many of the women were displaying beaded jewelry and other items that they were selling. Each visitor was accompanied by a male from the village; when I finished choosing the items I wanted to purchase, my male guide gathered them up and took me back into the village center and we bargained until we agreed on the total cost.

When I asked why his wife and mother-in-law were not doing the bargaining, he explained to me that they knew nothing about money and were better off just making the items; besides, they "couldn't speak English, so what good would they be?"

Social Stratification

When examining the role and experiences of women in developing countries, we also must understand how a society organizes or classifies individuals. Social stratification is the hierarchical arrangement of individuals in a society based primarily on economic and power factors. Societies often are stratified based on class, race, and gender; this stratification controls the distribution of power, wealth, and prestige.

People who have similar economic status, often based on income, occupation, and education, form a particular social class within society. Those in the upper class have more power, authority, and prestige than those in the middle class or lower class. Gender also defines the position of a person within the stratification system; men are granted higher social status than women in most societies simply because they are men. Finally, race or ethnicity also defines the position of a person in a society. Racial minority groups are often seen as having a lower position, with less power and authority, than the racial majority of a particular society.

This system for ranking individuals is important to understand and acknowledge when studying women in developing countries because women who are in higher social classes may have more rights than those in lower classes. Depending on the overall status of women in a particular country, women in the upper classes may have more access to education, economic opportunities, health care, and other areas critical to their quality of life.

Patriarchy

Some sociologists believe that male dominance is universal—that is, found in every culture throughout the world. They believe that some form of patriarchy is found in all cultures. Others believe that sexual differentiation is found in all societies but that females are not always the ones who are considered of lower status (Rogers 1978; Eitzen and Zinn 1991).

Patriarchy is defined as the "principle of male dominance that forms both a structural and ideological system of domination in which men control women" (Chow and Berheide 1994, 14). Walby (1996) sees it as a system in which "men dominate, oppress, and exploit women" (20). It is not a static condition or universal in its characteristics. The specific forms that patriarchy may take vary by class, race, and age. Patriarchy is most commonly seen and studied in relation to its role in the family. In the patriarchal family, men have the power to determine the status, privileges, and roles of women and children within the family. This power is also reinforced by traditional gender role belief systems.

Patriarchy can be both public and private. Private patriarchy generally is practiced in the family environment, while public patriarchy is practiced by the state and within public activities such as government and the economy. Historically, international relations theory and practice has primarily been developed by men who have based their theories on their own knowledge and experience as men. Women are often left out of this equation, and as a result their impact on society is not considered or valued. In many countries women are not encouraged to participate in the national government, although increasing numbers of countries have set aside a certain number or percentage of seats in legislative bodies for women (see Chapter 6). Patriarchy and patriarchal structures also influence the role of women in the economy, specifically their position in and control over income-generating activities.

Cultural Relativism

Cultural relativism is the principle that the beliefs an individual holds and the actions he or she takes should be examined in terms of the individual's own culture. In other words, the actions and behaviors of others should not be evaluated based on one's own culture. For example, Americans should not condemn the practice of arranged marriages in a developing country solely because it is not accepted practice in the United States.

Years ago, attempts by Westerners to study the problems and issues of women in developing countries often created resentment on the part of those women studied. Western researchers, including sociologists and anthropologists, were often viewed as coming into a developing country with a grant to study a particular issue;

they asked questions, and then returned home to write a report in the comfort of their own familiar worlds. Often, careers were boosted by these studies but little or nothing was provided to help improve the welfare and lives of the people who were studied. Many researchers asked questions that were meant to elicit intimate details of the lives of the people studied, but most had no idea of the impact this intrusion had on those involved. Outsiders who had little understanding of local culture came in and studied polygamy, purdah (the seclusion of women from the public, practiced by Muslims and some Hindus), veiling, dowry (in India, the money and/or goods that a bride's family brings to her husband and his family), brideprice, and child marriages and condemned these practices based on Western beliefs and traditions. Little if any attempt was made to understand these practices within their cultural context before condemning them. Many individuals in developing countries had difficulty understanding this attitude and resented the implication that their societies were viewed as primitive and problematic while Western societies were seen as more advanced and problem-free.

Research and development work conducted today is often more sensitive to the characteristics of other cultures. The world has become smaller in the sense that more people have traveled outside of their countries of origin, and the widespread availability and usage of the Internet, including social media, have enabled individuals to learn about other cultures and practices and gain a greater understanding of the differences as well as the similarities among various cultures. Development workers and social scientists today are generally more sensitized to cultural variations and understand the importance of respecting the cultural values and traditions in other countries.

History of Women in Development

The practice of incorporating women into the development process has evolved over time. From the first development programs in the 1960s, most development professionals did not even consider women in their planning of development activities. If women were considered at all, it was to the extent that if men were provided with training and development activities in developing countries, women's lives would be improved. The improvement of women's lives was not a focus or even an anticipated outcome;

it was a side effect. However, in the 1970s, many development program planners began to understand that women had to be included in the development process. Finally, in the 1980s, the focus shifted to gender and development, where development projects incorporated a gender perspective. The focus of these programs was on understanding the role that gender played in development and then developing programs that would benefit entire communities.

The United Nations

The United Nations played a major role in development projects in developing countries, along with the World Bank and the International Monetary Fund. In 1946, the Economic and Social Council of the United Nations (ECOSOC) established the Commission on the Status of Women (CSW) with a mandate to "prepare recommendations and reports to the Economic and Social Council on promoting women's rights in political, economic, civil, social and educational fields" (ECOSOC 1946). The CSW also was tasked with identifying urgent problems and recommending corrective action to the ECOSOC. The CSW was to play a major role in the drafting and review of several UN Conventions (see Chapter 6 for details on various Conventions relevant to women).

In 1967 the General Assembly of the United Nations adopted the Declaration on the Elimination of Discrimination against Women. The Declaration was a statement on the importance of granting various human rights to women. Eleven articles specified various rights that women should be granted (see Chapter 6 for a summary).

The Commission on the Status of Women was upgraded by the United Nations in 1972, becoming the Branch for the Promotion of Equality for Men and Women, led by Helvi Sipilä, the first woman named a UN Assistant Secretary-General. Following its recommendation to designate 1975 as the International Women's Year, one of CSW's mandates was to prepare for the First UN World Conference on Women, set up to coincide with the International Women's Year. Held in Mexico City in 1975, the conference was attended by delegates from 133 countries and focused on themes of equality, development, and peace. A parallel NGO forum, the International Women's Year tribune, attracted approximately 6,000 participants. Women from the Global North focused their attention on equality (during this time the focus of many U.S.

women was on ratification of the Equal Rights Amendment to the U.S. Constitution), while women from the Global South were more concerned with basic issues of survival. Global South women viewed the focus on equality as divisive. This difference in focus led to a major division between women from the North and the South and between women from capitalist countries and those from noncapitalist countries. Because this Conference was held during the United Nations's Second Development Decade, participants were already realizing the existence of growing gender disparities as a result of the development process (Friedlander 1996).

Following one of the recommendations of the first World Conference, the United Nations launched the UN Decade for Women: Equality, Development and Peace (1976–1985). This designation contributed to the growth of the international women's movement and changed the focus of development agencies from focusing on men to a realization that women had to be included in development activities. Another one of the major tasks of the Commission during this decade was the drafting of the Convention on the Elimination of All Forms of Discrimination against Women (CEDAW).

The Second World Conference on Women, held in Copenhagen, Denmark, in 1980, was attended by over 1,300 delegates from 145 countries, with over 8,000 women participating in the parallel NGO Forum. This conference reviewed progress in implementing the recommendations from the First World Conference on Women and updated the Plan of Action. Focused on employment, health, and education, the Conference also recommended that the governments of its member states ensure women's ownership and control of property and improve inheritance rights and child custody rights.

In 1985, the Third World Conference on Women, and the parallel NGO Forum, were held in Nairobi, Kenya. The Conference was attended by approximately 1,400 delegates from 157 countries, while over 13,000 people attended the parallel NGO forum. Its primary focus was to review the achievements of the UN Decade for Women. The role and format of development activities were questioned by many participants, including women from both the Global South and North. Conference delegates adopted the Forward-Looking Strategies for the Advancement of Women, which called for equal participation of women in all political, social, and economic activities, including equal access to education and training.

In 1995, the Fourth World Conference on Women was held in Beijing, China, and included over 6,000 delegates from 189 countries. The parallel NGO Forum attracted over 30,000 women. The Beijing Declaration and Platform for Action was adopted by the delegates and identified 12 areas of concern to women, including poverty, education, health care, violence, and human rights.

Since the 1995 Conference in Beijing, additional sessions have been held every five years to measure progress toward the goals set out in the Beijing Declaration and Platform for Action. In 2000, a special session of the UN General Assembly convened *Women 2000: Gender Equality, Development and Peace in the 21st Century* to review progress; the General Assembly agreed to conduct a full review in 2005. The 2005 World Summit was held at UN headquarters in New York and reviewed the progress made in meeting the Millennium Development Goals (MDG) established in 2000.

In 2010, the Commission on the Status of Women conducted a 15 year review of the progress on implementing the Beijing Declaration and Platform for Action and for reaching the MDGs. It was noted that gender perspectives were not currently being specifically addressed or identified in strategies developed for reaching the MDGs. Gender perspectives needed to be more clearly articulated and mechanisms developed to ensure accountability of States and other stakeholders. The commonalities and relationships between the Beijing Declaration and the MDGs were not understood which contributed to the limited progress in reaching the MDGs.

Development Agencies and Approaches

Running parallel to the UN conferences, and prior to understanding the important role played by women in development activities and the need to include women in the development process, the U.S. government, the World Bank, and other entities were involved in development activities in the Global South.

Early development activities in the developing world focused on the production and industrial sectors of the economy, which were predominantly male. The relationships between resources and individuals had not yet been examined. Governmental agencies and financial institutions believed that development activities should focus on the economics of development. In developing countries, this focus led to the involvement of men in development activities because, for the most part, men were the ones engaged in and responsible for the economic activities of families. The development agencies did not consciously exclude women from these activities; they simply did not recognize that development activities were male-oriented, and never considered that women might play a role in development activities.

Beginning in the early 1970s, and following publication of Ester Boserup's book on women in development (Boserup 1970), the focus of many development programs shifted from being male-oriented and excluding women to one of bringing women into the development process. This program focus was referred to as women in development (WID). WID challenged the gender bias in early programs, understood the importance of women's contributions, and focused on integrating women in development programs. Many programs were successful in reaching these goals and improved the general conditions of women; however, they often did not put women on an equal footing with men when it came to social and economic power. Women were still seen as secondary to men in the development process; they were not included in the initial phases of development but their contributions were acknowledged.

The U.S. government's experience in WID programs illustrates the problems with this approach. The Percy Amendment to the U.S. Foreign Assistance Act of 1973 required the U.S. Agency for International Development (USAID) to encourage foreign governments to include women in their countries' local economies, and established an Office of Women in Development in USAID to assist State Department employees in their work with foreign governments. Many people inside USAID were unclear on how to implement the required policies, while others believed this focus was the product of a few vocal women in the women's liberation movement and did not believe that it was important or necessary for women to be involved in the development process. However, by the early 1980s, many development experts believed that the WID approach was not effective in incorporating gender issues into the development process. Women saw the WID approach as patriarchal—with a focus on involving women in the market economy and looking for income-generating activities, but only to the extent they would support men's contributions to the economy.

In the late 1980s, the frustration over the issues with the WID approach led to the development of what was believed to be a more comprehensive approach to development—the gender and development (GAD) approach. GAD took WID one step further by emphasizing the need to understand the importance of gender roles in development activities. GAD saw the importance of encouraging the redistribution of power in social relations between men and women. Its proponents understood that women's role in the basic institutions of family, education, and work had to change to bring women into an equal relationship with men; both men and women had to equally prosper from development activities. Female-focused programs and activities had often been segregated from mainstream development activities in the WID approach, and the GAD approach aimed to mainstream women into development activities (Jaquette and Summerfield 2007). The overall goal was to put women and men on an equal footing.

The GAD approach is still being employed, although doubts exist concerning its effectiveness. When it first became popular, the word "gender" did not have an equivalent word in many languages; it was sometimes confusing to those in local communities, and some NGOs and other advocacy groups suggest that women are still being excluded from many development activities. Jaquette and Staudt (2007) suggest that the lessening interest in the GAD approach and the increasing "war on terror" and other militarization policies may present opportunities to rethink development approaches to incorporating and benefiting women.

Structural Adjustment Programs

During the late 1970s and early 1980s, as the governments of many developing countries incurred increasing debt, several governments turned to the International Monetary Fund (IMF) and the World Bank for help. The IMF and World Bank instituted structural adjustment programs to assist countries in rebuilding their economies and restructuring their debt. These programs were designed to help debtor nations by increasing their exports through higher commodity production in order to repay their loans while at the same time reducing the drain on government funds through job cuts, lowered wages, reduced services to citizens, and other cost-cutting measures.

In some countries, structural adjustment policies had harmful consequences for women's work and the well-being of children and families. Unemployment increased, with women losing the most jobs; education, health, and other social programs that were funded by the government lost funding or suffered reduced funding; and, in some instances, women's access to land and credit decreased (Kahne and Giele 1992; Murray 2008).

Overall, structural adjustment programs were detrimental to most developing countries, but the impact on women was devastating in many areas. More individuals entered informal income-generating activities during this period, and men were better positioned to succeed in these activities because they had more access to income to invest in these activities. Cutbacks in federal spending on social welfare programs were more likely to impact women because women and children were usually the recipients of these government programs (McMurtry 1998). For example, in Africa, structural adjustment programs required reductions in government spending; spending on infrastructure and social programs was frequently cut, and because women and children compose the majority of the poor in any society, they bore the burden of these cuts and were hurt the most. When governments cut back on spending on infrastructure, such as building and maintaining roads and providing telecommunications services, ease in transporting goods to markets suffered. In Africa, where many women are in agriculture, these policies made it even more difficult for rural areas to succeed in business. Health care services also suffered, as well as education. In a study on structural adjustment programs, Cornia, Jolly, and Stewart (1987) found that reductions in spending on social programs were detrimental to children. These programs also affected women as they attempted to care for their children without any support from the government.

Millennium Development Goals

In 2000, 189 government officials attended the Millennium Summit to discuss critical issues the international development community would face in the 21st century. The resulting Millennium Declaration provided a road map for international cooperation in confronting the world's major development challenges. The overall aim is to reduce extreme poverty; with eight specific goals established, the ultimate goal is to halve extreme poverty by the year 2015.

Two of the eight major goals focus attention on women, including promoting gender equality and empowering women (Goal 3) and improving maternal health (Goal 5). The remaining goals impact women to some degree, including eradicating extreme poverty and hunger (Goal 1), achieving universal primary education (Goal 2), reducing child mortality (Goal 4), combating HIV/AIDS, malaria and other diseases (Goal 6), ensuring environmental sustainability (Goal 7), and developing a global partnership for development (Goal 8).

However, all of the goals are impacted by the progress made on establishing gender equality around the world. Women play a prominent role in child welfare, are more susceptible to HIV/AIDS and other major diseases, and play a large role in natural resources management. In addition, all the goals are related in some way; progress in achieving one goal may help in achieving another goal. For example, by achieving universal primary education (Goal 2), maternal health may improve over the long term as girls mature and understand what they need to do to maintain their health. If women are empowered (Goal 3), they will understand the importance of keeping their children healthy and be able to determine ways to achieve that goal.

Overview of Women's Status and Experiences in the World Today

As the Millennium Development Goals indicate, progress has been slow in providing women with equal opportunities in the areas of family, education, work, and other critical aspects of their lives. Women still lag behind in many areas and are often still treated as inferior to men. This section briefly describes some of the experiences of women in developing countries based on their status as women. See Chapters 2 and 6 for additional discussion and details regarding these topics.

Family Relations

Marriage

Most women throughout the world are expected to marry at some time during their lives. In many developing countries, women are seen as property, having value to their birth families only to the extent that when they are married off, preferably at an early age, the family will receive money or goods for their "purchase." The wife in many families is expected to care for her husband and to bear children, preferably boys. Women often bear the major responsibility for taking care of the home; their tasks may include tending the family's garden; caring for live animals that the family may have; gathering fuel for cooking; gathering water for drinking, cooking, and bathing; caring for the children; and caring for and supporting their husbands. In many cases, women are also expected to find paying work to help support the family financially.

In many developing countries, arranged marriages are still a common practice. In these cases, parents make all arrangements to find a wife or husband for their child. The prospective bride and groom have little or no say in the wedding and often do not even have a chance to meet their future spouse until the day of the wedding. Cultural norms are changing, in that some families allow marriages based on love, that is, marriages in which the young man and young woman choose each other. As more girls are allowed to go to school, enter college, and find jobs, the opportunities expand for them to find their own mates. However, while many parents around the world expect to at least informally "approve" their future son- or daughter-in-law, many marriages in developing countries still require the approval of the parents, who are determined to ensure that their sons marry properly and successfully. Even in developed countries, parents often approve or disapprove of their child's choice of spouse.

Increasing attention is being focused on child marriage, its prevalence, and the serious effects it has on girls in developing countries. In some developing countries, girls are engaged when they are still very young, even 11 or 12 years old. The marriage may actually take place when they are older, but they will have no choice in the matter. Based on some estimates, 100 million girls will become child brides between 2004 and 2014 (Bruce and Clark 2004). Some young girls are matched with older men; especially in Middle Eastern countries and many African countries, older men prefer to marry young virgins, who they believe will protect them from becoming infected with HIV/AIDS.

In India and many countries in Africa, once a girl marries, she will be expected to live with her husband's family. Her family loyalties must change from her birth family to her new family. Emotionally, economically, and legally, a girl is property that is transferred to another family. In-laws may make life difficult for the new bride and may interfere in the relationship between her and her husband. The wife may be required to help her husband's parents with many of the household chores, especially if she does not have outside employment or other income-generating activity.

In several Islamic countries, women's behavior is severely restricted. The practice of purdah, a Persian word meaning "curtain," is an institutionalized system that requires women to cover their bodies and faces and to remain in seclusion from the rest of society. Purdah has three major parts: women are physically separated with their own living space; they are socially segregated from all but their immediate kinship circle; and they must cover their bodies and their faces whenever they appear in public places. Purdah keeps women secluded and isolated from the rest of society by confining them to the surroundings of their home, family, immediate kinship circle, and neighborhood (Dankelman and Davidson 1988).

Preference for Males

Even before young women are engaged and married, they understand the place they hold in their families and society. From the time they are born, many girls do not hold an honored place within their families. Many families, especially in developing countries, prefer boys over girls. Girls are biologically stronger than males in their early years, and they are estimated to have a mortality rate lower than males (1 to 1.15) (Royston and Armstrong 1989). Research conducted by the United Nations in the early 1980s indicated that while mortality rates for girls are generally lower than rates for boys, rates for girls were 1.5 times higher than boys in Sri Lanka and Pakistan, 1.4 times higher in Bangladesh, and 1.3 times higher in Colombia (UNFPA 1989). However, more recent research indicates that in much of the world girls now have a lower mortality rate than boys. Only in a few countries, such as India and China, are their rates higher. Current rates in Bangladesh, Pakistan, Sri Lanka, and Colombia indicate that girls have a lower mortality rate than boys (WHO 2010).

Boys are expected to become wage earners to support their own families as well as to provide support to their parents in old age. In many developing countries, the extended family is still common, with the male usually bringing home his bride to live in their own home or in the home of his parents. The preference for males also often extends to access to health care and education. Families are more likely to provide their sons with all available health care and with an education. Girls are seen as providing service to their families by staying home and helping their mothers with housework, child care, and income-generating activities if available.

Education

Education is recognized as an inalienable right for every person by the Universal Declaration of Human Rights and the International Covenant on Economic, Social, and Culture Rights. Both have been adopted by the United Nations and its member nations. Governments around the world recognize the importance of educating their citizens—education enhances economic, political, social, and cultural development and provides benefits to the community as well as the nation. Women who are well educated have more control over their lives, including reproduction, and have fewer children than women with little or no education.

While governments see value in educating all citizens, the reality is that many women in developing countries have not had access to education. As young girls, they are less likely to attend school than boys, especially in many sub-Saharan African and South Asian countries. Many possible reasons exist for this discrepancy. First, cultural or religious beliefs may keep parents from enrolling their daughters in school. Second, parents may believe that it is important for their sons to attend school in order to become successful in life, but they expect their daughters will get married and move into their husband's homes and therefore not provide the parents with any return on their investment. Third, parents may also hold their daughters out of school for their safety; girls attending school may be threatened with violence, including physical assault, emotional abuse, sexual abuse, or rape. Fourth, in many developing countries, while primary education is free, students may have to pay for uniforms, school supplies, and other accessories, and their families may not be able to afford these costs. Finally, parents may need their daughters to stay home and take care of younger siblings, help with housework and cooking duties or, in rural areas, spend time gathering water and fuel.

Within schools, attitudes of the teachers toward the value or lack of value of educating girls, gender biases in the curriculum, male teachers who may prey on young female students, few female teachers to act as role models, gender-based violence, and lack of adequate bathroom facilities and other hygiene and sanitation provisions may make daily school attendance difficult. Families living in rural areas may have a more difficult time sending their children to school; students may have to travel some distance to get to school and their safety along the way, especially for girls, is often not ensured. Families living in urban areas are more likely to have access to schools as well as to income to pay for their children's education, and are more likely to understand the importance of an education.

Even if girls complete primary school, they are less likely to enter and complete secondary school. Girls may need to take on more responsibility at home. In many countries, by the time a girl reaches puberty her parents may have arranged her marriage and see no reason for continuing her education. Safety may also be a factor, as girls may experience growing levels of school-based gender violence; teachers may require sexual relations in exchange for good grades or to remain enrolled in school. For example, in one study of girls in three African countries, while attending school, almost 50 percent of women in Uganda reported some level of sexual, physical, or psychological abuse from male teachers (African Child Policy Forum 2006). In some instances, a girl may also find herself pregnant and not able to continue her education. Schools may not have adequate bathroom facilities for girls who are menstruating and the girls may be too embarrassed to attend school during that time.

Once a girl completes her primary and secondary education, she may have limited options in terms of finding paid employment. Studies have shown that paid employment opportunities for women, especially in developing countries, are expanding very slowly, with paid employment outside of the agricultural sector difficult to find (United Nations 2009). Geographical location also is a factor; if a woman is from a rural area or indigenous group, there may be even fewer opportunities for gainful employment. In difficult economic times, men are usually seen as the "breadwinners" of the family and may be given preference over women in hiring and retention decisions. In addition to trying to find employment, women at this stage in their lives may have recently gotten married and started a family. Their priorities may be higher in terms of raising a family than in finding paid employment.

Even though a woman may not find paid employment, she and her community still benefit from her education. Research has demonstrated that an educated woman is more likely to understand the value of an education and encourage her children, including daughters, to go to school (Grown, Gupta, and Kes 2005; Murray 2008; UNICEF 2007). An educated woman is also more likely to participate in civic affairs, at the local community as well as the national level. Many studies have demonstrated that educating girls and young women provides many benefits to them, their families and the larger society. These benefits include later marriages and pregnancies, healthier children, smaller families, and lower infant mortality rates. Young women who go on to higher education may come back to their local communities as teachers, thereby providing positive female role models for young girls, which may encourage them to stay in school. Educated women also contribute to their countries' economic growth by entering the paid labor force, which can lead to increased job creation. They also play important roles in improving public health and have the opportunity to play a central role in their countries' civic affairs.

Health Care

Most women will face a variety of health issues related to their reproductive systems at some point in their lives. During pregnancy women can experience vitamin deficiency, high blood pressure, miscarriage, and anemia, among other problems. Lack of prenatal care endangers the lives of both the mother and the child. Contraceptives may pose their own risks, but lack of access to contraceptives may create unwanted pregnancies and result in children that cannot be adequately cared for. Abortion services are not always available. Maternal mortality rates are higher in developing countries than in developed countries, often because of lack of access to medical care, numerous pregnancies, poverty, and overwork. The practice of female genital mutilation or female genital cutting in many societies can lead to several health problems, including excessive bleeding, painful menstruation, painful sexual intercourse, infection and even death for some young girls. Sexually transmitted diseases, including AIDS, threaten the health and lives of many women, including those forced into prostitution. During wars and internal conflicts, women often are raped by soldiers.

Knowledge of health care issues that affect them as well as access to health care is often lacking for women in developing countries. Access to health care may be limited for several reasons, including lack of infrastructure; lack of services for referral, poverty, unavailability of midwives; the lack of acceptance of traditional birth attendants by community maternal health programs; lack of information about health care and the need for it; lack of self-esteem; and the position of the woman in the family and her ability to make her own decisions concerning health care.

Medical facilities, hospitals, and clinics, along with medical staff, including physicians, nurses, midwives, and traditional birth attendants are often only available in major cities. If facilities are not located in the same village or town, women need transportation to get to these facilities; many do not have access to cars or bicycles, are not on a bus route, or do not have the money to spend on transportation. Some women do not have the time to go to a doctor or another medical practitioner, they cannot get time off from work, or they cannot leave their children alone. Some do not have money to pay for medical services. Some women live in rural areas that do not provide easy access to medical facilities. Lack of communications, for example, telephone service, also plays a role in women's ability to gain information concerning their medical conditions or to make appointments.

If midwives or traditional birth attendants (women from the local village who are untrained in modern medicine) are not available, maternal and child mortality levels may increase. For example, in Kenya, a skilled person was only present at 41 percent of all births, and maternal mortality was over twice the world average (Population Reference Bureau 2005). However, in Matlab, Bangladesh, maternal mortality decreased by 68 percent over three years when midwives staffed two health clinic sites (Fauveau 1991). Midwives in Ghana were trained in advanced lifesaving techniques and midwifery skills, and as a result, mortality has been reduced significantly. Midwives have developed good supportive relationships with community and traditional practitioners in Ghana, which has contributed to improved maternal and child health. These cooperative, mutually respectful relationships among all health care workers are critical to the success of health care programs.

The sex of the health care provider also plays a role in whether or not a woman will seek health care. For example, most doctors in Egypt are male; custom dictates that women, once past puberty, should not be seen by any male other than a close relative. Even in an emergency situation, many women must get their husband's permission to seek treatment. A woman's reputation could be ruined if she seeks out a male doctor for treatment of any kind; many will question her purity and accuse her of sexual misconduct (el Saadawi 1980; Krieger 1991). Islamic married women in Cameroon cannot be touched by a male without the husband's permission. Women interviewed in one study claimed that they would rather die than seek medical care without their husband's approval (Alexandre 1991).

Lack of knowledge concerning the human body and the need for health care in certain circumstances also limits the ability of women to seek help. In some cases, women do not recognize their or their child's need for medical attention. Sometimes women deny, or refuse to acknowledge, their pregnancy in its early stages, when prenatal care may be critical to the health of the mother and the fetus. Sometimes women are afraid to tell their husbands they are pregnant again, especially if birth control is not available or not encouraged for religious or cultural reasons and the family cannot afford another child.

Nutrition

Because most women put in long hours and play many roles, as wife, mother, and income earner, they are vulnerable to malnutrition. Poverty also influences a woman's nutritional status. The men and boys in a family often are fed before girls and women because boys and men are perceived as more valuable and therefore deserving of as much food as they need to stay healthy and satisfied.

As a result of numerous pregnancies, low food intake, and high work demands, women may not able to meet the nutritional needs of their bodies. They may experience deficiencies of specific vitamins and minerals or a condition of chronic malnutrition may exist. Women tend to suffer from anemia as a result of iron deficiency or stunted growth as a result of lack of protein and calories. As women age, their health may deteriorate as a direct result of poor nutrition throughout their lives.

During pregnancy, many women have difficulty meeting their additional nutritional needs. Pregnant women may have a deficiency of iron and become anemic, which may lead to infections and problems with the health of the fetus. Four of the major causes of maternal mortality are related to poor nutrition: hemorrhage, infection, obstructed labor, and eclampsia (Koblinsky, Timyan, and Gay 1993).

Occupational Health

Women's occupational health is also at risk in many developing countries. While few statistics are available to determine the size of the problem, many health hazards do exist. For example, women working in agriculture may be exposed to dangerous pesticides and other chemicals used to enhance crop size. Women working at home maybe exposed to eyestrain and more serious vision problems as a result of close production work. Poor lighting may contribute to this problem. They may also be exposed to dangerous fumes emitted from various fuel sources when cooking indoors. Many countries do not have safety laws that protect workers from common dangers in the workplace, including exposed wiring, lack of fire protection equipment such as sprinkler systems, and crowded conditions without adequate exits. Locked doors have proven deadly in several developing countries; fires have started somewhere in the building and women have not been able to get out.

Contraceptives

Family planning programs provide individuals and families with the ability to safely control their fertility. In many countries, government policies and laws determine the availability of contraceptives to the general population. These policies and laws may be based on the need to reduce population growth, or on religious beliefs, cultural traditions, or political expediency.

The use of contraceptives challenges the belief that men have the right to control women's fertility and sexuality. In areas where contraception resources are available, the level of education that a woman has achieved influences her willingness to use contraceptives. The more education a woman has, the more likely she is to use some form of birth control. Educated women are more likely to understand the way contraceptives work and their side effects and are less likely to be inhibited about discussing their use with their sexual partners and about actually using them.

Even where family planning policies are in effect, some countries prohibit the advertising of services, prevent trained medical personnel from distributing contraceptives, or in some other way prohibit their use. In some countries nurses are not allowed to insert intrauterine devices (IUDs) or distribute oral contraceptives. If women do not have the consent of their husbands or if adolescent girls do not have the permission of their parents (rarely given), contraceptives are not provided. In many developing countries, the decision to use contraceptives is often made by the husband. The prevailing belief may be that a woman's fertility is the property of the husband; the husband is the only one allowed to determine whether or not to use birth control and what type to use.

The cost of contraceptives may also be a factor in whether or not a woman uses them. Other problems include the availability of contraceptives, the distance one has to travel to procure them, the poor quality of services provided in procuring them, fear of negative health consequences and side effects, limited choice of method, prohibitive cost, or the woman's belief that she is not at risk of becoming pregnant.

Abortion

Abortion is one of the most controversial topics today throughout the world. Many countries outlaw abortion because it goes against the particular religious beliefs of the country. Other countries allow abortions when the life of the mother is in danger or when the pregnancy is a result of rape or incest (see Chapter 6). In developed countries as well as developing countries, discussions and policies concerning abortion are usually controversial.

Induced abortion is probably the oldest and perhaps the most widely used form of fertility control (Royston and Armstrong 1989). According to Murray (2008), approximately 50 million pregnancies are terminated each year by induced abortions. Approximately one-half of these abortions are illegal and most often occur in developing countries with restrictive abortion laws, while the other half are legal abortions most often performed in countries with more liberal laws that allow abortions. Physical results of unsafe abortions include hemorrhage, uterine perforation, cervical trauma, and even the death of the woman. Other costs include psychological trauma, guilt, expense, and the stigma associated with having an abortion. See Chapter 2 for a discussion of the issues surrounding abortion and other family planning options.

Maternal Mortality

Women's work is often devalued or considered less valuable than men's work. This belief often leads to gender discrimination in the distribution of basic resources, including food and health care, and may lead to early death. Women often die from many of the same causes as men, but one gender-specific cause of maternal mortality is childbirth. Hemorrhage, obstructed labor, infections, hypertension, and complications from induced abortion are the major causes of maternal death during pregnancy, labor, and delivery. Maternal deaths in developing countries account for a high proportion of all deaths of women in their reproductive years. According to the World Health Organization, in 2005 there were approximately 500,000 maternal deaths and 99 percent of those occurred in developing countries (WHO 2009). While statistics on other mortality rates indicate declines over the years, maternal mortality rates have stayed about the same or shown only small declines (see Chapter 2 for additional discussion).

Female Genital Mutilation

Often referred to as female circumcision or female genital cutting, the practice of female genital mutilation (FGM) has seen increased attention in recent years. Even in the United States, many states have outlawed the practice, considering it a form of child sexual abuse (see Chapter 3 for further discussion). Physical complications from this surgery are often severe, and may include hemorrhage, tetanus, blood poisoning, and shock from the pain of the operation.

The World Health Organization (1996) has designated four types of FGM: Type 1, known as clitoridectomy, involves the removal of the prepuce, and may include removal of the clitoris. Type 2, known as excision, includes removal of the clitoris and the labia minora. Type 3, referred to as infibulation, includes removal of the clitoris, labia minora, and labia majora and the stitching of the remaining labia to narrow the vaginal opening. Type 4 includes all other forms of genital alteration, including pricking or piercing of the clitoris or labia, cauterization, or incisions in the vaginal wall.

FGM is primarily found in Africa and a few countries in the Middle East and Asia. In many rural parts of Africa, traditional midwives often perform the circumcision, although barbers and male priests are also known to perform it. In urban areas, doctors, nurses, or midwives perform the procedure and are known to use anesthesia and antiseptics.

According to common belief, circumcision continues today primarily because it has always been done—it is the custom of many cultures. Reasons for continuing the practice include the protection of women from unwanted sexual intercourse, the protection of women from their own sexuality or from an uncontrolled sexual appetite, to keep young girls virgins, to enhance fertility, to enhance femininity, to keep married women faithful, to prevent women from masturbating, and because many men will only marry a woman who has undergone this procedure.

Long-term effects of circumcision include loss of any sexual feeling, chronic urinary tract infections, painful intercourse, pelvic infections, and severe scarring that can result in hemorrhaging during childbirth. Women often must be cut open on the wedding night and when giving birth in order to make sexual relations and childbirth possible.

Sexually Transmitted Diseases

Sexually transmitted diseases, including gonorrhea, syphilis, HIV, and AIDS, affect both men and women throughout the world. In developing countries, these diseases can cause more problems than in more developed countries, due to lack of medical facilities and treatment options, lack of medications, expense of medications, and the stigma associated with contracting any of these diseases, especially HIV and AIDS. Many women in developing countries do not seek timely medical attention for many reasons, including the unavailability of doctors or nurses, especially in rural areas, poverty, lack of time, cultural inhibitions, problems in communicating with male doctors, and feelings of shame over their condition (Koblinsky, Timyan, and Gay 1993).

For some women, the inability to deny sex to their husbands creates an additional vulnerability to sexually transmitted diseases. In many countries, men are allowed, even expected, to seek sex outside of their marriage. If they contract a sexually transmitted disease, they are often unaware of their infection and eventually transmit the infection to their wives.

Child marriage also contributes to the spread of sexually transmitted diseases, especially HIV and AIDS. According to a WHO study, one-half of all new infections of HIV occur in young people between the ages of 15 and 24 (WHO 2006). The majority of these young people are female, since girls are physiologically more susceptible to infection. In many areas of Africa, girls and young women make up 48 percent of those living with AIDS (UNAIDS 2006).

Prostitution and Sex Trafficking

Prostitution is big business in many countries. Previously, several Southeast Asian countries were known as places in which women could be found for "rest and recreation" activities for foreign military personnel. Currently, these countries and several others have expanded these services to include wealthy businessmen and tourists as clients; men traveling alone are creating a new market for prostitutes. Developing countries often encourage these activities either openly or quietly behind the scenes because foreign currency benefits the countries' economies.

Women participating in prostitution may do so voluntarily or may have been coerced into this activity. Some women choose to become prostitutes because they find that it can be financially lucrative for them and their families. In other cases, young girls and women may be forced into it; parents may sell their young daughters to traffickers or other individuals believing that they will have an opportunity to earn income for the family. Many women who migrate to urban areas in search of employment may be coerced into it by employment agencies that act as fronts for prostitution rings, crime rings, or other groups that are trafficking in women (Hyland 2001).

Prostitution places women in danger. The most common danger is from sexually transmitted disease, including gonorrhea, syphilis, and AIDS, but physical violence also endangers women. Male sexual aggression may lead to beatings and other physical harm. In Bangkok, a study sponsored by the United Nations found that two-thirds of women in Bangkok were afraid of being raped or physically assaulted while walking on the city's streets. The researchers found that hospital statistics of rapes and assaults supported this fear (Buendia 1989).

Violence against Women

Throughout the world, women are threatened with violence, including violent acts committed against them by their husbands. In many developing countries, women are expected to obey their husbands and the husbands often have customary if not also legal authority to discipline and control their wives in whatever way they see fit. In the 1980s in Bangladesh, Stewart (1989) found that the murder of wives by their husbands accounted for 50 percent of all murders in the country. Almost 75 percent of all women murdered in Papua New Guinea were killed by their husbands (Bradley 1988).

Many women have died in India as a result of the practice of dowry. The custom of the woman's family providing a dowry to the husband has been prohibited by law since 1961. However, the practice itself, along with bride-burning or dowry deaths, has grown in recent years. Providing a dowry may help elevate the economic status of the husband and his family, and may be encouraged by greed. When the husband decides that his wife's family has not provided him with an adequate dowry, he may resort to burning his wife alive. Police often have a difficult time proving that the woman was intentionally murdered, primarily because the husbands often make the death look like a cooking accident.

Rape may be one of the most underreported crimes against women throughout the world. The stigma and shame that are often associated with rape appear universal. Estimates in developing countries are believed to be even less accurate than in developed countries because the report rate in developing countries is even lower than in developed countries. In both developed and developing countries, statistics indicate that most women who have been raped know their assailant. In countries that highly value a woman's virginity, including many Asian, Middle Eastern, and African countries, women who have been raped have lost all value. Women are driven to suicide, beaten, or murdered as a result of the dishonor that they have brought upon their families.

In some countries, rape is used as a weapon against the women of one's enemies. Because female sexuality is seen as sacred by many cultural traditions, rape becomes a show of force against one's enemy. Hindu fundamentalists have raped Muslim women as a way of attacking the Muslim population in India; Hutu rebels raped Tutsi women in 2000 as part of the state-sponsored genocide against the Tutsis; and women have been raped in Bosnia, Burma, Kenya, Rwanda, Darfur, and other countries as part of wars and internal conflicts. Rape in this setting humiliates the male members of the women's family and often dishonors the family.

In many countries, marital rape is not considered rape. In India in the early 1980s, many women's groups demanded that forced intercourse by a husband with his wife without her consent should be considered rape, but the Criminal Law (Amendment)

Act of 1983 stated that "sexual intercourse by a man with his own wife, the wife not being under fifteen years of age, is not rape" (Calman 1992, 121). Today in India, however, marital rape is considered rape and prohibited by law, but is still widespread.

Women have a difficult time leaving violent husbands, no matter what country they live in. In many developing countries, leaving is virtually impossible. For many of these women, returning to their birth families is not an option. The women's parents may have died or may be living with a son or economically dependent on a son and have no room and no economic resources to provide to the woman. In some cases, parents may talk to their son-in-law about his violent behavior and request that he stop. Marriage is often seen as a permanent union and women are expected to suffer within the marriage.

Employment

Most women's work is unpaid and not recognized as having any economic value. In employment, women face discrimination and multiple challenges. Access to jobs may be limited within certain cultures that restrict the position of women. The general economic conditions of the area in which they live affect women's standard of living and ability to find work outside the home. Women often earn less than men in many occupations and are usually found in lower-level jobs. Changing economic policies have affected women and their position in the economy of many developing countries. Women's lack of access to assets such as land and other forms of collateral hurts their ability to get loans to start businesses. However, in many areas, despite the many restrictions faced by women, women are increasing their participation in the workforce and assuming greater economic responsibility for their families.

In the past, women have traditionally had trouble obtaining credit from banks and other lending institutions. In many developing countries women have not been allowed to own property; husbands or fathers have had total ownership and control of property. Therefore, women have been unable to provide any form of collateral to back up a bank loan. However, by the 1980s, some institutions had begun to realize that women are usually excellent credit risks. NGOs and several small business lenders have demonstrated that providing loans to women entrepreneurs is good business. The Grameen Bank in Bangladesh, the Self-Employed

Women's Association (SEWA) Cooperative Bank in India, and Banco Solidario in Bolivia have pioneered efforts to provide loans to poor women who have no collateral.

Women play a major role in the agricultural activities of many developing countries, including many African countries, although very few women hold title to land; for example, they own less than 20 percent of all the land in Africa (Cotula 2006). Nevertheless, many governments now recognize this role that women play in the local economy. In the 1980s in Kenya, a national agricultural extension system specifically targeted women. Extension agents reported that over half the farmers they meet with were women (Herz 1989). This experience influenced extension efforts in other African countries, including Cameroon, Somalia, Nigeria, and Zimbabwe, where women are now seen as farmers in their own right.

In Asia, many women are involved in rice farming activities, especially in the production and post-harvest phases. Their roles vary widely, depending on economic, religious, and social factors within each country. Women can benefit from technological advances in agriculture as long as they have some control over the income received, and this varies from country to country. In Java, women are allowed to own land and control household finances, while women in Bangladesh have had little input or control over agriculture-related decisions (Stoler 1977; Abdullah and Zeidenstein 1982).

Industry is one of the fastest growing sectors in developing countries. Women in many developing countries have found employment in export-oriented industries, including garment and circuit board production. In Bangladesh, the export garment business has opened up 500,000 jobs for young women (UBINIG 1991). Even though pay is low, hours are long, health hazards exist, and job security is nonexistent, many women move from rural areas specifically to take these jobs. Many women find that employment frees them from oppressive social and cultural traditions.

Women have increased their participation in industry in recent years; however, this has tended to reinforce sexual stratification in the labor market. Unless training and other incentives are provided to women, they will continue to remain in low-paying, dead-end, and often hazardous jobs. The mechanization of tasks may also reduce the number of women employed in this sector, unless other industries move in to provide new jobs. When women, especially rural women, participate in wage labor, they are often vulnerable to discrimination, primarily in the form of lower wages. Many employers also find that rural women are usually more docile and less likely to complain about working conditions, low wages, or other problems with their jobs.

In addition to employment in industrial facilities, many industries operate in the form of small workshops, and women work in their own homes. Wages are usually lower in these cases, women receive fewer fringe benefits, and job security remains nonexistent.

Women participate heavily in several service sectors, including community services, such as health, education, and social welfare, as well as commerce and domestic service. Tourism is a major employer of women in many developing countries.

Informal activities account for a larger percentage of female employment than employment in the formal sector in most developing countries. Many reasons for this trend exist. The informal labor market is usually easier to enter, in part because it usually requires fewer skills than the formal market. Informal work can be done at home or at times of the day that enable women to take care of their families and work at the same time. Cultural patterns and expectations about women and work also make it easier for women to enter the informal labor market.

Outwork, or subcontracting work that can be done in the home, is becoming more popular for women, especially in developing countries. Employers are able to cut costs and avoid paying benefits to many of these workers. Women who work these jobs provide their own tools—for example, sewing machines—and can set their own hours, as long as they meet quotas set by their employers. The drawbacks for women include low wages, little or no benefits, and no formal organization or union to protect their rights.

Women in many countries are beginning to see the benefits of organizing among themselves. One of the best-known groups is India's Self-Employed Women's Association (SEWA), established in 1972 by a group of garment vendors, head-loaders (individuals who are hired to transport loads on their heads), and vegetable sellers. SEWA has organized over 40,000 women workers in Gujarat and five other states in India, helping them to get licenses, organize industrial and service cooperatives, and obtain legal help. Women members receive assistance in obtaining loans and banking services. The group also advocates for women's rights.

Women's Rights as Human Rights

Long before the phrase "women's rights are human rights" was used prominently at the Fourth World Conference on Women in Beijing, social reformers, writers, philosophers, and others were writing about the lack of human rights available to most women. In 1792, Mary Wollstonecraft, a British feminist, wrote *Vindication of the Rights of Women,* in which she challenged the prevailing attitudes of the day concerning human rights. Both liberals and conservatives at the time advocated for rights for men, but did not think that women needed these same rights. Later, in 1869, John Stuart Mill wrote *The Subjugation of Women,* in which he advocated equal opportunities for women and suggested ways to eliminate the basic causes of women's oppression. Today, even though many international documents exist to protect women and their rights (see Chapter 6), women in many areas of the world are not aware of their rights or are denied these rights by common practice, by cultural traditions, or by law. In many cases, women are not aware of the fact that they have certain rights, or of how to get access to information on how to gain their rights. Many NGOs as well as governmental agencies today emphasize the belief that women's rights are human rights and should not be separated from the global attempts to gain equal rights for everyone.

Empowerment of Women

Changing laws to grant women certain rights in many countries does not necessarily mean that the laws will be followed. Traditions are difficult to change; the laws may not be followed, or they may not be enforced. Passing laws is relatively easy compared with changing attitudes. Possibly the best, most effective way to empower women is to do it on an individual basis. Provide a woman with the means to support her family—through microloans, for example—and her family will see the benefit to everyone of this policy. Husbands will see the value in supporting their wives in these endeavors, and sons will see the advantages of allowing their mothers to financially support their families, which may change the way the sons later view their wives and daughters.

References

Abdullah, Tahrunnesa, and Sondra Zeidenstein. 1982. *Village Women of Bangladesh: Prospects for Change.* Oxford: Pergamon Press.

African Child Policy Forum. 2006. *Violence against Girls in Africa: A Retrospective Survey in Ethiopia, Kenya and Uganda.* Addis Ababa: African Child Policy Forum.

Alexandre, Marie. 1991. "The Role of Gender: Socio-Economic, Cultural, and Religious Pressure on the Health of Women in Cameroon." Paper presented at the 18th Annual NCIH International Health Conference, Arlington, VA.

Boserup, Ester. 1970. *Women's Role in Economic Development.* London: Allen and Unwin.

Bradley, Christine. 1988. "The Problem of Domestic Violence in Papua New Guinea." In *Guidelines for Police Training on Violence against Women and Child Sexual Abuse.* London: Commonwealth Secretariat, Women and Development Programme.

Bruce, J., and S. Clark. 2004. *The Implications of Early Marriage for HIV/ AIDS Policy.* New York: Population Council.

Buendia, Hernando Gomez, ed. 1989. *Urban Crime: Global Trends and Policies.* Tokyo: U.N. University.

Calman, Leslie J. 1992. *Toward Empowerment: Women and Movement Politics in India.* Boulder, CO: Westview Press.

Chow, Esther Ngan-ling, and Catherine White Berheide, eds. 1994. *Women, the Family, and Policy: A Global Perspective.* Albany: State University of New York Press.

Cornia, Giovanni Andrea, Richard Jolly, and Frances Stewart. 1987. *Adjustment with a Human Face,* vol. 1. Oxford: Clarendon Press.

Cotula, Lorenzo. 2006. *Gender and Law: Women's Rights in Agriculture.* Rome: FAO Legal Office.

Dankelman, Irene, and Joan Davidson. 1998. *Women and Environment in the Third World: Alliance for the Future.* London: Earthscan Publications.

ECOSOC Resolution E/RES/2/11, June 21, 1946.

El Saadawi, Nawal. 1980. *The Hidden Face of Eve.* Translated and edited by Sherif Hetata. London: Zed Press.

Eitzen, D. Stanley, and Maxie Baca Zinn. 1991. *Conflict and Order: Understanding Society.* Fifth ed. Boston: Allyn and Bacon.

Fauveau, Vincent. 1991. "Mortality Impact of a Community-Based Maternity Care Program in Rural Bangladesh." Presentation at the 18th

Annual NCIH International Health Conference, Arlington, VA.

Friedlander, Eva, ed. 1996. *Look at the World through Women's Eyes: Plenary Speeches from the NGO Forum on Women, Beijing '95.* New York: Women, Ink.

Grown, Caren, Geeta Rao Gupta, and Aslihan Kes. 2005. *Taking Action: Achieving Gender Equality and Empowering Women.* Sterling, VA: Earthscan.

Herz, Barbara. 1989. "Women in Development: Kenya's Experience." *Finance and Development* 26(2): 43–46.

Hyland, Kelly. 2001. "Protecting Human Victims of Trafficking: An American Framework." *Berkeley Women's Law Journal* 29–71.

Jaquette, Jane S., and Kathleen Staudt. "Women, Gender, and Development." 2007. In *Women and Gender Equity in Development Theory and Practice: Institutions, Resources, and Mobilization,* edited by Jane Jaquette and Gale Summerfield. Durham: Duke University Press, 17–52.

Jaquette, Jane S., and Gale Summerfield, eds. 2007. *Women and Gender Equity in Development Theory and Practice: Institutions, Resources, and Mobilization.* Durham: Duke University Press.

Jiggins, Janice. 1994. *Changing the Boundaries: Women-Centered Perspectives on Population and the Environment.* Washington, D.C.: Island Press.

Kahne, Hilda, and Ganet Z. Giele, eds. 1992. *Women's Work and Women's Lives: The Continuing Struggle Worldwide.* Boulder, CO: Westview Press.

Koblinsky, Marge, Judith Timyan, and Jill Gay, eds. 1993. *The Health of Women: A Global Perspective.* Boulder, CO: Westview Press.

Krieger, Laurie. 1991. "Male Doctor, Female Patient: Access to Health Care in Egypt." Presentation at the 18th Annual NCIH International Health Conference, Arlington, VA.

McMurtry, John. 1998. *Unequal Freedoms: The Global Market as an Ethical System.* West Hartford, CT: Kumarian Press.

Murray, Ann Firth. 2008. *From Outrage to Courage: Women Taking Action for Health and Justice.* Monroe, ME: Common Courage Press.

Population Reference Bureau. 2005. *2005 Women of Our World.* Washington, D.C.: Population Reference Bureau.

Rogers, Susan Carol. 1978. "Women's Place: A Critical Review of Anthropological Theory." *Comparative Studies in Society and History* 20(1): 123–162.

Royston, Erica, and Sue Armstrong. 1989. *Preventing Maternal Deaths.* Geneva: World Health Organization.

Stewart, Denise. 1989. *The Global Injustice.* Ottawa: Canadian Council on Social Development.

Stoler, A. 1977. "Class Structure and Female Autonomy in Rural Java." In Wellesley Editorial Committee, Bunster B. Ximena et al., *Women and National Development: The Complexities of Change.* Chicago: University of Chicago Press.

UBINIG. 1991. *Bangladesh's Textile and Clothing Industry: The Role of Women.* Working Paper prepared for UNIDO (United Nations Industrial Development Organization) and presented at a seminar in Dhaka on 7 October.

United Nations. 2009. *2009 World Survey on the Role of Women in Development: Women's Control over Economic Resources and Access to Financial Resources, including Microfinance.* New York: United Nations.

UNAIDS. 2006. *Global Summary of the AIDS Epidemic.* Geneva: UNAIDS.

UNFPA. 1989. *State of the World Population Report.* New York: UNFPA.

UNICEF. 2007. *A Human Rights-Based Approach to Education for All.* New York: UNICEF.

U.S. Department of State. 2009. Country Reports. Available at http://www.state.gov/g/drl/rls/hrrpt/.

Walby, Sylvia. 1996. "The 'Declining Significance' or the 'Changing Forms' of Patriarchy." In *Patriarchy and Economic Development: Women's Positions at the End of the Twentieth Century,* Valentine M. Moghadam, ed. New York: Oxford University, 1996, 19–33.

World Health Organization. 1996. *Female Genital Mutilation: Report of a Technical Working Group.* Geneva: WHO.

World Health Organization. 1999. *Abortion in the Developing World.* New Delhi: Vistaar Publications.

World Health Organization. 2003. *The World Health Report 2003: Shaping the Future.* Geneva: WHO.

World Health Organization. 2005. *WHO Multi-Country Study on Women's Health and Domestic Violence against Women: Initial Results on Prevalence, Health Outcomes and Women's Responses.* Geneva: WHO.

World Health Organization. 2006. *The World Health Report 2006: Working Together for Health.* Geneva: WHO.

World Health Organization. 2009. *Women and Health: Today's Evidence, Tomorrow's Agenda.* Geneva: WHO.

World Health Organization. 2010. *World Health Statistics.* Geneva: WHO.

2

Problems, Controversies, and Solutions

This chapter examines specific problems that women in developing countries face in their daily lives in the areas of education, marriage and family, and employment, as well as some controversial issues involving women such as female genital mutilation, abortion, honor killings, and property rights and inheritance. We will also explore general solutions to these ongoing problems and issues that have emerged within local cultures as well as in law and government.

Problems

Many women in developing countries face problems in their daily lives that most women in developed countries do not encounter. Some of these problems include the lack of educational opportunities, a cultural preference for male children rather than female children, dowry demands, child marriages, lack of access to health care facilities and treatment, the inability to own or manage real property, and limited employment and other income-generating opportunities. This section examines these problems and offers several possible solutions.

Tradition

One of the primary factors that influences many of the decisions governments make about the rights of their citizens, especially the role of women in society, is the country's cultural and religious traditions. These traditions play an important role in the position of women in many developing countries. Individuals, communities, and entire nations rely on these traditions to structure, organize, and maintain order in their communities and societies. Traditions play a central role in guiding people in the proper and expected way to behave. For example, in the United States it is traditional for young people to socialize and make their own decisions regarding their marriage partners. However, in many developing countries the parents play a major, or the only, role is choosing their child's marriage partner.

Who decides which practice is "correct" or "fair"? Should we study the divorce rate in each country to see which system offers more long-lasting marriages? Should we interview a representative sample of married couples in both countries in an attempt to understand which system appears to work better? For the most part each tradition has its positive and negative aspects, and we must have some grasp of the power of tradition in order to begin to understand the experiences of women in developing countries.

A growing number of programs administered by foreign governments and international nongovernmental organizations (NGOs) working in developing countries are taking a human rights perspective when advocating on behalf of women in those countries. That is, they look at the current status of women in a particular area and examine whether tradition or statutes infringe on the individual's rights as a human being. Cultural tradition alone is no longer considered a valid reason for denying women their basic human rights.

While many researchers and NGOs view women's lives from the perspective of human rights, governments in many countries believe they have the right to dictate the treatment of their citizens and male members of many societies believe they have the right to control their family members. This issue is loaded with emotion; supporters of local/national control believe they have the best interests of everyone in mind and that outsiders should stay out of the nation's affairs. Their detractors believe that human rights are universal and that the treatment of women in many countries demonstrates a clear denial of their basic human rights.

As discussed in Chapter 1, cultural relativism often influences the supporters and detractors of the policies and practices of individual countries toward their citizens. It is difficult to analyze and make recommendations for future policies and programs regarding the treatment of women without understanding the underlying reasons for the past and current treatment of women. Local tradition, especially in many rural communities, may be the only practice people know; it defines who they are and what they can do and provides general order to the community. Changing traditional practices can be difficult and frightening, especially if the changes are in conflict with local traditions. Changes also take time, especially when they are seen as drastic; individuals and communities must be able to understand how the proposed changes will benefit them.

Local and national governments often see tradition as an important means of controlling their citizens and local practices often have their roots in religious observances and practices, which provide the local governments and communities with an incentive to maintain the status quo. Changing traditions and practices also may be seen as conceding control to Western influences. Individuals and governments in many countries resent and decry the influence of Western society, especially when it takes the form of consumerism and what may be viewed as the out-of-control behavior of Western society, particularly as it plays out in the United States. Many view the adoption of human rights legislation as an adoption of a "Western" lifestyle.

Understanding the role and importance of a country's cultural and religious beliefs and practices in the treatment of women is critical to understanding the challenges that women face in their everyday lives regarding the care of their families and their own health and welfare.

Education

Estimates from various governmental agencies and nongovernmental agencies such as the United Nations, the World Bank, UNICEF, and UNESCO suggest that there are between 600 and 700 million girls and women around the world, but primarily in developing countries, who are illiterate. Illiteracy is a major problem and governments and international organizations are working to reduce it, especially among women.

In 2000, 189 government officials attended the Millennium Summit, sponsored by the United Nations, to discuss critical issues the international development community would face in the 21st century. The resulting Millennium Declaration provided a road map for international cooperation in confronting the world's major development challenges. Millennium Development Goal (MDG) No. 3 is to achieve universal primary education by the year 2015; the means for achieving this goal are left up to participating governments. Other agencies and organizations are also advocating for universal primary education. In 2000, and in addition to the MDGs, the World Education Forum met in Dakar, Senegal, and drafted the Dakar Framework for Action, which committed the world community to achieving education for all (EFA), including girls and women, indigenous communities, and other often marginalized groups. Among the goals of EFA are providing free and compulsory universal primary education, meeting the learning needs of young people and adults, increasing adult literacy, especially for women, and achieving gender parity and equality.

Progress is being made toward the goal of universal primary education. According to the United Nations, 88 percent of children in developing countries are enrolled in school; however, the common belief is that the goal will not be met by 2015 (United Nations 2009). One reason for this failure is that getting education out to remote rural areas is difficult and costly. Also, in many areas, education for girls is seen as unnecessary, and it places a burden on parents who need their daughters to assist with younger children, household work, and income-generating activities. In other, often rural, communities, parents do not believe that girls need to be educated; many girls will be married by the time they enter puberty or soon after, and the cost of educating them is seen as a waste of limited financial resources. Members of some communities are hostile to the idea of girls going to school; for example, in Kunduz province in Afghanistan in April 2010, over 80 girls in three schools became ill, and authorities believe this may have been the result of the actions of local militants who do not believe that girls should be educated (CNN.com/Asia 2010). Earlier, in 2009, several young women in Afghanistan were attacked with acid while in school (Abawi 2009).

While most governments believe that education is important, the financial resources to support education may not be available. The ongoing financial crisis that began in 2007–2008 in the United States and spread to many countries around the world has exacerbated the problems many governments are facing in their attempts to fund the building or expansion of schools and the hiring of teachers. The global recession has created an added economic burden that has led many families to choose between sending their children to school or keeping them home to help with necessary domestic work and income-generating activities. If a family has to limit the number of children they send to school, they are most likely to choose to send their sons, and keep their daughters home.

In order to reduce illiteracy and encourage parents to send their daughters to school, education must be viewed as a basic right for all individuals. This approach is necessary for the elimination of gender-based discrimination in schools and in educational policies. Many policy makers and researchers believe that it is the most effective means for addressing the many deep-seated and widely held cultural values and norms that prevent women from having access to educational opportunities. Several successful programs, such as Campaign for Female Education (CAMFED), work with community leaders and other community members to teach the importance of educating the girls in their communities. Since 1993, CAMFED has educated over one million children in Ghana, Malawi, Tanzania, Zambia, and Zimbabwe (see Chapter 7).

The quality of education must also be improved. Most of the recent efforts regarding universal primary education have been focused on helping children get into school. Efforts must shift to improving the quality of the education that students receive. Many students leave school without the skills necessary to be productive, successful adults. There is little point in providing students with the opportunity for an education without helping them to succeed in life. Improvements must be made to school curricula to make them comprehensive and useful, learning materials including books and other resources must be available to all students, and teachers must be trained to constructively interact with students to encourage learning and to understand the need to remove gender bias from the curriculum.

Schools must be made safe for all students, but especially girls, which can be accomplished through stronger school infrastructure, teacher training, improved working conditions for teachers and staff, training and hiring of female teachers, development of codes of conduct for students and teachers and enforcement provisions for them, and effective discipline for those who violate the code of conduct.

Statistical data from developing countries should also be improved to more accurately measure successes as well as identify failures so they can be corrected. Current statistics are often unreliable; inconsistent methods of gathering data, differing interpretations of data collected, difficulties getting to rural and other remote areas of a country, and other factors contribute to this unreliability. Consistent measures of school enrollment and attendance must be established in order to determine the true picture of how many girls are actually in school. For example, there is a big difference between being enrolled in school and actually attending school; parents may enroll their daughters, but then hold them out because they are needed at home or for cultural or religious reasons.

It is often more difficult to educate women as adults. By the time girls become young adults, most of them have family responsibilities, which can include child care, growing food for the family, income-generating activities, and other household duties. Several programs that provide loans to women to start their own businesses also provide basic literacy training, including financial and other business-related classes. Microfinance programs such as the Grameen Bank have extensive training programs to provide basic literacy education for the recipients of its loans along with business courses to aid recipients in developing and maintaining their small businesses.

Finally, if education is viewed by parents as preparing children for the working world, to earn income to support a family, then many families will not understand the value of educating their daughters. If, on the other hand, education is seen as contributing to the health and welfare of society in general, the obvious benefits to educating women are enormous. An educated woman is more likely to understand the importance of medical care and immunizations for her children and the dangers of HIV/AIDS to herself and her family, and will have the ability to contribute to her local community and the larger society.

Marriage and Family

The family environment is central to a woman's life, especially in developing countries, and it has been a focus of study and concern for many researchers, policy makers, and NGOs. The position and role that a woman plays in the family, preferences for male children, arranged marriages, dowry, domestic violence, and selling female children into prostitution are some of the critical issues facing women today.

Preference for Male Children

Male children are preferred in many countries, even in the Global North. Male children are valued for a variety of cultural, religious, social, and economic reasons, while female children are seen as a burden—they will cost the family money to raise them and to pay for their marriages, whether through the cost of a wedding to be paid for by the girl's parents or the provision of dowry to the family of the groom. Even in the United States and other developed countries, the birth of a girl is not always greeted with as great a joy as when the child is a boy.

As a result of the widespread belief that female children are a burden on their families and on society, families, for a variety of cultural and economic reasons, may choose to abort a female fetus, or murder a female child either passively through the denial of food and other necessities of survival or actively through the murder of the child. In rural areas of many developing countries, limited access to education, health care, and economic resources for families and lack of access to abortion may lead to female infanticide. In urban areas, sex-selective abortions are often the choice of families who have access to ultrasound technology and do not want to give birth to a female child.

Female infanticide is still a major concern in several developing countries. India and China are the most well-known countries that may tacitly allow the intentional killing of female infants, and China's one-child policy has led to numerous abortions of female fetuses and female infanticide. Along with sex-selective abortions, female infanticide demonstrates the low status of women in and the patriarchal nature of these countries. While China has enacted legislation that bans female infanticide, the practice continues in many areas. India has also banned infanticide, but it is currently practiced in many parts of the country and the perpetrators are rarely if ever prosecuted. India's child sex ratio according to the 2001 census was 927 girls to 1,000 boys (John et al. 2008). Local traditions and customary laws are the guiding standard for many local communities, while national laws, even if known and understood by the local community, are often not followed. According to Sen (2001), the number of girls "missing" through sex-selective abortion or infanticide may range from between sixty and one hundred million.

Several ways to combat the preference for males in many countries have been suggested. First, laws that provide girls and women with equal rights should be universal. Public education campaigns should be undertaken to educate individuals and communities about the valuable contributions girls and women make to society, and the importance of equal rights for all. Countries should pass laws, if they have not already done so, outlawing infanticide and sex-selective abortion. In countries with one-child only policies, exceptions should be made if the first child is female. Finally, communities might consider incorporating preferential policies for families that have no sons, such as guarantees for social security for the parents (Bannister 2003).

Child Marriage

Child marriage is also a major issue in many developing countries, even though it is considered a violation of human rights. This practice is most often found in sub-Saharan Africa and South Asia. According to UNICEF (2005), over 64 million women between the ages of 20 and 24 were married before they were 18 years old and approximately 14 million girls between the ages of 15 and 19 gave birth each year.

Why are so many children, primarily girls, married when they are still children? The parents of many of these children consent to the marriage of their daughters to adult males for financial or social reasons. They believe their daughters will be protected by the adult husbands, will be provided with a means of support, will relieve the parents of having to support children who are viewed as burdens to them, will be protected from sexual assault, or will be protected from pregnancy outside of marriage. The adult husbands may value these young brides because they are virgins and therefore less likely to have been exposed to HIV/AIDS or other sexually transmitted diseases. Young brides will have a potentially longer life to produce more children and will be expected to be more obedient to their husbands' wishes because they are younger and have not yet been exposed to an education in which they are taught to think critically or understand their rights.

While the Universal Declaration of Human Rights includes the right to "free and full" consent to a marriage, a child who is promised in marriage by her parents does not have that right. The Convention on the Elimination of All Forms of Discrimination against Women includes the right to protection from child marriage (Article 16), and the Convention on the Rights of the Child indirectly links child marriage with other rights, such as the right to be protected from harmful traditional practices and the right to protection from all forms of abuse. In many countries, however, these conventions are not supported by statutory or customary law.

Over the past several years, statistics indicate that the median age at marriage is rising around the world, including in developing countries (UNICEF 2005b). Several authors suggest that this increase is due to the growing number of girls attending school and the growing labor force participation by women (Mathur, Greene, and Malhotra 2003; UNICEF 2005b).

Women who marry when they are still children are exposed to a variety of reproductive health issues, especially if they become pregnant while still very young. They and their babies are more likely to die from complications during pregnancy or during childbirth. A young girl's body is not mature enough to sustain the rigors of pregnancy and childbirth, and her child is more likely to be born prematurely and have a low birth weight (Save the Children 2004). Early marriage often eliminates the opportunity to attend school, to gain an education or vocational training, and to find rewarding employment. Girls who are married young are more likely to become socially isolated because they have not had an opportunity to develop friendships with other women. They are also more likely to contract HIV than unmarried young girls (Clark, Bruce, and Dude 2006).

In a study by UNICEF (2005b), researchers found that women who were married by the age of 18 were more likely to be from rural areas and from poor families and were unlikely to have had any education or to have had only limited education. In many of the countries studied, women who were already married by age 18 were less likely to use contraception than women who were married when they were over 18. One explanation for this statistic is that men may choose young girls to marry in order to have a longer period of childbearing, resulting in the birth of a larger number of children for their young wives than for those women who marry later in life.

Effective means to eliminate the practice of child marriage include providing girls with access to education, alleviating poverty and other social problems that create pressure for parents to arrange marriages for their young daughters, developing public awareness programs to educate families on the negative effects of early marriage, and advocating for the passage of legislation to prohibit the practice. However, providing financial incentives may be one of the most effective means to help lift a family out of poverty and eliminate the major reason for a family to arrange for a child marriage. Microfinance programs that help women support themselves and their families have been successful in lifting participants out of poverty. Other programs have been developed that have shown some success; for example, the government of Bangladesh instituted a program that encouraged the secondary school enrollment of girls by offering parents compensation for the loss of their daughter's labor and covering the cost of school fees and books if the parents signed an agreement to refrain from arranging a marriage for their daughters before they turned 18 (Amin and Huq 2008).

Domestic Violence

Violence against women and girls takes place throughout the world, cutting across cultures, class, education, income, race, and ethnicity. Domestic violence is probably the most common and also the most difficult to measure and to address because of its private, hidden nature, but some studies estimate that between 10 and 50 percent of women in every country have experienced physical, including sexual, violence from a husband or family member (WHO 2005).

The reasons for and causes of domestic violence are complex and often difficult to measure, but they all stem from gender inequality and unequal power relations between men and women. Cultural reasons include definitions of appropriate sex roles; belief in male superiority; marriage customs, including dowry; belief that what happens behind closed doors in the family setting is a private matter between family members; and norms that allow men proprietary rights over women. Other reasons include the legal view that women have less status than men, statutory and customary laws that support men's superiority over women, limited understanding by women of their legal rights, and less legal standing of women in court systems. Economic factors include women's limited access to credit, employment opportunities, and education and training; laws that discriminate against women in land ownership and property rights; and women's general financial dependence on men for care and support (UNICEF Innocenti Research Centre 2000).

The physical costs to women are enormous. In addition to broken bones, the acquisition of sexually transmitted diseases including HIV/AIDS, gynecological problems, and internal injuries, women also suffer from other physical ailments as a result of the stress associated with living with recurring abuse, including headaches, ulcers, and high blood pressure that, when left untreated, can lead to strokes and heart attacks. Psychologically, women can suffer from low self-esteem, depression, anxiety, and the constant fear of another attack.

One of most serious acts of violence is referred to as "femicide," defined by Diane Russell as the murder of women simply because they are women (Russell 1990). Femicide can result from domestic violence, rape, actions to protect the family honor, dowry practices, or female infanticide. Measuring the extent of femicide is difficult; data collection is often unreliable and many family members and jurisdictions hide the occurrences by defining these deaths in some other way. For example a husband might be angry with his wife so he sets her on fire while she is in the kitchen; he subsequently claims that it was a tragic kitchen fire. Studies conducted in Australia, Bangladesh, Canada, Kenya, Thailand, and the United States have documented incidents of femicide as a result of domestic violence (United Nations 1996).

In order to eliminate domestic and other violence against women, the power relationships between men and women must change, and women must have equal rights. Health care clinics and personnel must be available to all women, especially in rural areas of developing countries, to recognize and treat injuries from acts of domestic violence. The education system must begin to teach children at an early age about human rights and the proper relationships between men and women.

Public awareness campaigns must provide information regarding treatment for victims of domestic violence as well as legal enforcement of statutes and international conventions. Men can participate in public awareness campaigns, teaching other men that violence is not acceptable. Governments must outlaw all forms of domestic and other violence and support those laws with sufficient law enforcement officers who are required to uphold the law no matter what cultural norms and customary laws suggest. Problems with the reliability of data hamper researchers' ability to gather and interpret data regarding violence against females and better data collection and tracking systems must be adopted to accurately measure the incidence and prevalence of domestic violence acts.

Dowry

Dowry is defined as the financial and material goods that a bride's family provides to the groom's family as payment for the marriage of their daughter into the groom's family. Despite the passage of the Dowry Prohibition Act in India in 1961, which banned the payment of a dowry, and a later amendment in 1983, which prohibited dowry deaths, dowry demands and dowry murders persist in India.

Families of both brides and grooms continue to believe in and practice dowry for a variety of reasons. Because male children are valued over female children, the bride's family may believe that the cost of the dowry is worth moving her out of the family so that she is no longer their responsibility. In India's strong patriarchal society in which men traditionally control all aspects of women's lives, female children are generally considered a burden rather than an asset. They are seen as unable to provide income to their birth family or support their parents, and, if unmarried and living at home as young adults, they may bring shame to their family, as outsiders may view them as women who are unwanted or of no value to any man. For the groom's family, demanding and receiving dowry provides them with financial benefit along with any additional value the bride may provide to the groom's family. It indicates to the family that the groom is a worthy husband, and provides compensation to the groom's family in the event that the wife is an "economic liability" in their view, that is, if she does not bring value to the family by bearing sons or providing income to the family. If the groom's family chooses to provide the bride with only limited amounts of food and other necessities, they gain additional financial benefit by minimizing their expenses.

In India, the Dowry Prohibition Act of 1961 prohibited the request, payment, or acceptance of any sum presented as a requirement for marriage. The penalty for demanding dowry is up to two years in prison and a 10,000 rupee fine. If a person is caught and convicted of advertising that a dowry must be provided, he or she could be imprisoned for between six months and five years and also be liable for a 15,000 rupee fine. In 1983, authorities amended the Act to include additional protection for women; a husband or the relative of a husband could receive a punishment of up to three years in prison and a fine if convicted of subjecting the wife to cruelty, such as any action likely to seriously injure her or drive her to suicide. In 1986, the Indian Penal Code was amended to provide a penalty for causing the death of a woman within the first seven years of her marriage if it can be demonstrated that she had been subjected to cruelty during the marriage.

Despite these and other laws designed to protect women from domestic violence and murder, many families of brides continue to pay dowry to their husbands and their families. In a country steeped in tradition, these practices are difficult to overcome, especially in rural areas of the country. Many families are not aware of the law and of the recourse available to wives and their families of origin. There are few incentives for the bride's family to report dowry requests or dowry murders to the authorities because cultural traditions or customary laws condone these practices. In many cases, the authorities are aware of what is going on but have little reason to intervene.

Demands for dowry may continue during the marriage in order to enhance the husband's social status or simply to gain additional material goods. The husband or his family may need additional funds, goods, or property, and ask the wife's family to provide these items. The wife's safety may be threatened if her family does not comply or the husband or his family may threaten to return her if her family does not pay.

Health Care

Problems women face regarding health care generally relate to reproductive health issues, including access to contraceptives and abortion, high rates of maternal mortality, prevention and treatment of sexually transmitted diseases including HIV/AIDS, and health care during pregnancy and childbirth. This section examines issues surrounding the provision or lack of availability of health care to women and consequences that result when women are denied access to basic health care. The issue of abortion is examined in the following section on controversies.

Two major factors impact the availability of health care to women in developing countries: the availability of health care workers and facilities and the cultural norms that may not allow women to have control over their lives or their health care decisions. The shortage of health care workers, including doctors, nurses, and midwives, according to the World Health Organization, covers all areas except Europe, and the shortfall is approximately 4.3 million skilled medical personnel. A survey conducted by WHO estimates that Africa has over 24 percent of the world's disease but only 3 percent of its health care workers, while North America, the Caribbean, and Latin America account for only 10 percent of the global disease but have 37 percent of the world's health care workers (WHO 2006).

Health care workers frequently prefer to work in urban areas because of the availability of higher income, better equipment and facilities, better living conditions, and the active social life present in urban areas. Women—and men—living in rural areas often do not have access to health care because of a lack of local facilities or the limited staffing of those facilities, lack of transportation to reach existing facilities, lack of income to pay for the services provided, and other poverty-related reasons.

Cultural and religious practices also influence the ability of a woman to seek out health care. Some religious and cultural traditions dictate that a woman cannot be examined by a male physician or is only allowed to go to the doctor when accompanied by her husband or other male relative. In patriarchal cultures the woman may have no power to decide on her own whether to seek medical or other care, and may not have access to financial resources to pay for that care.

Family Planning

According to various estimates, approximately 67,000 women die each year as a result of unsafe abortions, and 97 percent of these women are living in developing countries (Sedge et al. 2007). Many of the rest of the 20 million women who have had unsafe abortions are faced with the resulting health issues caused by these unsafe procedures. If family planning services were more widely available, many women would have other options beside an unsafe and illegal abortion.

Family planning services provide one of the most cost-effective means to improve the health of women in developing countries; in areas where family planning services are available and utilized, rates of maternal and child mortality and transmission of HIV/AIDS between mother and child are lowered and women are more likely to actively participate in their health and pregnancy decisions. Yet family planning information and services are unavailable to many women, especially in developing countries. What factors limit women's access to these services?

First, women have to be allowed to learn about and use family planning services if they are available. Young girls in many cultures are not taught about their bodies, especially their reproductive systems, because cultural traditions valuing modesty and virginity deny them this knowledge (Murray 2008). Many women do not have the ability to control their reproductive choices because they live in cultures in which their husbands make all the decisions about sexual relations, pregnancy, and family responsibilities. When women are provided with knowledge concerning family planning, have these services available, and are able to use contraceptives, their chances for living a healthy life are greatly improved.

Second, the many barriers to accessing family planning services must be removed. In addition to limited knowledge about the use and value of contraceptives and cultural and religious beliefs that are contrary to any type of family planning, the ability to travel to health care facilities must be improved. Many developing countries lack the infrastructure to make travel to these facilities simple and inexpensive. Even if a woman has control over the decision to use contraceptives, if she does not have control over the family's resources she will be less likely to be able to travel to a health care facility.

Maternal Mortality

Pregnancy and childbirth are dangerous periods for a woman in a developing country. Although maternal mortality has received increased attention throughout the world and many efforts have been made to lessen the danger to women, pregnancy and childbirth remain one of the most dangerous threats to a woman's health and life, and to the health and life of her child. According to a UNICEF report on maternal and child mortality, approximately 1,500 women die each day as a result of complications from pregnancy and childbirth (UNICEF 2008a).

Millennium Development Goal No. 5 is to improve maternal health and to reduce the 1990 maternal mortality rate by 75 percent by 2015 and to achieve universal access to reproductive health care by 2015. In 1990, the maternal mortality rate for all developing regions was 480 per 100,000 live births. In 2005, the rate was 450 maternal deaths for every 100,000 live births. Based on current trends, this goal will not be met.

As in other areas of concern regarding the status and conditions of women in developing countries, statistics on maternal mortality are inconsistent, often unreliable, and difficult to gather. Since 1990, the World Health Organization, UNICEF, and the UN Population Fund (UNFPA) have cooperated in pooling resources to determine a more accurate estimate of maternal mortality around the world. In 2006, these organizations were joined by the World Bank. Other researchers have also been working on data collection techniques to create better, more accurate estimates. Even the statistics for developed countries are not reliable or consistently measured.

Maternal mortality rates that are provided vary from region to region, suggesting that some regions of the world are more successful than others in reducing mortality. South Asia reduced its rate from 650 to 500 maternal deaths per 100,000 live births, East Asia and the Pacific reduced their rate from 220 to 150, and Latin America and the Caribbean reduced their rate from 180 to 120 maternal deaths per 100,000 live births. The area having the most difficulty in reducing maternal mortality is sub-Saharan Africa; the rate in West and Central African countries stayed the same between 1990 and 2005 (1,100 maternal deaths for every 100,000 live births), while Eastern and Southern African countries were able to reduce their rates slightly, from 790 to 760 maternal deaths per every 100,000 live births (WHO, UNICEF, UNFPA, and World Bank 2007).

Most maternal deaths occur between the third trimester and the first week after giving birth. Several conditions can cause death at this stage, including infections, eclampsia, post-partum hemorrhage, and problematic or prolonged labor. Complications from an abortion can also contribute to the death of a woman. These conditions are exacerbated by the lack of skilled health care personnel and equipment in many developing countries. Other factors may contribute indirectly to the woman's death, including anemia, iodine deficiency, malaria, diabetes, and HIV/AIDS (UNICEF 2008a).

Other factors also play a role in contributing to maternal mortality. Prenatal care is accessed by fewer than half of all pregnant women in South Asia and sub-Saharan Africa (United Nations 2009). Limited access to health care personnel and facilities is a reality for many women in developing countries, especially in rural areas. Without trained health personnel to monitor their pregnancies and provide guidance regarding proper nutrition and other important pregnancy-related health issues, women may encounter a variety of problems. Many women may not have access to healthy food to provide proper nutrition. Without any education or knowledge about their bodies, women may be unaware of the problems that can arise during a pregnancy or are unaware of ways to remedy these problems. Poverty and gender discrimination also are factors limiting women's access health care facilities and services.

Several suggestions have been made regarding ways to improve the chances of survival for pregnant women in developing countries. A crucial one regards providing access to family planning so that women and their husbands can make conscious decisions regarding children; women must have a choice when it comes to becoming pregnant. Easily accessible prenatal care including general health guidance as well as information specific to pregnancy is critical because having medical personnel available to guide and monitor a pregnancy can make a huge difference in whether a woman survives her pregnancy and delivers a healthy baby. Provision of other medical and health-related services such as immunizations, nutritional counseling and vitamins, and insecticide-treated mosquito netting to protect against malaria will also help to keep the expectant mother healthy. Emergency obstetric care should be available within a reasonable distance in case women experience serious symptoms. The presence of a skilled medical professional, a doctor, nurse, or midwife at the time of delivery offers women a safety net in case an unexpected problem arises. Finally, postnatal visits to ensure that women understand how to care for their children and to answer any health questions they have about themselves and what they are experiencing will give many women confidence.

There are also nonmedical suggestions for improving maternal survival. Women and their families need access to water and sanitation to keep them healthy. Providing girls with access to education can empower them to understand their bodies and take charge of their health, along with many other benefits. Training in life skills and what to expect during their pregnancies will provide women with the knowledge to understand their experiences and the ability to cope when situations arise in which they need to seek medical help.

The experience of Sri Lanka has been studied by many NGOs and foreign governments because of that country's success in reducing maternal mortality, among other improvements the government was able to make in the lives of its citizens. During the early 20th century the Sri Lankan government focused on offering universal and improved health care to its citizens, and then added specific provisions to improve the lives of women and children. Between 1947 and 1950, the rate of maternal mortality was reduced by half. Maternal mortality was cut in half again thirteen years later, and continued to be halved every 6 to 11 years. Overall, Sri Lanka's maternal mortality rate dropped from 340 to 43 per 100,000 live births between 1960 and 2005 (Padmanathan et al. 2003; UNICEF 2008b).

Prostitution and Sex Trafficking

Prostitution and sex trafficking continue to be major issues concerning women in developing countries. The total number of people trafficked (men and women, for sex and other reasons) is estimated at 12.3 million (U.S. Department of State 2010); the number of female sex trafficking victims is estimated by the United Nations to be between two and four million every year. Sex trafficking is defined as "a commercial sex act [that] is induced by force, fraud, or coercion or in which the person induced to perform such an act has not attained 18 years of age" (U.S. Department of State 2010). While some women may voluntarily become involved in prostitution, the majority are coerced into this activity.

Locating and protecting victims of all forms of trafficking, including sex trafficking, is difficult. When they arrive in their destination country, they are often unable to speak the language, do not understand cultural practices, and are not aware of organizations that might be able to assist them. They are often captives of their traffickers, not allowed out or given opportunities to escape. If they were tricked into believing that they were traveling to a new country with the promise of paid employment, they may be embarrassed and reluctant to admit to anyone that they have been victimized.

Large organized crime syndicates are involved in many trafficking operations. They use many tactics to prevent victims from leaving, including debt-bondage, violence or threat of violence, food and sleep deprivation, threats of rape, or threats of deportation. When victims have entered a country illegally, they are less likely to be able or willing to go to the authorities for protection. In fact, traffickers may threaten victims with reporting them to the local authorities if they do not adhere to the traffickers' demands (Program for Appropriate Technology in Health 2002).

Many laws have been enacted to prevent all forms of trafficking, including the Protocol to Prevent, Suppress and Punish Trafficking in Persons, Especially Women and Children (the Palermo Protocol), which supplements the UN Convention against Transnational Organized Crime. This protocol focused the world's attention on the problems and extent of human trafficking and helped nations begin to work together to combat all forms of trafficking. Most countries have also enacted laws to criminalize trafficking within their borders. In order to effectively combat all forms of trafficking, these laws must be enforced and programs developed to assist trafficking victims.

HIV/AIDS and Other Sexually Transmitted Diseases

Throughout the world, HIV/AIDS is one of the primary causes of death and disease among women in their reproductive years (UNICEF 2009). Sub-Saharan African women have been particularly hard hit; girls between the ages of 15 and 24 are three times more likely than boys their age to be infected with HIV (UNAIDS 2004). Why are women more likely to be infected with HIV/AIDS than men and what can be done to protect them?

A variety of biological and cultural/social factors play a role in women's increased vulnerability. Physiologically, during vaginal intercourse, a woman has a greater amount of soft tissue that can be exposed to the virus. If a woman has unprotected sexual intercourse with her husband or other male partner, she is at increased risk; condoms may not be available to her, her husband may not want to use a condom, or she may not be able to refuse sexual intercourse.

The highest rates of HIV/AIDS are generally found in countries and cultures that experience the highest gender inequality, where women are subordinate to men and are generally unable to control the incidence of sexual intercourse with husbands or partners. In fact, in many of these cultures men are encouraged, or at a minimum not discouraged, from having sexual relations with women outside of their marriage. For example, over 90 percent of the 1.7 million women living with HIV/AIDS in Asia were infected by their husbands or partners while in long-term relationships (UNAIDS 2010).

Women, especially in many areas of developing countries, may have other sexually transmitted infections (STI) that have not been treated, either because doctors and health care facilities are not locally available or because these infections have few symptoms and women are unaware that they are infected (Lamptey et al. 2006). STIs may lower a woman's ability to fight off additional infections such as HIV/AIDS.

Women and girls can also be infected as a result of forced sexual encounters. The incidence of sexual assault on girls in school is increasing; one reason why girls leave school without completing their educations is because of sexual assaults on them, especially by teachers. One study conducted in South Africa determined that teachers perpetrated 33 percent of the sexual assaults on girls under the age of 15 (Jewkes et al. 2002).

Girls who are married while still in their teens are more likely to become infected with STIs, including HIV/AIDS. They are likely to have unprotected sexual intercourse with their husbands, who in many cases have more sexual experience than they do, which increases their chances of becoming infected. Older men who marry young girls are likely to be the patriarchs of the family and their wives are not in a position to insist on the use of condoms.

Treatment of HIV/AIDS may be difficult to find and too expensive to use. Cultural prohibitions against women going to male physicians may hinder a woman's ability to receive treatment. Prevention is also difficult in many areas of the world. Aside from the physical options to prevent HIV/AIDS, such as the use of condoms and refusal to have sexual relations with someone who insists on not using protection, there are also societal causes that need to be addressed. Governments and NGOs must continue their promotion of gender equality in all areas and must increase women's economic independence and encourage legal reforms regarding discrimination against people living with HIV/AIDS, as well as upholding the principle of human rights for all.

Women and Work

Women's contribution to the economy in developing countries is undervalued because their domestic work, including agricultural work growing crops to feed their families, is not viewed as income-generating work. In some cases, when women find employment working for someone else they provide income to their families, but they may also suffer from hazardous working conditions, especially in developing countries. The growth of microcredit programs has helped many women to support themselves and their families through the creation of income-generating self-employment opportunities.

According to the ILO (2009), three billion people were employed throughout the world in 2008 and 40 percent of them were women. Worldwide, 17 percent of women are employed in industry, 40 percent in services, and 43 percent in agriculture. Within sub-Saharan Africa, 71 percent are in agriculture, 23 percent in the service industry, and only 6 percent in industry.

Ability to Work Outside the Home

For many women in developing countries, working outside the home is not an option. In some cases, they spend most of their time on household tasks, such as child care, cooking, crop farming (growing food for the family's consumption), and in rural areas, gathering water and fuel for cooking. In other cases, women are not allowed to work outside the home for religious or cultural reasons; their husbands may forbid them to do so, or may allow them to work only in specific areas or for a limited amount of time. Again, in rural areas, there may be a limited amount of income-producing jobs.

When examining women's opportunities for employment outside the home in the paid employment sector, we must account for differences in urban and rural areas. Urban areas offer many more job opportunities for women, while in rural areas, income-producing jobs may be scarce and the competition for them fierce. In rural areas, women often spend more time on fulfilling their families' basic needs, including gathering fuel for cooking, gathering water, caring for children, cooking, and other basic tasks. Even if jobs are available, many women may not have the time or energy to work outside the home.

According to the ILO (2002), the majority of new employment opportunities have occurred in the informal sector of the economy. These jobs are the most insecure and lowest paying, usually without benefits and without protection through government legislation, labor agreements, or other types of agreements or legislation. Informal sector jobs are generally jobs that are "under the radar" in terms of what are considered primary income-producing work and include domestic labor or piece-rate work, such as making a set number of items for a set price (Chant and Pedwell 2008; Carr and Chen 2002). According to one study, the average number of jobs for all nonagricultural employment in developing economies/countries in the informal sector is 24 percent, with rates of 70 percent in sub-Saharan Africa and 47 percent in the Middle East and North Africa (Charmes 2009). In developing countries, women account for 60 percent of all workers in the informal sector (Chen et al. 2005). Poor women who work in the informal sector are exposed to health and safety risks, dangerous working conditions, sexual and other types of violence, lack of infrastructure, unequal pay, and other potentially harmful conditions (Chant and Pedwell 2008). Women who work in the informal sector often have no alternative in terms of finding work and therefore employers are able to take advantage of them, not only paying them exploitative wages but also endangering their lives through poor working conditions and violence (United Nations 2009b).

Gender Gap in Pay and Positions

Women overall are paid 16 percent less than men for the same work, and the gap would be larger if salary information from the informal sector were available and included in these statistics (International Trade Union Confederation 2008). The percentage varies from country to country, but the evidence clearly demonstrates that women are discriminated against solely because they are women when it comes to salary. Even educated women in developed countries often do not fare better because of their education.

Microenterprise

Microfinance has become in recent years a powerful tool for helping poor individuals, primarily in developing countries, gain access to capital in order to create income-generating projects. Loans ranging from $25 to $100 in some of the poorest regions of the world have changed lives by giving their recipients the opportunity to lift themselves out of poverty and create profitable self-employment opportunities. Many of the programs that have been set up to provide these loans also provide education and training to their recipients, including training on setting up a small business, basic financial information, marketing techniques, and other related training.

But how successful are these programs? They tout individual successes in their public relations materials but only a few rigorous studies have been conducted to measure their success rate and the results are mixed. When a poor family is attempting to start a small business from their home other factors can come into play and influence the success or failure of the program. For families living in poverty, a microloan to start a business can bring income to the family and provide the basic necessities. However, if a serious illness strikes the loan recipient or another member of the family, any economic gains the family realized could be gone.

Several programs have been established that play a large role in providing microloans to individuals. The Grameen Bank provides services to poor landless women in Bangladesh. More than two-thirds of all villages in Bangladesh are covered by this bank, which provides banking and other financial services as well as skills development. Formed by the Self-Employed Women's Association of India, the SEWA Cooperative Bank has one main office and mobile credit officers. The bank works with rural credit groups and provides individual loans and group lending to rural associations. The Banco Solidario in Ecuador is a commercial bank that offers a variety of services, financial as well as nonfinancial, to clients. Programs are continually being established to offer a wide range of microloans, literacy training, and business development help.

Women's World Banking (WWB) is a global network of over 50 institutions that provides credit, savings, and business services to women. The network offers technical assistance and the local affiliates provide direct financial services to their clients. FINCA International is another affiliate network of nongovernmental organizations in Latin America, the Caribbean, and Africa. Affiliates provide credit through village banks; the main offices provide loan capital and technical assistance. The World Council of Credit Unions, located in Washington, D.C., is a network of 17,000 credit unions in 67 developing countries. Another affiliate network is Friends of WWB/India, an NGO with a national network of grassroots NGOs that provide financial services to poor rural women. The organization offers technical assistance and loan support to NGOs and organizes credit and savings groups.

Land Ownership and Property Rights

Women play a pivotal role in agricultural activities around the world. They run farm activities as well as work on farms, but often they have no rights to the land they farm. They often have no access to credit to help support their agricultural activities. Governments of several countries, such as Mali and Liberia, have enacted legislative reforms to provide ownership rights to women. But have changes to laws in these countries actually been put into practice? Are women better off now than they were 10 or 20 years ago, before governments enacted laws giving them the right the own land?

Women have an increased burden in the rural areas of many developing countries; in addition to all their household duties, many husbands have migrated to urban areas in search of jobs and income to support their families, leaving their wives responsible for working the land. In many areas, women are responsible for growing food crops, that is, food to feed their families, while men are more involved in the growing of cash crops, meaning crops that will be sold to provide income for the family. In other areas, women are heavily involved in both food and cash crops. In many cases, this may be an important distinction when it comes to providing women with the rights to land ownership, because when women own the land and grow cash crops, they are viewed as a business, thereby providing value to themselves, their families, and their communities. They are empowered by being able to decide what is grown, how much is grown, and are able to set the price for their crops.

International laws provide for women's rights to land and other natural resources. For example, the Universal Declaration of Human Rights states that women have the right to own property (Articles 2 and 17) and the right to adequate food (Article 25). The Convention on the Elimination of All Forms of Discrimination against Women (CEDAW) gives women the right to own property (Article 15), the right to "equal treatment in land and agrarian reform" (Article 14[2][g]), and the right to adequate living conditions, which include water rights (Article 14[2][h]). The International Covenant on Economic, Social and Cultural Rights provides women with the right to adequate food (Article 11).

In 1998 the Sub-Commission on the Promotion and Protection of Human Rights of the United Nations passed Resolution 15, which encouraged governments to repeal laws that discriminated against women in the acquisition of land. This resolution declared that such discrimination was a violation of human rights law. Principle 20 of the Rio Declaration noted the critical role that women play in the management and development of natural resources, stating that their participation is critical to the success of sustainable development.

Various regions of the world have also adopted resolutions and conventions to encourage individual countries to reform their positions on women's access to land and other natural resources. For example, the Protocol on the Rights of Women in Africa encourages a gender perspective in legislation enacted in all African countries including equal spousal rights with regard to property and the rights of women to acquire property, to have access to land, to have equal property rights upon divorce, and to have the right to inherit land upon the death of a spouse or other family member. However, while this Protocol and other African legal documents encourage women's equal rights when it comes to land and other natural resources, other instruments do not provide women with these same protections and do not discourage discrimination against women. For example, the African Charter on Human and Peoples' Rights guarantees the right to property without discrimination (Articles 2 and 14); however, it does not specifically refer to equal spousal rights in marriage and it promotes the protection of traditional African values in local communities (Articles 17[3] and 18[2]).

With this international encouragement of anti-discrimination laws to provide land ownership rights to women, are women better off today than they were before these types of laws were enacted? While legislation has given women rights in many areas of land and resource ownership and management, traditional practices have not always gone along with these changes.

In Africa, Asia, Latin America, and other developing regions, customary or traditional law exists alongside statutory law. Statutory laws have given women greater property rights regarding land acquisition and ownership, management decisions, and inheritance, but customary laws and practices have often made these rights difficult to enforce. For example, in Mali, statutory law provides women with equal property rights; however, traditional and customary laws give men the edge in property matters. In Tanzania, all property is owned by the government but statutory law provides both men and women with the right to use and transfer land. Implementation of the law is difficult, however, in large part because many women are unaware of it (U.S. Department of State 2009).

In Central and South America, the American Convention on Human Rights (ACHR), entered into force in 1978, provides the right to use and enjoy property without discrimination based on sex, as well as the equality of rights within marriage. However, in practice, the vast majority of women do not own land in many countries—for example, less than 25 percent own land in Brazil, Mexico, Nicaragua, and Peru (Mason and Carlsson 2005). Some women have started social movements within their countries to fight for property and land rights and have often been successful; some of these movements include Moviemento dos Trabalhadores Sem Terra in Brazil, the Federación Hondureña de Mujeres Campesinas in Honduras, and the Asociación Nacional de Mujeres Campesinas e Indigenas in Colombia (FAO undated).

Women's legal rights to ownership of land in Central and South America can also vary among and within countries. For example, in Mexico civil laws vary from state to state, while in Brazil civil laws are created at the national level and apply across the country. But even though women may have rights through international law and the statutes in their own country or state within the country, community and local norms and customary laws often dictate their reality. For example, studies reveal that in rural areas in Mexico the eldest male son is usually the one who inherits the land upon the passing of the father, while daughters often inherit only if they do not receive any dowry at the time of their marriage (Quintana et al. 1998).

In the Middle East and Northern Africa, the Arab Charter on Human Rights recognizes every person's right to own private property without discrimination based on gender, but in practice this provision is not enforced by the individual states. Most land ownership and land succession practice is based on Shari'a law, which generally discriminates against women in its focus on the male as the unquestioned head of the family. The position of women is somewhat better in countries such as Tunisia, which has enacted laws that, while incorporating the Shari'a standards, provide some relief to women. Women are allowed to control their own property although succession rights are still given to the male in the family (FAO undated).

In sub-Saharan Africa, the African Charter on Human and People's Rights guarantees the right to property without discrimination and directs individual African states to eliminate all discrimination against women. In reality, however, few women hold title to land in sub-Saharan Africa and when they do own land, they usually own less land than men; this limited amount of land ownership is based on legal factors as well as cultural factors and customary laws.

Property rights and natural resources law vary widely across Asian countries. For example, in Pakistan and Bangladesh, the law is predominantly based on Shari'a law, while in Central Asian countries such as Kyrgyz Republic and Uzbekistan land inheritance goes to the head of the household, and in India, land succession largely depends on location and religious affiliation. In many of these countries, statutory law is generally not enforced when it comes to land ownership and succession; rather, customary and religious laws and practices dictate the right of ownership and succession.

Overall, property ownership and succession rights in developing countries do not often favor women. Customary and religious laws provide guidance over statutory laws. In order to change laws and practices that discriminate against women regarding land and property issues, women must become involved in local, state, and national governments in order to influence legislation. They need to have basic access to education in order to become knowledgeable regarding land and natural resources issues in their local communities and countries. Public education activities should focus on educating men on the benefits of providing these rights to women, empowering them, for example, to become more involved in every stage of crop production. Local social movements such as those in Latin America may be effective in turning public opinion in favor of women's rights. The statutory laws already enacted must be enforced, which will require a change in perception of the customary and religious laws and practices.

Information and Communications Technologies

Information and communications technologies (ICTs) comprise a variety of information, telecommunications, and network technologies. They are tools used to handle information, that is to produce, store, process, distribute, and exchange information. Information technologies involve computers, including hardware and software. Telecommunications technologies include older tools, such as telephones, radios, and television. Network technologies include the Internet, mobile phones, satellite communications, VoIP (Voice over Internet Protocol), and other developing broadband connectivities (Association for Progressive Communications 2003).

The growth of ICTs has been enormous and rapid in recent years. In the last two decades, the Internet and other ICTs have changed the way many people receive and send information and communicate with each other. Mobile phone technology advances and the widespread availability of the Internet have led to increasing numbers of users, and the number of people using social networking sites has increased dramatically. The effects of these technologies can be seen around the world.

At the UN World Conference on Women in Nairobi in 1985, participants realized the importance of technology and its potential to assist women around the world; however, media representations of women had a history of not fulfilling that potential. According to the Forward-looking Strategies for the Advancement of Women (1985), "It is expected that the ever-expanding communications network will be better attuned than before to the concerns of women and that planners in this field will provide increasing information on the objectives of the Decade – equality, development and peace – on the Forward-looking Strategies, and on the issues included in the sub-theme – employment, health and education" (para. 30).

Participants at the Fourth UN World Conference on Women in Beijing in 1995 also saw opportunities for women in the growing technology industry. A review of the monitoring process set up in Nairobi demonstrated that women's concerns were not resolved; while recognizing the potential for empowerment of women, participants noted that the content, structure, and access to these technologies were not reaching women. Largely as a result of these concerns, the UN began to focus more attention on gender-sensitive ICT policies and projects. It developed the WomenWatch website in 1997 to provide a central source for gender-related information and resources and to promote gender equality and women's empowerment.

By 2000 the WomenWatch website was getting approximately 10,000 hits per month. However, women's participation in ICTs was limited. According to a UN report, women "have been slow to enter ICT-based professions worldwide and have been largely excluded from designing and shaping information technologies.... Traditionally, gender differences and disparities have been ignored in policies and programmes dealing with the development and dissemination of improved technologies." (UN 2001, 295) Women did not benefit from advances in ICTs and were actually found to be disadvantaged by them.

The United Nations held its first World Summit on the Information Society (WSIS) in 2003. Its goal was to develop a plan for addressing issues raised by evolving ICTs in order to develop an information society available to everyone for the sharing of information. While the importance of gender equality in ICTs has been emphasized in subsequent sessions held in 2009 and 2010, reports continue to suggest that more attention should be given to those individuals and organizations working in the areas of women's rights, women's empowerment and gender equality in ICTs. (WSIS 2010).

The term *digital divide* was coined to describe the wide gap in access to ICTs between industrial nations and developing countries. Industrialized nations have made great advances in the availability of many ICTs, while many developing countries are struggling to make these technologies available to their citizens. Traditional forms of ICTs, including television, radio, and telephones are available in most urban areas of developing countries, and somewhat less likely to be found in many rural areas. Newer digital technologies are also found in many urban areas, but less likely in rural areas of developing countries.

There is also a gender divide within the digital divide, in which men are more likely than women to have access to and use ICTs, even though these can be powerful tools in helping women overcome poverty, empower them, and aid in business development. Girls and women living in countries where they have limited access to education also have limited access to ICTs. Many developing countries have little infrastructure for ICTs especially in rural areas or in poor urban areas where the majority of women live. Accessibility to ICTs, especially computers and the Internet, is limited for many women in developing countries because of social and cultural norms that discourage or forbid them from visiting cybercafés or other types of information centers, where access to the Internet is available.

However, accessibility of ICTs to women in developing countries has expanded in recent years. NGOs are developing programs to provide these resources to women. For example, the Grameen Bank developed the first cell phone network in Bangladesh, Grameen Phones, and provided cell phones to women who are able earn a living by selling phone airtime to local villagers. The Asian Women's Resource Exchange (AWORC), an Internet-based network, encourages increased access to ICTs through the development of partnerships and other cooperative approaches. The International Institute for Communication and Development (IICD), a nonprofit organization, uses ICTs to improve the lives of individuals in developing countries. IICD partners with local NGOs and other public and private agencies to provide modern media, including cell phones and computers, for use in education, health, agriculture and government activities. Many NGOs in developing countries have their own websites to provide information to interested individuals and organizations.

The increased accessibility and availability of ICTs have demonstrated their power to improve the lives of many women and men. Politically, this effect is especially clear in the civil unrest seen in 2011 in many countries in North Africa and the Middle East. News reports were filled with images of young people on the streets communicating via cell phones, using Facebook, and tweeting their friends. In response, some governments cut Internet access to rein in protestors, but many individuals were able to continue communicating through Facebook and other social media tools. While women of all ages participated in these civil resistance, including Gigi Ibrahim and Nawal El-Saadawi in Egypt, it is unclear the impact that regime change will have on women. But it is clear that ICTs are changing the way the world communicates.

ICTs clearly have a role in creating social mobilization and change and providing greater access to information throughout the world. They have the ability to empower women, by providing educational and business opportunities, information, and networking opportunities. Yet they are not available equally to women and men in developing countries. Governments and NGOs must develop policies and strategies for making ICTs accessible to all, because men can continue their dominance and control over women if they are allowed to use existing ICTs to reinforce that dominance (Primo 2003). Policymakers must include a gender perspective when developing ICT policies (Buskens and Webb 2009). The use of ICTs in educational settings must be expanded; they can be effective tools in improving the relevance of education in today's digital environment and the quality of education.

Female Refugees and Victims of War

Another issue is the safety of women during periods of internal strife within countries and in refugee camps. Even though women do not normally instigate wars or other conflicts, they are most often the victims; they face additional complications in caring for their families, and they may be separated from family members, displaced from their homes, and raped, tortured, or even killed. In fact, they are often targeted for rape and murder in order to humiliate their male family members and to demonstrate that their enemies have total control. The majority of civilians killed in wars and other conflicts are women and children (Murray 2008).

Women and girls are often targeted for rape and other sexual violence in these armed conflict situations. There are three major reasons for this specific violence. Enemies use rape as a tactic to terrorize women and their families into leaving certain territories. Male family members of victims are humiliated, which serves to break down social norms. When women and girls become pregnant and give birth to a child fathered by a racial or ethnic enemy, the enemy views it as a means to start a new race by purging what they consider the "inferior" race (Nikolic-Ristanovic 2000).

As women and their families flee conflict they are exposed to additional dangers. Finding a safe haven is difficult, predators prey on refugees as they are escaping the violence, and the basic necessities of life are frequently unavailable or in short supply. The Office of the UN High Commissioner for Refugees (UNHCR) is actively involved in protecting women and children in refugee situations. They recognize that everyone is exposed to violence during conflict and war but that women and girls are often targeted because of their sex and their status in society. Sexual violence, including "rape, forced impregnation, forced abortion, trafficking, sexual slavery, and the intentional spread of sexually transmitted infections, including HIV/AIDS is one of the defining characteristics of contemporary armed conflict. Its primary targets are women and girls" (UNHCR 2008, 7).

The UNHCR has developed a five-point action plan to help refugee women gain empowerment in situations of internal displacement. Women are to be included in decision-making in these situations, a system of registration and documentation is to be provided, ways to combat sexual and gender violence are to be developed and implemented, women are to be participants in food distribution, and sanitary materials are to be provided (UNHCR 2008). Women and girls are to be provided with equal access to education, health care, and economic opportunities, and the UNHCR is to develop and implement programs to help shift the power relations between men and women, giving women and girls equality.

As the primary international agency working to protect refugees, the UNHCR examines the role that cultural traditions play in the treatment of women and girls in refugee situations. Because women and girls often have less access to education and less exposure to social situations, spending the majority of their time working in domestic and agricultural activities, they are less likely to seek out and interact fully with authorities and humanitarian workers. Domestic violence is often hidden from humanitarian workers, who must find ways to detect violence and threats of violence and protect women and children. A coordinated approach must be developed with partners, including other agencies and NGOs, to provide protection to women (UNHCR 2008).

Women also play a role in fighting wars and other internal conflicts. In some countries women have played active roles in wars and insurgency movements. More recently, they have participated in terrorist attacks as suicide bombers, willingly or unwillingly giving up their lives. In some cases they may be coerced into these roles with the understanding that authorities would not normally suspect a woman of being a terrorist and willing to kill innocent people. In recent events in Tunisia, Jordan, Yemen, and Egypt, we see women out in the streets protesting repressive regimes and encouraging new governments.

Controversies

Providing all women with basic human rights creates major controversy around the world, not just in developing countries. Emotions run high in debates over many issues regarding women's rights, including the right to have control over one's body, especially in the areas of abortion and female genital mutilation. Protecting young girls from female genital mutilation (FGM), also referred to as female genital cutting, is opposed by many traditionalists. Saving a family's honor by murdering a wife, mother, or daughter who has brought shame to the family is still tradition in many developing countries. This section describes these and other major controversies faced by women in developing countries today.

Female Genital Mutilation

Estimates vary concerning the number of women who have undergone this procedure, ranging from 92.5 million in Africa (Pathmanathan et al. 2003) to 130 million around the world (Population Reference Bureau 2001). It is still practiced in many African countries, several countries in the Middle East, and in parts of Asia, including Indonesia and Malaysia.

The movement to prevent FGM began in African countries in the 1960s and continues today. The Inter-African Committee on Traditional Practices Affecting the Health of Women and Children, as well as many professionals, including physicians and nurses, gather information concerning FGM and advocate an end to this practice. The African Charter on the Rights and Welfare of the Child calls for an end to harmful social and cultural practices. The Programme of Action of the International Conference on Population and Development as well as the Convention on the Rights of the Child also condemn traditional practices that may negatively impact the health of children.

Over the past ten to twenty years, an increasing amount of attention has been focused on FGM and local, national, and international NGOs and governmental bodies have stepped up their efforts to eliminate this practice. Although gathering reliable data is often difficult, based on available statistics the World Health Organization reports that small decreases in the incidence of FGM have been observed recently, and that when the practice does occur, it is increasingly being performed by health care professionals. But FGM remains widespread and the average age at which girls undergo the practice is declining, meaning that the number of girls undergoing this before the age of five is growing (World Health Organization 2009).

Most NGOs view this practice as a human rights violation, similar to other traditional practices that are harmful to women in developing countries. In March 2010, the Economic and Social Council of the United Nations adopted a resolution condemning the practice, recognizing that FGM is a violation of the human rights of women and girls. The practice is seen as an example of the continuing inequality between the sexes and a violation of the individual's right to health, security, and life, as well as the right to be free from torture and cruel, inhumane, or degrading treatment.

There are no known health benefits to the practice but many problems associated with it, including the pain and trauma it causes, and the fact that it interferes with the natural functioning of the female body. FGM leads to long-term health problems including infections, chronic pain, decreased sexual enjoyment, and problems during pregnancy and childbirth. Babies born to women who have undergone the procedure are more likely to die during or immediately after childbirth (WHO Study Group on Female Genital Mutilation and Obstetric Outcome 2006).

While some supporters of the practice argue that it is similar to male circumcision, studies have demonstrated that the benefits from male circumcision include lowering men's risk for contracting HIV/AIDS (Bailey et al. 2007). In fact, many supporters refer to it as female circumcision or female cutting in an attempt to equate it and its effects with male circumcision. However, more and more NGOs and other groups fighting the practice believe that it should be called female genital mutilation because its only effect is to mutilate a girl's body.

If FGM is so harmful and a violation of girls' and women's human rights, why is it still practiced today and why does it appear to have the support of many people, including women? FGM demonstrates the deeply entrenched nature of gender inequality, demonstrating society's control over women. In countries where it is widely practiced, both men and women support it, and those who do not agree are often harassed, condemned, and ostracized; great pressure is put on those detractors to support the practice (WHO 2008). A study conducted by UNICEF revealed a strong correlation between a woman's ability to have control over her life and her belief that the practice of FGM should be ended (UNICEF 2005c).

Some families who practice FGM and other long-held traditions are immigrating to other countries, including the United States, Canada, and many European countries; they frequently continue practicing their cultural traditions in their new country, and many of these countries are now enacting legislation to prohibit what they view as harmful practices. France has had issues with Muslim women wearing burqas, and the government is especially concerned with this practice when the women are driving because of the problem of limited vision. See Chapter 3 for a discussion of issues facing the United States and other countries.

Abortion

Abortion is an emotional topic for many people throughout the world. In the United States, demonstrators picket clinics where abortions are performed, threaten the lives of workers in those clinics, and even murder doctors who perform abortions. Most people see this as a black or white issue; there is no middle ground. On the one hand, supporters of abortion argue that a woman's body is her own, that she should have control over what happens to her, and that basically this is a human rights issue. Meanwhile, detractors believe that abortion is murder; that the fetus should also have rights, specifically the right to life; and that women should have considered the risk of becoming pregnant before engaging in sexual activities.

For women in developed countries such as the United States, abortions are generally readily available. Women may choose not have abortions due to their religious beliefs, the insistence of their husbands or boyfriends that they carry the fetus to term, the cost of an abortion, the embarrassment or scorn of their families or friends, or other personal reasons. However, the option is available to them. Women in developed countries also are more likely to have access to contraception and therefore are able to limit their chances of becoming pregnant.

Women in developing countries may not have options. In rural areas of many developing countries, health clinics may not be available for basic health needs, much less for abortions. Religious beliefs may not permit abortions. Husbands in strong patriarchal societies may forbid their wives from aborting a fetus. Many developing countries, such as Nicaragua, Chile, Honduras, and other countries in Latin America, as well as Egypt, Angola, Senegal, Somalia, and other countries in Africa, have enacted laws banning abortions completely (see Chapter 6 for complete list). Other countries may permit abortion only to save the life of the pregnant woman, or to protect a woman's mental health, on socioeconomic grounds, or without restrictions.

But abortions are performed around the world, in every country, whether or not it is legal to do so. In some countries, statutory laws allow abortions but customary laws do not. In other countries, abortion under certain circumstances may be allowed, but in actuality, abortion services are available only in urban areas or in limited rural locations.

Unsafe abortions are a major health concern throughout the world, but especially in developing countries. Unsafe induced abortions are the leading cause of female mortality. These are the most preventable maternal deaths. Abortions by themselves are not responsible for women's deaths; abortions that are unsafely performed are the cause of death. According to a World Health organization study conducted in 2003, approximately 70,000 of the 500,000 maternal deaths were the result of illegal abortions (WHO 2003). Unfortunately, in countries that have made abortion illegal, women who find themselves pregnant sometimes go to extreme measures to terminate a pregnancy.

According to one report, only 22 percent of the world's 190 countries allow abortion, and only 6 percent of developing countries do (WHO 1999). Abortion policies vary from country to country; each country's policy is influenced by several factors, including religion, birth rates, and population policies. Countries with large numbers of Muslims or Roman Catholics tend to restrict or prohibit abortion. Countries may watch their birth rates and, as they drop, institute laws restricting abortion.

Honor Killings

One of the most extreme forms of domestic violence is the killing of a woman allegedly to save her family's or community's honor. It is most often practiced in the Middle East and South Asia. Many of these countries have statutory laws against honor killing, but traditional or customary law permits the practice. Considering it a harmful cultural practice, several countries, including Kuwait and Iran, have prohibited it, but have minimized the penalties associated with it.

In Egypt, the law does not specifically prohibit honor crimes and no reliable statistics exist regarding its extent but it is believed to occur, especially in rural areas. In Iran, a husband is allowed to kill his wife if she is caught in the act of adultery and if he is certain that she was a willing partner. In Iraq in 2008, 117 women reportedly died as a result of honor killings; Iraqi legislation considers killing to preserve the family's honor as a mitigating circumstance when sentencing (U.S. State Dept. 2009). In Jordan, the criminal courts established a special criminal court tribunal to hear all cases involving honor crimes and have issued some serious sentences for those found guilty; however, the government has made no changes to its current statutes to improve sentencing guidelines, which allow judges to consider honor killings as "crimes of passion" even when premeditated. While honor crimes are prohibited by law in Kuwait, the Kuwaiti penal code allows the crime to be reduced to a misdemeanor. In Lebanon, a male can receive a reduced sentence if he can prove that the victim was involved in a socially unacceptable sexual relationship. In India and Pakistan, honor killings continue to be a problem, with 73 crimes reported in India and over 600 in Pakistan in 2009 (U.S. State Dept. 2009).

As is clear from the above examples, honor killings may be considered crimes, but perpetrators are often able to get off with light sentences or even their freedom if they can prove it was a crime of passion. NGOs are working with the governments in many countries to create public awareness campaigns to educate the public regarding this practice and to convince them that honor killings truly are crimes. Tracking the number of incidents and determining the number of victims is difficult; few governments keep statistics on these crimes, which may be disguised as other types of crime. Meanwhile customary law and tradition continue to permit and, in many cases, encourage the murder of women for "dishonoring" their families.

Solutions

It is easy to say that laws should be enacted and enforced to ensure that women receive equal rights with men and protection against discrimination. However, in many cases and in many countries, governments have enacted laws and signed UN Conventions but continue to allow abuse and other discriminatory behaviors. Governments must enforce the laws that have been enacted, overriding customary law and traditions.

In order to protect women from discrimination and provide them with equal rights in all aspects of their lives, governments can take several additional actions. First, they can enact laws that prohibit discrimination against women and grant them equal rights. However, even when these actions are taken, customary laws and traditions frequently permit citizens, including family members, to abuse women, deny them their rights, and even murder them. Public awareness campaigns must be initiated to educate the public on the wrongness of denying women equal rights and to highlight the benefits of providing these rights. Public attitudes must be changed to encourage equal treatment for women.

Women must be provided with access to education and economic opportunities to give them more power to determine the course of their lives. Existing NGOs should work with governments to change public attitudes about the detrimental effects of denying women access to education, health care, and employment opportunities. Successful NGOs should be showcased, demonstrating to men and women that women, given freedom and opportunity, are able to contribute to society, support their families, and improve the standard of living without detracting from the quality of men's lives.

References

Abawi, Atia. 2009. "Afghan Girls Maimed by Acid Vow to Go to School." CNN.com/Asia. Available at http://www.cnn.com/2009/WORLD/asiapcf/01/22/acid.attacks/index.html?iref=allsearch.

Amin, Sajeda, and Lopita Huq. 2008. "Marriage Considerations in Sending Girls to School in Bangladesh: Some Qualitative Evidence." *Policy Research Division Working Paper No. 12.* New York: Population Council.

Association for Progressive Communications. 2003. *ICT Policy: A Beginner's Handbook.* Johannesburg: APC.

Bailey, R. C., S. Moses, C. B. Parker, K. Agot, I. Maclean, and J. N. Krieger. 2007. "Male Circumcision for HIV Prevention in Young Men in Kisumu, Kenya: A Randomized Controlled Trial." *Lancet* 369: 643–656.

Bannister, Judith. 2003. *Shortage of Girls in China Today: Causes, Consequences, International Comparisons, and Solutions.* Washington, D.C.: Population Reference Bureau.

Buskens, Ineke and Anne Webb, eds. 2009. *African Women and ICTs: Investigating Technology, Gender and Empowerment*. New York: Zed Books.

Carr, Marilyn, and Martha Chen. 2002. *Globalization and the Informal Economy: How Global Trade and Investment Impact on the Working Poor.* Working Paper on the Informal Economy No. 1. Geneva: ILO.

Chant, Sylvia, and Carolyn Pedwell. 2008. *Women, Gender and the Informal Economy: An Assessment of ILO Research and Suggested Ways Forward.* Geneva: ILO.

Charmes, J. 2009. "Concepts, Measurement and Trends." In *Is Informal Normal? Towards More and Better Jobs in Developing Countries,* edited by Johannes Jutting and Juan de Laiglesia. Paris: Organization for Economic Cooperation and Development (OECD).

Chen, Martha, Joann Vanek, Francie Lund, and James Heintz, with Renana Jhabvala and Christine Bonner. 2005. *Progress of the World's Women 2005: Women, Work and Poverty.* New York: UNIFEM.

Clark, S., J. Bruce, and A. Dude. 2006. "Protecting Young Women from HIV/AIDS: The Case against Child and Adolescent Marriage." *International Family Planning Perspectives* 32(2): 79–88.

CNN.com/Asia. 2010. "Taliban Suspected of Sickening Female Afghan Students." Available at http://www.cnn.com/2010/WORLD/asiapcf/04/25/afghanistan.school.illness/index.html?iref=allsearch.

Food and Agriculture Organization. N.d. *Gender and Law: Women's Rights in Agriculture.* Rome: Food and Agriculture Organization.

International Labour Organization. 2002. *Decent Work and the Informal Economy.* Report VI, 90th Session of the International Labour Conference. Geneva: ILO.

International Trade Union Confederation. 2008. *The Global Gender Pay Gap.* Brussels: ITUC.

Jewkes, R., et al. 2002. "Rape of Girls in South Africa." *Lancet* 359: 319–320.

John, Mary E., Ravinder Kaur, Rajni Palriwala, Saraswati Raju, and Alpana Sagar. 2008. *Planning Families, Planning Gender: The Adverse Child Sex Ratio in Selected Districts of Madhya Pradesh, Rajasthan, Himachal Pradesh, Haryana, and Punjab.* New Delhi: International Development Research Centre.

Lamptey, Peter R., Jami L. Johnson, and Marya Khan. 2006. "The Global Challenge of HIV and AIDS." *Population Bulletin* 61(1): 1–24.

Mason, K. O., and H. M. Carlsson. 2005. "The Development Impact of Gender Equality in Land Rights." In *Human Rights and Development,* edited by P. Alston and M. Robinson. Oxford: Oxford University Press.

Mathur, S., M. Greene, and A. Malhotra. 2003. *Too Young to Wed: The Lives, Rights and Health of Young Married Girls.* Washington, D.C.: International Center for Research on Women.

Murray, Ann Firth. 2008. *From Outrage to Courage: Women Taking Action for Health and Justice.* Monroe, ME: Common Courage Press.

Nikolic-Ristanovic, Vesna. 2000. *Women, Violence and War: Wartime Victimization of Refugees in the Balkans.* Budapest: Central European University Press.

Pathmanathan, Indra, et al. 2003. *Investing in Maternal Health: Learning from Malaysia and Sri Lanka.* Washington, D.C.: The World Bank.

Population Reference Bureau. 2001. *Abandoning Female Genital Cutting: Prevalence, Attitudes, and Efforts to End the Practice.* Washington, D.C.: Population Reference Bureau.

Primo, Natasha. 2003. *Gender Issues in the Information Society.* Paris: UNESCO.

Program for Appropriate Technology in Health. 2002. *Reproductive Health and Rights: Reaching the Hardly Reached.* Washington, D.C.: PATH.

Quintana, R. D., L. Concheiro Borquez, and R. Perez Aviles. 1998. *Peasant Logic, Agrarian Policy, Land Mobility, and Land Markets in Mexico. North American Series, Working Paper 21.* Madison: University of Wisconsin.

Russell, Diana E. H. 1990. *Rape in Marriage.* Bloomington: Indiana University Press.

Save the Children. 2004. *Children Having Children: State of the World's Mothers 2004.* Westport, CT: Save the Children.

Sedge, G., S. Singh, S. Henshaw, E. Ahman, and I. Shah. 2007. "Induced Abortion: Estimated Rates and Trends Worldwide." *Lancet* 370: 1338–1345.

Sen, Amartya. 2001. "Many Faces of Gender Inequality." *Frontline* 18(22), October/November.

World Health Organization. 2005. *WHO Multi-country Study on Women's Health and Domestic Violence against Women.* Geneva: WHO.

World Health Organization. 2006. *World Health Report 2006: Working Together for Health.* Geneva: WHO.

World Health Organization. 2008. *Eliminating Female Genital Mutilation: An Interagency Statement—OHCHR, UNAIDS, UNDP, UNECA, UNESCO, UNFPA, UNHCR, UNICEF, UNIFEM, WHO.* Geneva: WHO.

World Health Organization. 2009. *Women and Health: Today's Evidence, Tomorrow's Agenda.* Geneva: WHO.

WHO Study Group on Female Genital Mutilation and Obstetric Outcome. 2006. "Female Genital Mutilation and Obstetric Outcome: WHO Collaborative Prospective Study in Six African Countries." *Lancet* 367: 1835–1841.

WHO, UNICEF, UNFPA, and the World Bank. 2007. *Maternal Mortality in 2005: Estimates Developed by WHO, UNICEF, UNFPA, and the World Bank.* Geneva: WHO.

United Nations. 1985. *Forward-looking Strategies for the Advancement of Women* (A/CONF.116.28/Rev.1). Available at http://www.un.org/womenwatch/confer/nfls/Nairobi1985report.txt.

United Nations 2001. *From Beijing to Beijing+5.* New York, NY.

United Nations. 2009a. *The Millennium Development Goals Report 2009.* New York: United Nations.

United Nations. 2009b. *2009 World Survey on the Role of Women in Development.* New York: United Nations.

United Nations ECOSOC. 1996. *Report of the Special Rapporteur on Violence against Women.* E/CN.4/1996/53. New York: ECOSOC.

UNAIDS. 2004. *2004 Report on the Global AIDS Epidemic: 4th Global Report.* Geneva: UNAIDS.

UNAIDS. 2010. *Annual Report 2009.* Geneva: UNAIDS.

UNHCR. 2008. *UNHCR Handbook for the Protection of Women and Girls.* Geneva: UNHCR.

UNICEF. 2005. *The State of the World's Children 2006.* New York: UNICEF.

UNICEF. 2005b. *Early Marriage: A Harmful Traditional Practice.* New York: UNICEF.

UNICEF. 2005c. *Changing a Harmful Social Convention: Female Genital Mutilation/Cutting.* Florence: Innocenti Digest.

UNICEF. 2008a. *The State of the World's Children 2009: Maternal and Newborn Health.* New York: UNICEF.

UNICEF. 2008b. *Sri Lanka: Annual Report 2007.* Colombo: UNICEF.

UNICEF. 2009. *ChildInfo: Monitoring the Situation of Children and Women.* New York: UNICEF.

UNICEF Innocenti Research Centre. 2000. *Domestic Violence against Women and Girls.* Florence, Italy: UNICEF Innocenti Research Centre.

U.S. Department of State. 2009 Country Reports. Available at http://www.state.gov/g/drl/rls/hrrpt/.

U.S. Department of State. 2010. *2010 Trafficking in Persons Report.* Washington, D.C.: U.S. Department of State.

WSIS. 2010. WSIS *Forum 2010: Final Executive Briefing*. Available at http://www.itu.int/wsis/implementation/2010/forum/geneva/report/final_exec_briefing_full.html

3

U.S. Concerns

This chapter examines issues and controversies of central concern to the United States regarding women in developing countries. It will consider immigration, both legal and illegal, including immigration policies; trafficking of women and children into the country; asylum requests from women in developing countries, specifically the reasons women give when asking for asylum or refugee status; and the current immigration and court rulings regarding asylum. It will also review the history of the Mexico City Policy, often referred to as the Global Gag Rule, along with its effect on women in developing countries. Finally, it will look at the effects of the United States' failure to ratify the Convention on the Elimination of All Forms of Discrimination against Women (CEDAW).

Of course, the basic issues of survival and the prevention and elimination of discrimination and violence against women throughout the world are also of concern to the United States. The government, through the Department of State and its Agency for International Development and other aid programs, helps support vital programs to assist women in developing countries gain access to education, health care, and the other critical needs discussed in Chapter 2. This chapter, however, will focus on internal issues and concerns of the United States as they relate to the lives of women who leave developing countries, whether voluntarily or involuntarily.

Immigration

Policies regarding immigration to the United States have frequently been a controversial topic, with strong views on all sides of the subject concerning the numbers of immigrants allowed to enter and from which countries. Economic conditions in other countries, a relative abundance of jobs available in the United States, at least historically, and the persecution of various individuals and groups by governments or others in power in developing countries encourage many individuals and families to attempt to enter the United States.

From the 1965 Immigration and Nationality Act, which eliminated country-specific quotas and increased the total number of immigrants permitted to enter the country, to the Refugee Act of 1980, which broadened the definition of allowable refugees and allowed 125,000 refugees annually, lively debate has surrounded the issue of immigration in the United States. The 1986 Immigration Reform and Control Act legalized approximately 2.7 million unauthorized aliens and instituted penalties against employers who knowingly hired illegal aliens in an attempt to stop the flow of illegal immigrants into the country. The 1990 Immigration Act raised the annual limit on immigrants from 270,000 to 700,000 during the years 1992 through 1994 and to 675,000 from 1995 on, allowed unlimited visas for immediate family members of U.S. citizens, and stipulated that the 125,000 allowed refugees would not be counted as part of the total number of allowed immigrants.

In 1996, the Illegal Immigration Reform and Immigrant Responsibility Act of 1996 (Public Law 104-208) (IIRIRA) was enacted to place more responsibility on immigrants, including those requesting asylum, and on the authorities responsible for enforcing the law. It emphasized heightened border enforcement; increased penalties for transporting undocumented aliens into the country, both willingly and for involuntary servitude; described acceptable practices for examining, arresting, imprisoning, and removing deportable aliens; delineated allowable parameters of alien employment; solidified the government's role in assisting aliens; and contained various other stipulations.

IIRIRA makes the asylum process more difficult for many aliens by, among other requirements, (1) barring aliens from applying for asylum if they are able to move to a third country that has a fair asylum process and where their freedom would not be threatened;

(2) requiring applications for asylum to be filed within one year of entering the United States, with certain exceptions; (3) not allowing reapplication if an alien's first application has been denied unless the circumstances have changed; (4) denying asylum to certain convicted criminals and those who have participated in persecuting others; (5) requiring certain applicants to submit fingerprints and photographs; and (6) authorizing application fees.

The act also specifically defines female genital mutilation (FGM), requires that information be provided to all aliens who are issued immigrant or nonimmigrant visas concerning the harm to physical and psychological health caused by FGM, prohibits the practice on anyone under the age of 18 years, and subjects anyone who performs FGM to fines and/or imprisonment of not more than five years. The IIRIRA also addresses the "mail-order bride" business. It requires international matchmaking organizations to provide information to foreign spouses regarding immigration regulations; this information is to be provided in the spouse's native language and explain conditional permanent residency and domestic violence statutes. It also requires the explicit disclosure that matchmaking organizations are not regulated by the U.S. government.

Asylum

Every year, thousands of people apply for political asylum or refugee status in the United States. In order to qualify, an individual must first meet the definition of a refugee: "[A]ny person who is outside any country of such person's nationality or, in the case of a person having no nationality, is outside of any country in which such person last habitually resided, and who is unable or unwilling to return to, and is unable or unwilling to avail himself or herself of the protection of that country because of persecution or a well-founded fear of persecution on account of race, religion, nationality, membership in a particular social group, or political opinion ..." (Immigration and Nationality Act, Section 101[a][42]).

The United States may grant asylum to individuals who are currently in the country and, for specific reasons, are unable or unwilling to return to their native country. Individuals seeking asylum are required to request it at an airport or other port of entry or file an application within one year of their arrival in the United States. If circumstances change in their home countries or their personal circumstances have changed within the year before they ask for asylum and those circumstances have changed their eligibility for asylum, they may be granted additional time to file their applications. Additional time may also be allowed if extraordinary circumstances exist that prevent individuals from filing their applications within one year. Once individuals are granted asylum, they can apply for a Green Card and eventually for U.S. citizenship. As of 2011, the annual cap on the number of people granted asylum is 10,000.

Refugee Status

The U.S. government can grant individuals located outside of the United States refugee status if their lives or freedom are being threatened or if they are being persecuted. Individuals also must prove that their home governments are unwilling or unable to protect them from persecution. Most frequently, applicants for refugee status are referred to the U.S. Refugee Program by officials of the UN High Commissioner for Refugees; other individuals are referred by U.S. embassies or consulates. When they enter the United States, authorization is given allowing them to become employed. After they have been in the country for one year, they are eligible for an adjustment in their status to lawful permanent resident. They are eligible for U.S. citizenship after five years.

Determination of Asylum

Two primary ways exist to obtain asylum. Affirmative asylum cases are processed through the U.S. Citizenship and Immigration Services (USCIS). Applicants apply for asylum affirmatively by completing an application for asylum and sending it to a USCIS Service Center. Interviews are conducted in a nonadversarial manner by USCIS asylum officers located in one of eight Asylum Offices throughout the country, or in an office closer to the individual's residence. The USCIS attempts to interview the applicant within 43 days of the filing of the application and a decision is generally rendered within two weeks of the interview.

Defensive asylum cases are initiated when an applicant is defending herself or himself against removal from the United States; they are processed by Immigration Judges from the Executive Office for Immigration Review (EOIR). The Immigration Judge (IJ) holds a hearing in adversarial proceedings for the applicant's claims as well as the government's arguments against the granting of asylum. An applicant reaches this stage following the denial of his or her application, or upon his or her arrival at a U.S. port of entry without proper travel documents, or because he or she was placed in the expedited removal process and found to have a credible fear of persecution or torture by an asylum officer.

Once a case is heard by an IJ and a ruling issued, the applicant can appeal a negative ruling to the Board of Immigration Appeals (BIA), and then to the appropriate U.S. Circuit Court of Appeals if the BIA issues a negative ruling. Federal courts have generally deferred to the immigration judges but in some cases have overturned the BIA determination.

Derivative Asylum

Many asylum seekers want protection for their families as well as for themselves. Once a person has been granted asylum, he or she is allowed to apply for derivative asylum for a spouse and for children under the age of 21 years. Stepchildren are eligible for derivative asylum if the applicant and the spouse were married before the child turned 18 years old. Adopted children are required to have been adopted before they turned 16 years old and the applicant must have been the legal parent of the child for at least two years. The applicant must seek derivative asylum within two years of the date he or she was granted asylum.

Reasons for Asylum

Women in developing countries often have a number of reasons for wanting to apply for asylum in the United States or another developed nation. They may suffer persecution simply because they are female: they are beaten or sexually assaulted by their husbands or other male family members, they are raped and then blamed for causing their families dishonor, they or their daughters are victims of female genital mutilation, trafficked for sexual purposes or forced labor, or exposed to other physical dangers or life threatening situations. However, current asylum law does not allow an application based solely on gender; an individual must request asylum based on alleged persecution based on her race, religion, nationality, particular social group, or political opinion. U.S. laws and the Department of Homeland Security are reluctant to recognize the unique types of persecution that women in developing countries face, such as female genital mutilation, or rape or torture, especially in conflict situations, even though international law does recognize these issues (Goeller 2007).

Female Genital Mutilation

Fear of female genital mutilation is one reason women and other family members apply for asylum, and immigration officials and courts have supported several requests for asylum in recent years, often considering FGM as severe harm that constitutes persecution of a particular social group.

Several BIA and appellate court cases have reviewed asylum cases regarding FGM, with mixed results. The case *In re Fauziya Kasinga* provided a key ruling on FGM as a legitimate reason for a claim of persecution under the asylum regulations. Fauziya Kassindja (her name was incorrectly recorded by immigration authorities) was a 19-year-old citizen of Togo, a member of the Tchamba-Kunsuntu tribe. Young girls in Togo usually undergo FGM at age 15 but she was protected by her father, who opposed this practice. Upon his death in 1993, her aunt became the family matriarch and forced Kassindja into a polygamous marriage in 1994 at the age of 17. Her 45-year-old future husband, who had three other wives, required that she undergo FGM prior to the consummation of the marriage. She did not want to undergo the procedure and, with the help of her sister, fled to Ghana and then to Germany. There she was befriended by a Nigerian who suggested she purchase his sister's British passport and travel to the United States. She purchased the passport and landed at Newark International Airport on December 17, 1994, where she immediately requested asylum.

Kassindja filed her completed application for asylum in April 1995 and was detained by the INS until April 1996. In her request for asylum, she claimed that because Togo was a small country, her husband and aunt would have little trouble finding her with the help of the police. She would not have been able to find any safe place in her country or in Ghana because her family and her husband could track her within Togo or to Ghana with the help of the authorities. She did not want to remain in Germany because she did not speak German, nor did she have any relatives in Germany. She did have an aunt, uncle, and cousin in the United States.

The immigration judge determined that Kassindja's reasons and support for her application were not credible and denied her request for asylum. She appealed the decision to the Board of Immigration Appeals (BIA), who found Kassindja to be a credible witness. The BIA adopted the description of FGM as defined in the record and agreed that "this level of harm can constitute 'persecution' within the meaning of section 101(a)(42)(A) of the Act, 8 U.S.C. § 1101(a)(42)(A)(1994)" (*In re Fauziya Kasinga* 1996, 365). Further, they found that "the particular social group to be the following: young women of the Tchamba-Kunsutu Tribe who have not had FGM, as practiced by that tribe, and who oppose the practice" (*In re Fauziya Kasinga* 1996, 365). The BIA granted Kassindja's request for asylum. Following the ruling in Fauziya Kassindja's case for asylum and the outrage over the initial ruling in her case and her treatment by the INS, the BIA issued a determination in 1996 that asylum could be granted to a woman based on her fear of female genital mutilation. This case was a landmark in asylum law for women who feared FGM but it did not provide help for every woman.

The situation for women who had already undergone FGM was seen as different from women like Kassindja, who had not yet undergone the practice. In *Oforji vs. Ashcroft*, the Seventh Circuit Court of Appeals upheld the Immigration Judge's determination that because she had undergone FGM before coming to the United States, "there is no chance that she would be personally tortured again by the procedure when sent back to Nigeria" (*Oforgi vs. Ashcroft* 2003, 615). The opinion set a stringent standard for review, ruling that because she had already undergone the procedure there was no fear of further persecution. When she raised the fear that her two daughters, born in the United States and therefore U.S. citizens, would face FGM if they were sent back to Nigeria with her, and that she had no one to leave her children with, the court reasoned that the children had the legal right to remain in the United States and therefore had no bearing on Oforgi's argument for remaining in the country. She could not make a derivative asylum claim given the fact that her daughters were U.S. citizens, but the court recognized the dilemma faced by Oforgi. It indicated that the under the current law "a woman who is otherwise a deportable alien does not have any incentive to bear a child (who automatically becomes a citizen) whose rights to stay are separate from the mother's obligation to depart" (*Oforji vs. Ashcroft* 619).

In another Seventh Circuit case, *Olowo vs. Ashcroft* (2004), Olowo applied for asylum based on her inclusion in a social group composed of women who feared FGM, although she had already undergone the procedure. She also argued that her two daughters, who were legal permanent residents of the United States, would be forced to return to Nigeria with her and faced the prospect of being forced to undergo FGM. The court's decision was consistent with *Oforji vs. Ashcroft*; it ruled that Olowo could not make a claim for asylum based on her past experience with FGM and that, because her daughters had the option of legally remaining in the United States, they would be able to avoid FGM. The court also reasoned that if Mr. Olowo returned to Nigeria with his family, he would be able to protect his daughters from undergoing FGM. Alternatively, Mr. Olowo could stay with his daughters in the United States and therefore protect them from FGM.

Women who have already undergone FGM were having a more difficult time requesting asylum based on FGM because, as one court determined, FGM is an act that cannot be repeated; once a woman has undergone FGM, she will not be threatened with it again. As the Oforji and Olowo decisions make clear, some parents have argued that they have a derivative asylum claim because their children may face FGM if the parents are deported. When the children are U.S. citizens this becomes a difficult decision for the parent, but it does not expose the daughters to forced deportation with their parents.

Prior to the Oforgi decision in 2003, there were no court decisions regarding the deportation of a parent who feared that his or her daughter would be forced to undergo FGM upon return to her or her parents' native country. Following the Oforgi and Olowo decisions, and as more parents began to request asylum based on their fears that their daughters would be exposed to FGM, immigration judges, the BIA, and U.S. appellate courts began seeing more cases regarding persecution of women as victims of FGM and the follow-up requests for derivative asylum.

In *Abay vs. Ashcroft* (2004), Yayeshwork Abay and her nine-year-old daughter Burhan Amare were natives and citizens of Ethiopia and in 1996 requested refugee status in the United States based on Abay's fears that Amare would be circumcised. Abay had already been a victim of FGM, performed by her mother, and was afraid for her daughter. Abay's three other daughters were still living with her mother in Ethiopia; the mother had attempted to circumcise them but was stopped by Abay. However, Abay was afraid that she would not be able to prevent the circumcision of her other daughters once they were married or promised in marriage. She could still protect Amare. The IJ and BIA denied their request for asylum and the case was appealed to the U.S. Sixth Circuit Court of Appeals.

The court concluded that, given the evidence that FGM is condoned and practiced nearly universally throughout Ethiopia, the fact that Abay had been a victim, her mother had already attempted to subject her daughters to the practice, Abay could not protect her daughters from the wishes and actions of their future husbands, and Ethiopia does not enforce laws to prohibit certain harmful practices, "a rational factfinder would be compelled to find that Abay's fear of taking her daughter into the lion's den of female genital mutilation in Ethiopia and being forced to witness the pain and suffering of her daughter is well-founded" (642).

Other appellate courts have supported the findings of the Seventh Circuit and issued similar rulings. For example, in *Mohammed vs. Gonzales* (2005), Mohammed was 17 years old when she applied for asylum, claiming she had a fear of future persecution based on her membership in a social group (the Benadiri clan). Mohammed and her family fled Somalia for Ethiopia following the disappearance of her father and brother, the rape of her sister, and the militia's attempt to imprison all members of her clan. Following her arrival in the United States, Mohammed requested asylum. The Immigration Judge denied her request because she did not demonstrate that she was eligible for asylum, entitled to withholding or protection under the Convention against Torture. The BIA affirmed the decision of the IJ.

Mohammed appealed the decision of the BIA, claiming that her attorney at the time failed to present evidence of her past experience with FGM in order to establish past persecution. The Ninth Circuit Court of Appeals ruled that the BIA did not review all the evidence; the case was remanded back to the BIA to examine the evidence of past FGM. The court found that "persecution in the form of female genital mutilation is similar to forced sterilization and, like that other persecutory technique, must be considered a continuing harm that renders a petitioner eligible for asylum, without more" (3085). Further, the court determined that "genital mutilation permanently disfigures a woman, causes long term health problems, and deprives her of a normal and fulfilling sexual life" (3086).

Overall, the United States has made progress in asylum law, but according to Schubert (2007), still must protect the rights of women who do not want to return to their native countries because of their fear of FGM. She encourages further improvements in the law regarding asylum. As a member of the United Nations, the United States has a responsibility to protect all human rights while remaining sensitive to particular cultural practices. This need for sensitivity has created a dilemma for many people regarding FGM and other "cultural" practices because of the concern of labeling it an illegal and immoral act. Some individuals who have undergone the practice argue that it is a legitimate cultural practice. In fact, women who have undergone the practice are often the ones who arrange for their daughters to undergo FGM. Some argue that it should be referred to as "female circumcision" to remove the negative connotation.

The federal law that prohibits FGM provides that "no account shall be taken of the effect on the person on whom the operation is to be performed of any belief on the part of that person, or any other person, that the operation is required as a matter of custom or ritual" (18 USC § 116[c]). This prevents the perpetrator from arguing that it is a legitimate cultural or religious practice. International law and conventions, including the Convention on the Rights of the Child, protect children from inhumane treatment; in this respect, FGM violates international human rights law (Aherne 2006).

Domestic Abuse, Rape

Domestic abuse, including rape, is a frequent occurrence in many developing countries. It is most likely to occur in situations where the balance of power between the sexes is overwhelmingly in the male's favor and sex discrimination against women is considered legitimate. The first case to come before an immigration judge, the BIA, and ultimately, the U.S. Attorney General, was the *Matter of R-A-*.

The *Matter of R-A-* concerned the case of Rodi Alvarado, a native and citizen of Guatemala. Married at 16 to a 21-year-old former soldier, Alvarado was consistently physically and sexually abused by her husband. He controlled every aspect of her life; she attempted to flee several times from him, but each time he tracked her down and beat her, often to the point of unconsciousness. She enlisted the help of the Guatemalan police, who at first issued summonses to her husband; he ignored them, and the police did not follow up. Calls to the police did not result in any action. Alvarado went before a judge and complained, but the judge told her that he would not interfere in domestic disputes. Finally, with help, Alvarado was able to flee Guatemala for the United States, where she requested asylum.

The Immigration Judge ruled in Alvarado's favor, granting her asylum based on her past persecution and well-founded fears of future persecution. The IJ defined her membership in a social group as "Guatemalan women who have been involved intimately with Guatemalan male companions, who believe that women are to live under male domination" (*In re Alvarado*, 8). The IJ relied on the decision in the *Matter of Fauziya Kasinga* and ruled that Alvarado, "and others like her, are targeted for persecution specifically because they are women" (*In re Alvarado*, 8).

The INS appealed the IJ's ruling in the Alvarado case, and the BIA in 1999 reversed the grant of asylum to her. While they agreed that the abuse suffered was egregious and that the government of Guatemala had failed to protect her, they determined that she had not established that the harm she had suffered was because of her membership in a particular social group.

The BIA's decision received criticism from a variety of sources and prompted the intervention of U.S. Attorney General Janet Reno and the Department of Justice, who proposed new regulations that would address the issues in *Alvarado* and similar cases. The regulations were never finalized; however, Reno vacated the BIA's decision in 2001 and remanded the case back to the BIA until the proposed regulations became final. In 2003 U.S. Attorney General John Ashcroft certified the case to himself, asking the BIA to send the case to his office. In 2004 the Department of Homeland Security filed a brief with the Attorney General, providing an analytical framework for deciding claims such as Alvarado's and arguing in favor of granting asylum to Alvarado. Ashcroft did not take any action in the case and remanded the case back to the BIA.

In 2008 the Department of Justice regulations remained in draft form and U.S. Attorney General Michal Mukasey took jurisdiction of the case, ruling that the BIA did not have to wait for final regulations and could decide the case. The case was sent back to an Immigration Judge for final determination, and Alvarado was granted asylum in 2008.

In a Second Circuit Court of Appeals case, Carmen Gomez appealed the BIA decision denying her request for asylum on the basis of her membership in a social group consisting of young women who had been beaten and raped by guerrilla forces in El

Salvador (*Gomez vs. INS* 1991). Between the ages of 12 and 14, Gomez's life was threatened and she was raped and beaten by guerrilla forces, who also vandalized her home; this occurred on five separate occasions.

Gomez entered the United States illegally and made her way to New York, supporting herself with a variety of odd jobs. At one point, unable to pay her rent, she resorted to selling cocaine. She pled guilty to the criminal sale of a controlled substance and other indictments. The INS sought her deportation back to El Salvador; she requested asylum, and an Immigration Judge conducted a hearing on the INS request. The IJ ordered her deported to El Salvador and the BIA upheld the deportation order. The Second Circuit agreed with the IJ and BIA rulings, indicating that Gomez was unable to produce evidence that women who had previously been attacked by guerrilla forces could be identified as members of a particular social group and were in continuing danger.

In the case of L-R-, a woman from Mexico lived with a man to whom she was not married; when she became pregnant with their child she attempted to escape her partner's physical abuse. He found her, assaulted her, and forced her to return home. She complained to the police, who told her that her problems were private and they did not believe her life was in danger. She fled to the United States but did not apply for asylum within one year of her arrival because she did not know she could. She applied "within months" of her arrival. She claimed that her particular social group was "Mexican women in an abusive domestic relationship who are unable to leave." The IJ believed her fears and reasons for asylum were credible, but nevertheless denied asylum based on her failure to meet the requirement to apply within one year of arrival.

The case was appealed to the BIA and, in addition to the briefs filed by the parties, the Department of Homeland Security filed a supplemental brief. This brief acknowledged that the DHS believed that persons who have experienced domestic violence could be granted asylum and that "DHS accepts that in some cases, a victim of domestic violence may be a member of a cognizable particular social group and may be able to show that her abuse was or would be persecution on account of such membership. This does not mean, however, that every victim of domestic violence would be eligible for asylum" (DHS Brief, 12). The case was sent back to an IJ to allow LR to submit additional materials.

Religion

Applications for asylum based on religion are often difficult to prove for women in developing countries and these claims are not used as frequently as claims based on membership in a particular social group. In 2002, the Seventh Circuit Court of Appeals heard the case of *Nazani Yadegar-Sargis vs. INS,* in which the plaintiff was an Iranian woman who claimed her particular social group was Iranian women of the Armenian Christian faith who chose not to wear traditional Islamic dress. She argued that she was not able to freely practice her religion, and that the state would not protect her from harassment and other problems she faced by refusing to wear the traditional dress. The court ruled that, while Yadegar-Sargis had proved that she was a member of a particular social group, she did not prove that she suffered from persecution because of that membership; she was never detained, imprisoned, or physically threatened. The court agreed with the BIA ruling that while Ms. Sargis's experiences were deplorable, they constituted harassment, not persecution.

Forced Marriage

In 2006 the U.S. Court of Appeals for the Second Circuit heard the appeal of Hong Ying Gao, who had fled from China to the United States seeking asylum based on her membership in a particular social group, in this case "women who have been sold into marriage (whether or not that marriage has yet taken place)" (*Gao vs. Gonzales* 70). Prior to fleeing to the United States Gao had lived in Fujian Province, in an area where parents would routinely sell their daughters into marriage and the local residents and authorities supported and enforced these forced marriages. She was promised in marriage to Chen Zhi in exchange for a monetary payment; Gao's parents used this money to pay off their debts and promised their daughter to Zhi when she turned 21. Gao discovered Zhi to be bad-tempered, violent, and a gambler, and attempted to break the agreement. Zhi refused and followed her when she moved away from her district. Zhi continued to harass her family, insisting that Gao marry him, and discovered her new location. She fled to the United States approximately six months later.

The IJ determined that Gao's situation did not meet a protected ground such as membership in a particular social group but was only "a dispute between two families." The Judge also found that the record did not establish that the local authorities would not protect Gao and that she did not require asylum because she was able to safely move to another location. The BIA affirmed the IJ's determination. The Second Circuit Court of Appeals reversed the IJ and BIA rulings and remanded it back to the BIA for additional proceedings consistent with the Court's ruling. The Court defined Gao's particular social group as consisting "of women who have been sold into marriage (whether or not that marriage has yet taken place) and who live in a part of China where forced marriages are considered valid and enforceable." It also ruled that Gao established a nexus between the particular social group to which she belonged and the persecution she feared, and vacated the findings that Gao had not established that the government would not protect her and that she was able to safely relocate in another area. This decision was the first of its kind focusing on forced marriages.

Overall, women have generally had a difficult time gaining asylum in the United States because they are not able to apply simply on the basis of being a woman and because they face discrimination or violence in developing countries. Immigration authorities are increasingly accepting claims within the "membership in a particular social group" as a valid reason for granting asylum, but more must be done to allow women fearing further persecution in their native countries to claim asylum simply because of their gender. Even the UN High Commissioner for Refugees encourages the use of "membership in a particular social group" to protect female asylum seekers as long as they meet the definition of a refugee (UNHCR 1994).

Detention While Awaiting Asylum Determination

The history of detention of immigrants to the United States goes back to the 1890s, when the detention center at Ellis Island was opened. As a result of the passage of the Immigration and Nationality Act (INA) in 1952, detention facilities, including Ellis Island, were eventually closed. Immigrants who posed a danger to society or were considered a flight risk were still held in other federal facilities.

The United States supported the UN Refugee Convention adopted in 1951 and the follow-up Protocol adopted in 1951, and enacted the Refugee Act of 1980 to comply with these conventions. The government and many NGOs have been strong supporters of refugee rights around the world. Almost three million refugees have been admitted to the United States in the past 30 years by the U.S. resettlement program, which has served as a model for other nations (Acer & Chicco 2009).

In the 1990s the U.S. government changed its policy again and instituted detention in order to enforce its immigration policies. With the passage of the Antiterrorism and Effective Death Penalty Act and the IIRIRA in 1996 detention policies were expanded, including detention without bond for many groups of noncitizens. The numbers of detainees grew dramatically between 2001, when 95,000 individuals were detained, and 2009, when 380,000 individuals were detained (see http://www.detentionwatchnetwork.org). The IIRIRA gave inspectors from the Immigration and Naturalization Service (INS) stationed at airports and borders the authority to order the immediate deportation of persons arriving without proper documentation and to detain asylum seekers who qualify for the expedited removal process.

The U.S. Department of Homeland Security (DHS) became responsible for immigration and asylum matters in 2003 following the elimination of the Immigration and Naturalization Service (INS) and amid additional immigration policy changes. The Immigration and Customs Enforcement (ICE) division became responsible for immigration detention and their attorneys represent ICE in asylum hearings, generally opposing the asylum seeker's request. An asylum officer with the U.S. Citizenship and Immigration Services (USCIS) is responsible for interviewing individuals before they are allowed to request asylum.

Under the expedited removal process, individuals seeking asylum can be summarily deported if immigration officers determine that they have arrived in the United States without the proper travel documents. In the past, this decision-making power resided with immigration judges. Many individuals and families fleeing their countries because of some type of persecution do not carry official travel documents with them because their governments would not issue these documents; they have managed to travel to the United States without proper documentation.

The law prohibits asylum seekers who have genuine fears about returning to their native countries from being subjected to expedited removal; however, in practice they are sometimes quickly sent back to their native countries to face an uncertain future. If they are not returned to their native countries, they are faced with mandatory detention until their reason for requesting asylum is determined to be a "credible fear of persecution." If a U.S. asylum officer or immigration judge determines that their fears of persecution are not credible, they are deported; if their fears are determined credible, they are allowed to apply for asylum, but are still detained.

Although one of the DHS duties is to ensure that the United States lives up to its commitments to the international community regarding asylum, many asylum seekers have been detained for months, and sometimes years, in jails and other jail-like facilities without any freedoms. Handcuffed when detained and issued prison-like clothing, many asylum seekers are allowed to visit with friends and family members only through glass partitions; in essence, they are treated as criminals. According to a 2009 report by the General Accounting Office, the average daily population of people detained grew by almost 40 percent from 2003 through 2007 (Acer & Chicco 2009).

The U.S. Commission on International Religious Freedom (USCIRF) studied the facilities used by ICE and the conditions under which detained persons were kept and issued a report in 2005 indicating that the facilities in which detainees were kept were inappropriate for asylum seekers, and that the operating standards were similar to correctional standards (USCIRF 2005). The Commission recommended that asylum seekers should be detained in "non–jail-like" facilities and that standards should be developed that are tailored to the requirements of asylum seekers and survivors of torture.

ICE issued a report in 2008 describing the detention standards that had been developed and would be implemented in 2010 in response to the USCIRF report. These performance-based standards were developed to ensure that asylum seekers in detention are provided with humane treatment, including access to health care services; that their health care needs will be met in a timely manner; and that they are given access to counsel, due process, and other requirements necessary to meet humanitarian concerns.

However, according to a Human Rights First report (2009), the standards continue to be based on standards for correctional systems, such as not allowing detained asylum seekers to wear their own clothes, have access to outdoor activities, have freedom of movement within the facility, or have face-to-face meetings with their families and friends. They are also not permitted to have an immigration court custody hearing to determine their eligibility for release from detention.

Women requesting asylum as a result of their fears of persecution have often escaped from female genital mutilation, forced marriage, forced sterilization, rape, domestic violence, and other serious situations they face in their native countries. They often travel at great peril to the United States to request asylum, only to be detained under demoralizing conditions. Even though the United States has generally supported and protected female refugees and asylum seekers, including through the development of guidelines that help U.S. asylum officers assess women's claims, problems remain.

Women seeking asylum should not be detained if they meet the "credible fear" standard and appear to have a reasonable opportunity of gaining asylum. If they are detained, they should not be shackled and treated like criminals. Women who are responsible for the care of children who have traveled with them to the United States should have access to parole if they present no reason to believe they will flee, supervised release should be used where appropriate, and detention facilities should be improved along with services to detainees. Finally, women coming from countries where male authority is often absolute should be interviewed by female officers and interpreters in order to lessen their fear of male authority figures (Lawyers' Committee for Human Rights 2002).

Guestworker Programs in the United States

The current U.S. program for allowing guestworkers into the country is known as the H-2 program under the Immigration and Nationality Act. Approximately 121,000 guestworkers were brought into the United States by employers in 2005, including 32,000 for agricultural work. According to the Southern Poverty Law Center (SPLC), these workers are not in fact treated as guests but are abused and exploited, and do not have any rights similar to U.S. citizens. They are tied to the employers who brought them into the country, and often have little or no access to legal counsel. The SPLC indicates that they are frequently cheated out of earned wages; coerced into mortgaging their futures in order to be hired for low-wage, temporary jobs; become virtual captives as their employers seize their documents; live in squalid conditions; and are often denied health care (Bauer 2007).

Agricultural workers are brought in under the H-2A program, and nonagricultural workers come in under the H-2B program.

These workers are only allowed to work for the employers that brought them in and are not allowed to bring their families with them. While the H-2A program has some legal protections according to federal law and Department of Labor regulations, similar regulations do not exist for H-2B workers. Even though the majority of these workers are male, women from developing countries come in under these programs and suffer discrimination and sexual harassment. According to a study conducted in 1993 by Maria Elena Lopez Trevino, over 90 percent of female farm workers in California experienced sexual harassment on the job (Ontiveros 2003).

The Equal Employment Opportunity Commission (EEOC) investigated reports of female farm workers subjected to sexual harassment and sexual assault in Fresno, California, in 1995. The investigation determined that hundreds, possibly thousands, of women were forced to have sex with their employers in order to retain their jobs. In one case, the women referred to one field as the "field of panties" because so many women had been raped there by their supervisors (Tamayo 2000).

Women, and men, who come to the United States on H-2 visas have a right to protection from discrimination and abuse; the government must develop labor regulations that protect both H-2A and H-2B workers and afford them legal protection and available resources. The government must develop mechanisms to monitor employers in order to ensure that they comply with guest worker contracts and do not abuse or discriminate against their workers.

Trafficking

Trafficking is a major human rights concern in developing countries and in the United States. The first comprehensive law concerning trafficking in the United States was the Trafficking Victims Protection Act of 2000; its goals were to combat trafficking in persons, ensure punishment of traffickers, and protect victims of trafficking. Two categories of trafficking were defined: sex trafficking and labor trafficking. Sex trafficking includes prostitution, pornography, live sex shows, mail-order brides, military prostitution, and sex tourism. Labor trafficking includes domestic servitude, restaurant work, sweatshop and factory work, agricultural work, and construction.

As in other countries, victims of trafficking within the United States can be U.S. citizens or legal or illegal immigrants who are desperate to support themselves and their families; this desperation leaves them vulnerable to force, coercion, and fraud. Victims need a variety of services to overcome their victimization, including emergency, short-term, and long-term assistance; these needs encompass health care, financial help, housing, counseling, job training, legal assistance, and other key services. International victims within the United States may also need legal help with their immigration status.

Law enforcement authorities have had little success in catching traffickers and protecting victims. As a result, the Trafficking Victims Protection Reauthorization Act of 2003 provided civil remedies for victims; for example, the law gave victims a means to sue their traffickers in U.S. district court. These civil actions enable the victims to hold their traffickers accountable; large financial awards may serve as a deterrent to other traffickers, and these monies can assist victims in recovering from their experiences. However, to date very few cases have been filed against traffickers.

The government must find ways to successfully reach these victims and stop the trafficking. There are many barriers to locating and providing services to victims. Lack of public awareness of the extent of trafficking in the United States, the isolation of victims, their fears related to reporting the crime, and the stigma of sexual exploitation are some of the barriers. Cultural and language barriers also plague immigrants along with illiteracy, making it difficult to reach these victims.

Immigrants' Life in the United States

If women from developing countries who decide, for any reason, to settle in the United States are willing and able to adapt to U.S. culture, their lives may be relatively uncomplicated. If they choose or are required to hold to their cultural beliefs, however, life may be more challenging. For example, if their husbands or other family members require them to maintain cultural practices that are against the law in the United States, they have a difficult choice to make.

In particular, family members may insist that girls and women residing in the United States undergo female genital mutilation, as required by their cultural traditions or for religious or other reasons. The federal government enacted legislation related to FGM in 1995. The Federal Prohibition of Female Genital Mutilation Act defined the practice of FGM as a criminal offense except in instances to protect a person's health, directed the Immigration and Naturalization Service (INS) to provide information concerning the health effects of FGM to all aliens when issuing visas, and required the Department of Health and Human Services to gather information regarding FGM and conduct public awareness and education activities.

The Illegal Immigration Reform and Immigrant Responsibility Act of 1996 criminalized the practice of FGM in the United States, specifying that "whoever knowingly circumcises, excises or infibulates the whole or any part of the labia majora or labia minora or clitoris of another person who has not attained the age of 18 years shall be fined under this title or imprisoned not more that 5 years or both." Exceptions are made to protect the health of the minor or if the operation is performed for medical reasons on a woman who is in labor or who has just given birth. The legislation does not permit the practice on the basis of custom or ritual.

Several states have also enacted laws prohibiting FGM (see Table 3.1). Most states define FGM similarly to the federal legislation's definition. Many states also specify that performing FGM for religious, cultural, customary, or ritual reasons is prohibited.

TABLE 3.1
State Statutes Addressing Female Genital Mutilation

State	Statute	Year Enacted	Age Limit
Arkansas	Ark. Code. Ann. § 9-13-402 (2010). Definitions. Included in the definition of human rights is the protection of children from genital mutilation.	2005	Under 18
California	Cal. Penal Code § 273.4 (2009). Female Genital Mutilation Act. Cal. Health & Saf. Code § 124170 (2010). Establishment of education and outreach activities	1996	Not specified
Colorado	Colo. Rev. Stat. § 18-6-401(b)(I) (2010). Child abuse: specific reference to excision or infibulation, in whole or in part, of a child's labia majora, labia minora, vulva, or clitoris.	1999	Females under 16
Delaware	Del. Code Ann. Tit. 11, § 780 (2010). Female genital mutilation	1996	All ages
Florida	Fla. Stat. Ann. § 794.08 (2010). Female genital mutilation	2007	Females under 18
Georgia	Ga. Code Ann. § 16-5-27 (2010). Female genital mutilation	2006	Females under 18

Idaho	Idaho Code Ann. § 18-1506A (2010). Ritualized abuse of a child: person is guilty of a felony when he "actually or in simulation, tortures, mutilates or sacrifices any . . . human" as part of a ceremony, rite or any similar observance.	1990	Children under 18
Illinois	325 Ill. Comp. Stat. 5/3 (2010). Specifically defines child abuse as committing or allowing to be committed "the offense of female genital mutilation . . ." 720 Ill. Comp. Stat. 5/12-32 (2010). Ritual mutilation 720 Ill. Comp. Stat. 5/12/33 (2010). Ritualized abuse of a child 720 Ill. Comp. Stat. 5/12-34 Female genital mutilation	1998	All ages
Maryland	Md. Code Ann., Health-Gen. § 20-601 (2010). Female genital mutilation	1998	Females under 18
Minnesota	Minn. Stat. § 144.3872 (2009). Female genital mutilation; education and outreach Minn. Stat. § 609.2245 (2009). Female genital mutilation; penalties	1994	All ages
Missouri	Mo. Rev. Stat. §568.065 (2010). Genital mutilation of a female child; penalty	2000	Females under 17
Nevada	Nev. Rev. Stat. Ann. § 200.5083 (2010). Mutilation of genitalia of female child; penalties; definitions	1997	Under 18
New York	N.Y. Penal Law § 130.85 (2010). Female genital mutilation	1997	Under 18
North Dakota	N.D. Cent. Code § 12.1-36-01. Surgical alternation of the genitalia of female minor; penalty; exception	1995	Not specified
Oklahoma	Okla. Stat. Ann. Tit. 21, § 760 (2010). Female genital mutilation	2009	Not specified
Oregon	Or. Rev. Stat. § 163.207. Female genital mutilation Or. Rev. Stat. § 431.827 (2010) Female genital mutilation prevention and education activities	1999	Not specified
Rhode Island	R.I. Gen. Laws § 11-5-2 (2010). Felony assault: includes physical injury that "causes serious permanent disfigurement or circumcises, excises or infibulates the whole or any part of the labia majora or labia minora or clitoris of a person"	1996	All ages
Tennessee	Tenn. Code Ann. § 39-13-110 (2010). Female genital mutilation	1996	All ages
Texas	Tex. Health & Safety Code Ann. §167.001 (2010). Female genital mutilation prohibited	1999	Females under 18
West Virginia	W.Va. Code Ann. § 61-8D-3A (2010). Female genital mutilation; penalties; definitions	1999	Females under 18
Wisconsin	Wis. Stat. Ann. § 146.35 (2010). Female genital mutilation prohibited	1996	Not specified

Many immigrants may be concerned with these laws but nonetheless continue to practice FGM. Watson (2005) explained this anomaly as follows:

> Criminalizing, on its surface, seems a justifiable response for practices that are thought to harm or maim another. Nevertheless, the history of criminalizing, particularly of cultural practices, tends to divert the practice underground, and therefore, lead to more rather than less concerns. Criminalization of such practices is also seen as paternalistic—one society's attempts to evaluate their own practices as the correct or moral ones and negate another culture's practices as lesser or immoral. Statutes requiring educational initiatives rather than criminalization initiatives might be the most appropriate compromise. (435)

The U.S. Congress also enacted legislation as part of the 1997 Omnibus Appropriations Spending Bill requiring U.S. executive directors of international financial institutions "to oppose nonhumanitarian loans to countries where female circumcision was practiced and whose governments had not implemented any educational programs to prevent the practice" (Sec. 579, Omnibus Consolidated Appropriations Act, 1997).

Family Planning Policy

As part of U.S. foreign policy, the U.S. Department of State's Agency for International Development (USAID) makes funds available to foreign countries to assist in furthering the government's foreign policy initiatives. USAID and other government agencies will sometimes attach conditions to the funds given to foreign governments in order to ensure that they will be used to improve the well-being of citizens of developing countries or to encourage the spread and stability of political democracies (Crimm 2007). Abortion has always been a controversial issue, drawing strong emotions on both sides. In recent years, the government has been under increasing pressure from the religious right to overturn *Roe vs. Wade* and prohibit abortion in the United States. The Mexico City Policy, more familiarly known by its opponents as the Global Gag Rule, was a product of this pressure.

Historically, the U.S. government supported family planning services as part of larger global health and population initiatives. Beginning with the Foreign Assistance Act of 1961 and continuing up until the presidency of Ronald Reagan, government aid agencies' support to developing countries included aid to NGOs to provide family planning services. With the Foreign Assistance Act of 1961, research on international family planning and other population concerns was authorized by the U.S. Congress. Family planning policies and programs in developing countries were examined and their relationship to economic development was debated. Supporters of family planning believed that population growth should be limited if developing countries wanted to prosper. Detractors believed that a growing population would provide additional productive capacity and aid economic growth. Family planning was becoming a growing controversial issue.

At the International Conference on Population in 1974, the debate intensified. Many developed countries theorized that high rates of population growth detracted from economic development and interfered with development objectives. Many developing countries disagreed, believing that they would benefit from the additional people entering the work force and becoming productive citizens (Nowels and Veillette 2006). In the United States in 1974 debate over family planning led Senator Jesse Helms, with the urging of the religious right, to sponsor an amendment to the Foreign Assistance Act that prohibited NGOs from using federal funds to provide abortions as a method of family planning. At that time, NGOs were still permitted to use other income sources to provide abortions.

That policy changed at the 1984 International Conference on Population in Mexico City. Developing countries were beginning to believe that high population growth was detrimental to their economic development and a large number encouraged development of family planning programs, many of which included the provision of abortion services. The United States under President Reagan believed that high population growth might not be contrary to economic development and changed direction on policies regarding family planning and abortion. The Mexico City Policy, announced at the 1974 population conference, prohibited USAID from providing funding to foreign NGOs that perform or actively promote abortion as a method of family planning in other countries, even if their funding did not come from the U.S. government.

Politics and policies changed as the occupant of the White House changed. On January 22, 1993, President Clinton rescinded the Mexico City Policy, stating that the "excessively broad anti-abortion conditions are unwarranted. . . . [T]hey have undermined efforts to promote safe and efficacious family planning programs in foreign nations" (Woolley and Peters 2011). Clinton believed that this effort would help stabilize the world's population. At the 1994 Conference on Population in Cairo, U.S. government officials continued to proclaim that the U.S. government was supporting family planning and reproductive health services, including the provision of safe abortions.

However, President George W. Bush reinstated the ban on funding NGOs that promoted or provided abortion services on January 22, 2001. He implemented it by attaching conditions to USAID grant awards, and eventually extended the policy to include "voluntary population planning" assistance that was provided to developing countries by the U.S. Department of State. Bush made it clear that U.S. taxpayer funds should not be used to promote or pay for abortions. However, abortions would be permitted to save the life of the mother or in cases of rape or incest, and family planning counselors in developing countries would also be allowed to provide "passive" responses to questions regarding abortion in cases where pregnant women had already decided to have an abortion. Counselors were also allowed to refer pregnant women to abortion services when their lives were in danger, and in cases of rape and incest. On January 23, 2009, President Barack Obama rescinded the ban on funding NGOs that promoted or provided abortion services, stating that this policy and its restrictions were excessively wide-ranging and had undermined developing countries' attempts to provide safe and effective family planning programs.

Depending on the party affiliation of the current president and the political climate, the policy will likely go through several rounds of rescinding and reinstating as governmental leadership changes. The impact of this on-again-off-again policy on NGOs and developing countries has been devastating. NGO activities, including the providing of reproductive health care and family planning services, have been limited or halted. Some NGOs have closed their doors. NGOs in countries that have legalized abortion have been forced to lay off doctors, nurses and other health care professionals at great cost to their clients; they have cut back their outreach activities, especially in rural areas (Hoodbhoy et al. 2005). In many developing countries, the Global Gag Rule has halted efforts to reform abortion and reproductive health laws. Public awareness activities have been limited, especially in countries where safe abortions are legal and available, depriving many women of the knowledge that abortion is a safe and available option. It also prevents health care professionals from working to lower rates of maternal mortality that result from unsafe abortions (Skuster 2004).

NGOs that receive money from USAID are unable to counsel women on the full range of contraceptive services available to them. In many developing countries the NGOs are the only providers of health care services, including family planning services, to women, especially in rural areas. According to Crimm, it "is horrendous that the GGR [Global Gag Rule] exacerbates the harm to a large, vulnerable audience of women and children about whom this nation should be concerned" (Crimm 2007, 614).

Lack of Ratification by the United States of Key International Conventions

Over time, many countries have looked to the United States for direction in ratifying certain UN conventions and in determining their own governmental policies toward human rights. Citizens in many countries hoped, and continue to hope, that the United States will lead in the fight for women's rights. While the United States and its agencies annually spend billions of dollars assisting governments and NGOs throughout the world, the United States is one of the few countries that have not ratified several key conventions that support women's rights. The Convention that generally garners the most attention is the Convention on the Elimination of All Forms of Discrimination against Women (CEDAW); the Convention on the Rights of the Child is another important treaty not yet ratified by the United States. The lack of ratification of these two conventions is viewed as compromising the credibility of the United States as a world leader in the fight for human rights.

Convention on the Elimination of All Forms of Discrimination against Women

The United States is the only industrialized country in the world that has not ratified CEDAW; other countries include Iran, Sudan, Somalia, Iran, Nauru, Palau, and Tonga. President Jimmy Carter initially signed the Convention within one year of its adoption by the United Nations, but the United States is not bound by its provisions until it is ratified by the U.S. Senate. President Clinton pushed for ratification in 1994 and the Senate Foreign Relations Committee held hearings and recommended ratification to the full Senate. However, the Senate never held a final vote on the measure due to the opposition of Senator Jesse Helms, a noted conservative. President George W. Bush supported ratification early in his presidency and the Senate Foreign Relations Committee again held hearings in 2002 and recommended ratification. Again, a final vote on the Senate floor was never held.

Opponents to ratification include many members of the religious right and other conservatives. They believe that the Convention will threaten the laws and culture of the United States by undermining traditional "family values" and current statutes concerning the family, including parental rights. They believe it will also ensure access to abortion and contraceptives, legalize prostitution, and allow same-sex marriage. Some also believe that it will force employers to pay women a salary equal to men, which they argue will undermine the free market system. Other arguments include the observation that CEDAW does not include any mechanisms for enforcing its recommendations and policies. Many in the government, as well as opponents of CEDAW, believe that women are already protected in the United States from discrimination, including in the Constitution, and therefore do not require any Conventions or other documents to provide them with basic human rights and prevent discrimination.

Supporters believe that it is important for the United States to stand up and show its support for women's rights by ratifying the Convention. In addition, women in the United States, while enjoying many opportunities not available to women in developing countries, still experience discrimination and violence. Women still lag behind men in income, earning only 78 cents for every dollar earned by a man. Despite the passage of the Violence against Women Act, domestic violence currently affects at least 2 million women every year—possibly more since this is an underreported crime. The United States is ranked 41st out of 184 countries on maternal mortality. Based on these facts, supporters urge passage of this Convention. Ratification would also continue the bipartisan tradition in the United States of encouraging and promoting human rights around the world. No costs would be incurred by the government if it ratified CEDAW.

CEDAW provides a roadmap for governments and NGOs to work together to improve the lives of women and eliminate and prevent discrimination and violence against them. Women in many developing countries are successfully working with their governments to achieve gender parity in education, reduce violence against women, provide inheritance rights and property rights to women, and give women the right to vote, and ratification by the U.S. Senate would send a strong message of support to these women, their governments, and local NGOs.

The administration of President Barack Obama has indicated that it supports ratification of CEDAW. On January 5, 2011, a resolution was introduced to the U.S. House of Representatives supporting ratification by the U.S. Senate and indicating that "the full realization of the rights of women is vital to the development and well-being of people of all nations." The bill has 70 co-sponsors and has been sent to the House Committee on Foreign Affairs for further action.

The Convention on the Rights of the Child

The Convention on the Rights of the Child (CRC), adopted in 1989, has not been ratified by the United States; Somalia is the only other country that has not ratified this Convention. The CRC promotes and protects the health and well-being of all children, focusing on children's right to survival; to develop to their greatest potential; to be protected from abuse, neglect, and exploitation; and to participate in family and cultural life.

Similar to the arguments that opponents raise for not ratifying CEDAW, opponents argue that this Convention will override the U.S. Constitution and become the ultimate law of the land. However, just as with CEDAW, the U.S. Supreme Court has already ruled, citing the Supremacy Clause of the Constitution, that no agreement or treaty can override the U.S. Constitution. Again, there are no provisions or requirements for implementing the CRC; each country can determine how it chooses to enforce the CRC provisions. Finally, as with CEDAW, ratification can always be subject to certain reservations, understandings, and declarations—a practice that many other countries have used when ratifying a treaty.

Opponents also believe that the CRC will undermine parental authority by allowing minors to have abortions, choose their own religion, join gangs, and gain unrestricted access to any information they want, including pornography; they believe, furthermore, that it will provide children with the same rights afforded to adults and allow them to sue their parents. One of the major objections opponents have voiced against ratification is that it prohibits the use of capital punishment against children (Art. 37). In 2005, the U.S. Supreme Court found that the use of capital punishment against juveniles was unconstitutional, which effectively removed that argument.

Proponents believe that because the U.S. government, along with NGOs, will be responsible for how the CRC is implemented, there is no danger that the United Nations will override all U.S. laws and control the lives of its citizens, including children. The CRC describes and encourages the important role parents play in the lives of the children, and does not dictate how parents are to raise their children. Children are permitted to practice their religion free from government interference, but parents may guide their children in this respect. Since ratification, many countries have improved access to a variety of programs for children and their families, strengthened programs and policies regarding children's rights, and reformed laws affecting children.

References

Abay vs. Ashcroft, 368 F.3d 634 (6th Cir. 2003).

Acer, Eleanor, and Jessica Chicco. 2009. *U.S. Detention of Asylum Seekers: Seeking Protection, Finding Prison*. Washington, D.C.: Human Rights First.

Aherne, Meredith. 2006. "Olowo vs. Ashcroft: Granting Parental Asylum Based on a Child's Refugee Status." *Pace International Law Review,* Paper 249. Available at http://digital commons.pace.edu/intlaw/249.

Bauer, Mary. 2007. *Close to Slavery: Guestworker Programs in the United States*. Montgomery, AL: Southern Poverty Law Center.

Crimm, Nina J. 2007. "The Global Gag Rule: Undermining National Interests by Doing unto Foreign Women and NGOs What Cannot Be Done at Home." *Cornell International Law Journal* 40: 587–633.

Gao vs. Gonzales, 440 F.3d 62 (2nd Cir. 2006).

Goeller, Cara. 2007. "Forced Marriage and the Granting of Asylum: A Reason to Hope after Gao v. Gonzales." *William and Mary Journal of Women and the Law* 14: 173–195.

Gomez vs. INS, 947 F.2d 660 (2nd Cir. 1991).

Hoodbhoy, Mehlika, et al. 2005. "Exporting Despair: The Human Rights Implications of U.S. Restrictions on Foreign Health Care in Kenya." *Fordham International Law Journal* 29: 1.

In re Alvarado, No. A73753922 (Immigration Court 20 September 1996).

In re Fauziya Kasinga, 21 I&N. Dec. 357 (BIA 1996).

Lawyers' Committee for Human Rights. 2002. *Refugee Women at Risk: Unfair U.S. Laws Hurt Asylum Seekers.* New York: Lawyers' Committee for Human Rights.

Nowels, Larry. 2001. *CRS Report for Congress, International Family Planning: The Mexico City Policy CRS-3.* Washington, D.C.: Congressional Research Service.

Nowels, Larry, and Connie Veillette. 2006. *CRS Report for Congress, International Population Assistance and Family Planning Programs: Issues for Congress 2.* Washington, D.C.: Congressional Research Service.

Oforji vs. Ashcroft, 354 F.3d 609 (7th Cir. 2003).

Olowo vs. Ashcroft, 368 F.3d 692 (7th Cir. 2004).

Ontiveros, Maria. 2003. "Lessons from the Fields: Female Farmworkers and the Law." *Maine Law Review* 55: 157.

Qu vs. Gonzales, 399 F.3d 1995 (9th Cir. 2005).

Schubert, Katie Ann. 2007. "Female Circumcision in the United States: An Analysis of Laws and Policies." Master's Thesis Abstract, Graduate School of the University of Florida. Available at http://etd.fcla.edu/UF/UFE0021016/schubert_k.pdf.

Skuster, Patty. 2004. "Advocacy in Whispers: The Impact of the USAID Global Gag Rule upon Free Speech and Free Association in the Context of Abortion Law Reform in Three East African Countries." *Michigan Journal of Gender and Law* 11: 97.

Tamayo, William R. 2000. "Forging Our Identity: Transformative Resistance in the Areas of Work, Class and the Law: The Role of the EEOC in Protecting the Civil Rights of Farm Workers." *University of California Davis Law Review* 33: 1075.

Tarnoff, Curt, and Larry Nowels. 2004. *CRS Report for Congress, Foreign Aid: An Introductory Overview of U.S. Programs and Policy 2.* Washington, D.C.: Congressional Research Service.

UNHCR. 1994. *Memorandum: Female Genital Mutilation.* Geneva: UNHCR, Division of International Protection.

USCIRF. 2005. *Report on Asylum Seekers in Expedited Removal, Vol. 1: Findings and Recommendations.* Washington, D.C.: USCIRF.

Watson, M. 2005. "Female Circumcision from Africa to the Americas: Slavery to the Present." *The Social Sciences Journal* 42: 421–437.

Woolley, John T., and Gerhard Peters. N.d. The American Presidency Project (online). Santa Barbara, CA. Available atat http://www.presidency.ucsb.edu/ws/?pid=46311.

Yadegar-Sargis vs. INS, 297 F.3d 596 (7th Cir. 2002).

4

Chronology

The history of the status and rights of women in developing countries is rich in detail from its earliest moments. Because so many events affecting women have occurred throughout history, this chapter will focus only on recent history. Most of the events described here occurred after 1974, although several before 1975 are included to provide a perspective on women's lives and activism in developing countries. References at the end of this chapter provide additional sources of information concerning important dates in women's history.

1919 Women in Egypt participate in street demonstrations to protest the many oppressive policies of the British protectorate, marking the beginning of the fight for their rights as women.

1919 The Paris Peace Conference is held. The women's delegation to the conference lobbies for an 8-hour workday, a 44-hour work week, an end to child labor, support for social insurance and pensions, maternity benefits, equal pay, and minimum wages for housework. Most delegates believe that these proposals are too radical and they are quickly shelved. Delegates also urge Conference leaders to nominate women to positions of influence in the League of Nations, to eliminate traffic in women and children and state-supported prostitution, and to recognize universal suffrage.

1927 The All-India Women's Conference opens with discussions concerning women's education. Participants expand their focus to include the elimination of purdah, child marriage, and other problems that were first tackled by nineteenth-century reformers.

1928 Female delegates to the Conference of American States propose an Inter-American Commission of Women. This group is officially endorsed at the 1933 conference. The commission is the first regional intergovernmental body whose specific purpose is to advance women's rights.

1933 The first women's bank is founded in Indonesia.

1936 Victoria Ocampo leads the effort to form the Argentine Union of Women. The union's main goal is to stop a proposed "reform" of the Argentine civil code that would again consider married women as legal minors, and therefore not allowed to control their wages or work but rather dependent on their husband's permission.

1937 In response to requests from several women's organizations, the League of Nations establishes a Committee of Experts on the Legal Status of Women. This committee has the authority to conduct a comprehensive and scientific inquiry into the legal status of women in countries throughout the world.

1945 Legislation is passed that outlaws infibulation in Sudan. This law will be ignored by many people.

1946 The Sudanese Women's League is formed. This is the first modern women's organization in the Sudan.

1946 After leaders of 51 governments ratified the UN Charter the previous year, they meet in London for the first time to discuss their role in preventing future wars and in solving the worldwide economic crisis that followed World War II. Several women serve as delegates to the UN General Assembly as representatives

1946 (*cont.*) or alternates from their countries. The five representatives are Eleanor Roosevelt (United States), Minerva Bernardino (Dominican Republic), Jeane McKenzie (New Zealand), Evdokia I. Uralova (USSR), and Ellen Wilkinson (United Kingdom). The alternates come from Czechoslovakia, Denmark, France, Greece, the Netherlands, Norway, the United Kingdom, and the United States.

1946 The Commission on the Status of Women is established by the United Nations. It is one of the earliest intergovernmental agencies set up to monitor the implementation and status of women's rights throughout the world. Helvi Sipilä, a lawyer from Finland, is its chairperson.

1947 Rani Gaidinliu, an Indian freedom fighter; is released after spending 14 years in jail for her protests against the British occupation and rule of India. At the age of 16, she led a group of guerrilla fighters and was captured only after the British sent out a large number of troops.

1947 A group of women in Nepal found the Adharsa Mahila Sangh (Model Women's Organization) to fight child marriage. They also fight for the right of widows to remarry.

1950 Planned Parenthood International is founded by Indian family planning advocate Dhanvanthi Rama Rau.

1951 The marriage of girls under 12 is allowed in Sri Lanka as long as each wedding is approved by a religious court.

1953 The UN General Assembly elects Indian diplomat Vijaya Pandit as its first female president.

1953 The Federation of Ghana Women, a trade and business association, is founded by Dr. Evelyn Amartiefio.

1954 Divorce is legalized in Argentina; women have worked for decades for this legal reform. However, the law will be repealed the following year.

1954 Women in Nepal stage a protest over the lack of women in the King's Advisory Assembly. As a result, the government forms a second assembly and includes four female members in a total of 113 members.

1954 The National Federation of Indian Women, a broad-based, moderate feminist group, is founded in India.

1955 In India, legislation outlaws polygamy for Hindus but Muslim men are still allowed to marry up to four women. Both women and men may sue for divorce on the grounds of adultery, desertion, physical or mental cruelty, religious conversion, insanity, leprosy, sexually transmitted disease, disappearance for seven years, or persistent and long-term refusal of conjugal rights. Women are also allowed to sue for divorce from a husband who is found guilty of rape, sodomy, or bestiality. Women who marry before age 15 have until age 18 to divorce their husbands, as long as the marriage has not been consummated.

1955 Women band together in India to found Bharatiya Grammen Mahila Sangh. This organization offers family planning services, maternity and child care, and vocational training for women.

1956 In India, legislation is passed that outlaws sati, or widow-burning; reaffirms the father's right to custody of his children; allows equal inheritance rights to both Hindu sons and daughters; allows women to adopt children; and provides equal rights to adopted sons and daughters.

1956 Recognizing the need for an organized approach to family planning, the government of Egypt establishes the Supreme Council of Family Planning.

1956 Believing that girls should be able to go to school, Saudi Arabian queen Iffat, the wife of King Faisal, establishes a government school for girls.

1957 Lee Tai Young, Korea's first woman lawyer, establishes the Korean Legal Aid Center for Family Relations. She helps women who have a variety of legal problems, especially women who need help getting divorces from their husbands.

1957 The UN General Assembly approves the Convention on the Nationality of Married Women, which no longer ties a woman's nationality to that of her husband.

1958 Afghanistan's prime minister calls for women to reject the veil.

1958 Recognizing the need for family planning programs, the Nepal Family Planning Association is founded.

1958 Nigeria opens its first birth control clinic.

1958 The Economic and Social Council of the United Nations and the Commission on the Status of Women call on the World Health Organization (WHO) to study the persistent custom of female genital circumcision and the steps that governments plan to take to end the practice. The following year, WHO rejects this request because circumcision is based on local social and cultural practices and therefore is outside the realm of WHO's interest.

1960 The Commission on the Status of Women urges governments to affirm women's access to all levels of education. The Convention on Eliminating Discrimination in Education is adopted by the United Nations.

1960 Sirimavo Bandaranaike becomes the prime minister of Ceylon following the assassination of her husband,

1960 (*cont.*) Solomon Bandaranaike. She is the world's first female prime minister.

1961 The Dowry Prohibition Act is passed in India. This legislation makes the act of asking for a dowry illegal, but the law has little effect on actual practice throughout the country. "Presents" can still be legally offered to the groom's family by the bride's family. If a groom's family believes that these "presents" are not sufficient, they may still harass the bride and sometimes kill her. The practice, known as dowry murder, continues despite protests from India's many women's groups.

1961 The Mount Carmel International Center for Community Training is formed at a meeting in Haifa, Israel. The meeting is attended by women from 23 African and Asian countries who are inspired by Golda Meir's desire to help rural women in Third World countries. The center offers agricultural and business training for women.

1962 Feminists in Brazil win a change of the law that considers women legal minors; they are now considered adults.

1962 Thailand outlaws prostitution, primarily as a result of the efforts of Pierra Hoon Veijjabu, Thailand's first female physician.

1967 The Declaration on the Elimination of All Forms of Discrimination against Women is written by the Commission on the Status of Women. It is the first comprehensive measure concerning women's rights.

1968 Iranian politician Farrokhrou Parsa, who had become one of the first six women in the Iranian Parliament in 1964, becomes her country's first female cabinet minister. She is named minister of education.

1968 The idea that family planning is a human right is first recognized at the U N International Conference on Human Rights in Tehran, Iran.

1969 The government of Ecuador institutes a "malaria control" program throughout the country. In reality, this program is an excuse to sterilize peasant women.

1969 Several women are elected or appointed to office during this year. These women include Jordan's first female ambassador, Laurice Hlass; Ecuador's first female senator, Isabel Robalino; Venezuela's first female cabinet minister; Minister of Development Aura Celina Casanova; South Africa's first female judge, Leonora Neethling; and Puerto Rico's first female cabinet member; Secretary of Labor Julia Rivera de Vincenti.

1969 The first feminist group in Venezuela, the Movimiento de Liberacion de la Mujer (Women's Liberation Movement), is founded.

1970 In Libya, women who are employed receive a pay bonus when they get married. A new law mandates that women receive equal pay for equal work but restrictions are placed on women working under certain conditions. These restrictions are that women cannot hold jobs that are dangerous, cannot work at night in most cases, and cannot work more than 48 hours per week.

1971 Women in India win the right to have an abortion (one and a half years before *Roe vs. Wade* legalizes abortion in the United States).

1971 Women's rights forces continue to lose ground in Islamic countries. President Numairi of the Sudan is openly hostile to the radical Sudanese Women's Union and forces the dismantling of the group.

1972 Aida Gindy of the Social Development Division of the United Nations recognizes the need for more understanding of the role of women in economic development. She calls for and plans an Expert Group Meeting to discuss these issues. Sir Arthur Lewis, president of the Caribbean Development

1972 (*cont.*) Bank, presides over the meeting; he is joined by Inga Thorssen (Sweden), Aziza Hussein (Egypt), Annie Jiagge (Ghana), Vida Tomsic (Yugoslavia), Mina Ben Zvi (Israel), Laticia Shahani (Philippines), and Elizabeth Koontz (United States). Margaret Snyder is the Economic Commission of Africa (ECA) Observer. Members discuss common strategies to effectively integrate women into the development process.

1972 The Economic Commission of Africa establishes its own Women's Programme, explaining that women are neglected as resources and that their contributions to society are rarely seen or measured. Women's social and economic activities and contributions within their families, communities, and nations are not acknowledged or supported, which leads to missed opportunities for development and negative effects on productivity. The ECA Women's Programme is designed to help communities and nations recognize women's contributions.

1973 The Institute for Women's Studies in the Arab World is created as part of Beirut University College. Its goals are focused on academics and include creating and maintaining contacts with people throughout the world interested in women's issues, increasing awareness of the advances made by Arab women, and advocating for the integration of women into development activities.

1973 The United States Congress passes the Percy Amendment to the Foreign Assistance Act. The amendment requires that development assistance programs pay particular attention to integrating women into national economies in order to improve their status.

1975 The first regional conference on Gulf women is organized by the Kuwaiti Women's Social and Cultural Society, an NGO that works closely with government officials to encourage the participation of women in the development process.

1975 International Women's Year is proclaimed by the United Nations. A conference is held in June in Mexico City and is the first world conference of governments focusing on women. Delegates create the World Plan of Action, the first international public policy to improve women's status. The conference is the largest consciousness-raising event held on this subject and advances women's claim to full citizenship. The conference is significant because it marks the merger of two distinct agendas: the women's agenda, defined and developed by the Commission on the Status of Women (CSW), and the larger political agenda of the United Nations. Delegations from 133 nations and representatives from eight UN agencies, 12 UN programs, and 192 NGOs in consultative status attend the Conference on International Women's Year. Over 6,000 participants attend an unofficial parallel conference at the opposite end of Mexico City.

1975 In October, the World Congress for International Women's Year is held in Berlin. Almost 2,000 delegates, observers, and guests from throughout the world gather to unite diverse social forces to encourage the world's women to maintain peace and to fight for democracy and the fulfillment of their legitimate rights. Delegates come from 29 European countries, 33 Asian countries, 44 African countries, and 33 countries in North, Central, and South America, as well as Australia and New Zealand.

1975 The Committee on the Status of Women in India publishes its findings in a report entitled *Towards Equality.* This government report examines the ways in which the status of women affects their lives.

1976 The International Tribunal on Crimes against Women convenes in Brussels to discuss the violence against women that occurs throughout the world. Over one thousand women from around the world discuss the extent and prevention of violence, including rape, battering, genital mutilation, and imprisonment.

1976 The United Nations develops its World Plan of Action, which suggests ways to integrate both men and women into the development process. Among its recommendations are the development of women's bureaus, advisory committees, commissions, ministries, and government offices at all levels to monitor and promote the causes of women.

1976 Egypt becomes the first Arab nation to reverse the gains that women have made throughout the region. The government amends article 2 of the constitution to make the Shari'a, or Islamic, law the principal law of the country.

1976 At the National Conference of the Mozambican Women's Organization, members define the problems that face them in Mozambique: illiteracy, unemployment, tribalism, racism, prostitution, and forced marriage.

1977 The World Bank creates the post of Adviser on Women. The president of the World Bank pledges to monitor the impact of bank activities on women and to ensure that attention will be paid to the role of women in development activities.

1977 A ten-day Pan-African Conference on the Role of Trade Women is held in Nairobi. It is sponsored by the African-American Labor Center and the AFL-CIO. Issues debated include why more women do not actively participate in their unions and what can be done to increase women's participation.

1977 General Zia al-Haq seizes power in Pakistan. He rolls back all the gains that women had made under the first president of Pakistan, Mohammad Ali Jinnah, and requires that they wear Islamic dress, including the chador. (Jinnah had believed that women should not be confined and that Islamic law did not require their subjugation and confinement.)

1977 In Buenos Aires, Argentina, the Mothers and Grandmothers of the Plaza de Mayo publicly protest against

1977 (*cont.*) military rule and begin their search for missing relatives. The military government had set up a network of more than 340 secret concentration camps to hold those they perceived as enemies of the state. Over 30,000 people, including approximately 10,000 women, were kidnapped from homes, schools, and places of employment. Families were not notified of the kidnappings or of the location of their relatives. The protest in the Plaza de Mayo brings world attention to the abuses of the military government.

1979 In February, the World Health Organization holds a conference in Khartoum, the capital of Sudan, on traditional practices affecting the health of women. As a result of this conference, the practice of female circumcision is examined and many participants begin to question the reasons for this custom. Estimates suggest that as many as 30 million girls have been circumcised to some degree. Most participants are health officials of countries in which female circumcision is practiced. The conference participants unanimously condemn circumcision as a practice that is disastrous to the health of women in these countries and one that cannot be defended on either medical or humane grounds.

1979 Egyptian feminist Nawal El Saadawi publishes *The Hidden Face of Eve: Women in the Arab World,* in which she discusses female genital mutilation, rape, the Arab emphasis on female virginity before marriage, family honor, and women in Arab history.

1979 On March 8, 6,000 women march in Tehran, Iran, to protest the oppressive policies of Iran's new leader, Ayatollah Ruhollah Khomeini. They chant, "In the dawn of freedom, there is no freedom." On March 10, Iran's Palace of Justice is seized by 15,000 women protesting the loss of their rights. On March 13, two women attack Khomeini's spokesman. They do not win any reforms of the repressive policies.

1979 The market in Accra, Ghana, is destroyed by the government, which believes that the market women

1979 (*cont.*) are responsible for food shortages throughout the area. The women become scapegoats and are persecuted because many people believe that the women are wealthy and powerful. The women have no real power and no way to fight back.

1979 The first widely publicized demonstrations against dowry murder in India take place. Women march through neighborhoods in New Delhi to the home where one dowry murder has recently occurred; other demonstrators march to the homes where suspected dowry murders have occurred.

1979 The first global feminist meeting is held in Bangkok, Thailand.

1979 In Medellin, Colombia, a National Women's Congress is held. Representatives from 19 women's groups meet to discuss abortion and the abuse of sterilization procedures.

1979 The Hudood Ordinances are passed in Pakistan. These four laws govern adultery, fornication, rape, and prostitution. The testimony of women is banned in certain types of serious criminal trials, including trials for murder, theft, adultery, and rape. A woman must have four adult male witnesses who are Muslim to prove that she has been raped. However, if the accused rapist is found not guilty, the woman can be sentenced to 80 lashes for "false testimony."

1979 In Iran, Farrokhrou Parsa, Iran's first female cabinet member, is executed by firing squad as a result of her feminist views. She had believed that schoolgirls should not have to wear the veil. She had also advocated that schools use non-sexist teaching materials.

1980 The King of Saudi Arabia decrees that brides and grooms must be permitted to meet each other before the wedding. Most Saudi Arabian women are married by the time they are 16 years old and are bought by the groom with a bride price.

1980 The UN Children's Emergency Fund (UNICEF) pledges to assist community groups and organizations willing to work toward the prevention of female genital circumcision. As a result, several women's organizations are formed, including the Somali Democratic Women's Organization, the Women's Group against Sexual Mutilation (France), Le Mouvement Femmes et Société (Senegal), and the Babiker Bedri Foundation for Women's Studies and Research (Sudan).

1980 In Namibia, Ida Jimmy makes a speech at the South West African People's Organization (SWAPO) and is sentenced to seven years in prison for speaking out against the current regime. Gertrude Kandanga, deputy secretary of SWAPO's Women's Council, also is arrested and held in jail for one year without being charged with a crime or given a trial.

1980 A workshop on national liberation and development is held at The Hague, the Netherlands. Women from all over the world converge to discuss the liberation struggles in which they have been involved (for example, in South Africa, Angola, Namibia, Mozambique, and Zimbabwe). They examine their participation and the gains, if any, they have made in their own liberation struggles once national liberation has succeeded. Most often, they discover, women return to their old (subservient) status following the national struggle.

1980 The mid-decade Conference for the International Women's Decade is held in Copenhagen. It has two goals: to measure progress in the first half of the Decade for Women (1976–1985) and to develop strategies and programs for the remaining five years. Politics appears to enter into every major item of discussion; for example, the Iran delegation withdraws; Jihan el-Sadat, the wife of President Anwar Sadat of Egypt, discusses Middle East issues and prompts a walkout by Palestinian representatives; and the concept of sexism is not included in the draft of the Programme of Action because many women insist that it does not exist in their countries. At the

1980 (*cont.*) conclusion, four delegations—from the United States, Canada, Australia, and Israel—vote against the Programme of Action, while the rest of the Western delegations abstain. U.S. representatives believe that the conference is a diplomatic defeat and many others believe that the women's movement has been damaged beyond repair.

1980 Following the murders of two women by their husbands, Brazilian feminists establish the Center for the Defense of the Rights of Women.

1981 The government arrests Egyptian feminist Nawal el Saadawi because she has published articles that criticize President Sadat's policies. Many other feminists are also arrested because of their activities protesting government actions and policies. El Saadawi is held in prison for 80 days and released after Sadat is assassinated.

1981 The first All Latin American Women's Conference is held in Colombia. The conference is attended by 250 delegates from 25 countries and focuses on the status of women in Latin America.

1981 The first battered women's shelter is opened in Thailand by activist Kanitha Wichiencharoen.

1981 Peruvian feminists protest pornography and violence against women.

1981 In Geneva, a conference on Women and Health is convened. Over 250 women from 35 countries gather to discuss health issues of importance to women.

1981 Several NGOs appear before the UN Working Group on Slavery to argue that female circumcision and other traditional practices are human rights violations. The Working Group recommends that a study be conducted to examine the extent of this problem.

1981 The International Labor Conference adopts a new convention, the Workers with Family Responsibilities Convention (No. 156), as well as a new Workers with Family Responsibilities Recommendation (No. 165). This is the first time at the international level that child care is acknowledged as the concern of men as well as of women. Convention 156 requires that member states of the International Labor Organization develop national policies that will "enable persons with family responsibilities who are engaged or wish to engage in employment to exercise their right to do so without being subject to discrimination and, to the extent possible, without conflict between their employment and family responsibilities" (Article 3). Recommendation 165 elaborates the steps that can be taken to implement the convention. These include reduced working hours and overtime, flexible work schedules, parental leave of absence following maternity leave, and protection for part-time workers.

1982 Two women in Nicaragua become justices on the Supreme Court (Sandra Day O'Connor became the first woman on the U.S. Supreme Court in 1981).

1982 An Expert Meeting on Multidisciplinary Research on Women in the Arab World is held in Tunis. The meeting is sponsored by the UN Educational, Scientific and Cultural Organization (UNESCO). As a result of this meeting, the Association for the Development of Research on Women in the Arab World is formed.

1982 In Chile, the Movement of Women Slum Dwellers (MOMUPO) is founded with the purpose of uniting and coordinating the activities of grassroots women's groups. There are over 50,000 people in the Santiago area who belong to 500 organizations to fight poverty.

1982 The Islamic Ideology Council of Pakistan proposes passage of a Law of Evidence that would value a woman's testimony in court half as much as a man's.

1982 (*cont.*) It also recommends that the lives of murder victims who are women should be valued half as much as murder victims who are male.

1982 A pro-contraceptive campaign is begun in India to curb large population increases. Women are paid $22 to be sterilized and men are paid $15.

1982 Kenya outlaws traditional genital mutilation of women.

1983 UNESCO begins to implement strategies with member states and NGOs to encourage literacy programs among women in developing countries. It launches Equal Opportunities in Education for Women and Girls, a special program whose aim is to reduce gender inequities in all areas but especially in education.

1983 The second Latin American and Caribbean Feminist Meeting is held in Lima, Peru. The focus is decidedly feminist; topics include patriarchy and the church, feminist research, domestic work, women in exile, health, literature, development programs, sexuality, power, violence and sexual slavery, paid work, family, peasant women, psychotherapy, feminism, and general problems in daily life.

1983 Thirteen women's organizations send a memorandum requesting government action to the lieutenant governor of Delhi, India, claiming that the number of young women who have died as a result of burns in New Delhi grew from 311 in 1977 to 610 in 1982 (*Indian Express,* 3 December 1983).

1983 Several women's organizations publicly protest the Pinochet regime in Chile. The Manifesto of the Feminist Movement is written, including the slogan "Democracy in the Country and in the Home." Several organizations coordinate their activities in opposition to military rule.

1983 In Brazil, women are outraged when a woman who killed her husband is sentenced to 14 years in prison

1983 (*cont.*) while a man who murdered his wife is given a two-year suspended sentence. The court's position is that the man was defending his honor and therefore had a right to murder his wife.

1984 In Egypt, the Committee on the Conditions of Women is created by the Arab Lawyers Federation. This committee examines the status of women and encourages interest in human rights in general and women's rights in particular.

1984 The Women's Cultural and Social Society of Kuwait works to mobilize women and to encourage them to work with, and lobby, key government officials to extend voting rights to women. Members are primarily upper- and middle-class women.

1984 The first Regiona1 Meeting on Women and Health in Latin America is held in Colombia and includes 70 participants from 10 countries. This is one of many conferences in which women's health concerns are made known and protests are registered against male-dominated health policy decisions.

1984 The Inter-African Committee on Traditional Practices is formed. The committee's two major tasks are supporting the creation of national organizations to address the issue of female circumcision and other traditional practices and encouraging research into those practices that are harmful to women. The committee also proposes strategies for eliminating female circumcision.

1984 The Dowry Prohibition (Amendment) Act of 1984 is passed in India. The purpose of this act is to strengthen the Dowry Prohibition Act of 1961, which was ignored by most Indians. There are no provisions for enforcing the act, however.

1984 In Argentina, the world's first Housewives' Trade Union is created to provide support and advocacy for housewives.

1984 The International Tribunal and Meeting on Reproductive Rights is held in Amsterdam.

1985 The Tunisian Human Rights Organization creates a committee to defend the rights of women. The committee circulates a petition that supports women's equal access to work, education, civil and political rights, divorce, guardianship of children following the death of the husband, and improvement in the inheritance rights of single female children. A series of debates is organized on these issues and many of them are discussed on television and radio programs. The campaign concludes with a large demonstration to show popular support for the fight for women's rights.

1985 The lack of progress in improving women's health is a major concern at the annual meeting of the World Health Assembly, which consists of representatives of all member states of the World Health Organization. The group also notes that women's rights should be protected and recognizes the link between equal rights and women's participation in health activities.

1985 Nairobi, Kenya, hosts the final conference of the UN Decade for Women, 1975–1985, and the parallel NGO Forum '85. Approximately 1,900 official delegates and more than 14,000 NGO representatives arrive in Nairobi for these meetings. The main purpose of the meeting is to review and appraise the achievements of the Decade for Women and to adopt the major conference document, the *Nairobi Forward-Looking Strategies for the Advancement of Women.*

1985 The National Conference on Perspectives for Women's Liberation is held in Bombay, India. Almost 400 delegates from over 100 women's organizations throughout India attend the conference.

1985 Over 5,000 landless peasants from the Paraguayan Peasants' Movement (MCP) organize a mass public demonstration for their rights. Over 1,000 peasant

1985 (*cont.*) women participate in a demonstration to celebrate the formation of the Women's Commission of the MCP.

1986 The International AIDS Conference recognizes the impact of HIV and AIDS on women for the first time and begins to focus attention on the neglect of women in AIDS-prevention activities.

1986 The UN Economic and Social Council recognizes that family violence violates the rights of women.

1987 Eight international agencies and organizations launch the Safe Motherhood Initiative, which focuses on attempts to reduce the number of maternal deaths throughout the world by half by the year 2000. Organizers place high priority on improving the socioeconomic status of girls and women, providing family planning services to all women, offering high quality prenatal and delivery care for all women, and providing skilled obstetric care for emergency and high-risk cases.

1987 In Uruguay, the Women's Institute is established within the Ministry of Education and Culture to promote policies that help women improve their status and their lives in general.

1987 Women from Latin America and the Caribbean meet in Taxco, Mexico, to discuss major issues of concern to them. The 1,500 participants include women from government ministries, NGOs, and Catholic feminist organizations.

1987 The fifth International Women and Health Conference is held in Costa Rica.

1988 The Korean Women's Association United, a coalition of 24 women's organizations in South Korea, holds a news conference to announce the launch of a crusade against trafficking in women and to focus attention on the increasing number of women who are being

1988 (*cont.*) kidnapped off the streets and sold into prostitution. The coalition calls for the government to take action against this practice and to slow down the rapidly growing entertainment industry, thought by many to be the cause of the increase in prostitution.

1988 The NGO Working Group on Refugee Women holds a meeting of 150 representatives from refugee women's groups, NGOs, intergovernmental groups, and governments to discuss refugee women's issues and to determine how these issues can be more effectively addressed. Five major themes are the focus at the meetings: protection, health, education, cultural adjustment, and employment.

1988 May 28 is set aside by women's groups and organizations throughout the world as an international day of action for women's health. Protests and demonstrations, lobbying activities, and publicity events are held to focus attention on the need to provide women with accessible, humanized, and competent health services and to lower maternal mortality. This will become an annual event.

1989 The International Conference on the Implications of AIDS for Mothers and Children is held in Paris, France. Two conclusions are reached at this conference concerning women and children with AIDS. First, AIDS prevention programs for women and children do not exist in most countries. Second, countries that have prevention programs for women often focus on female sex workers—that is, prostitutes and others involved in promiscuous sexual activities—rather than on women in the general population who are at risk of contracting AIDS.

1990 Recognizing the importance of education, especially in developing countries, the United Nations declares International Literacy Year.

1990 The South Asian Association for Regional Co-operation declares the Year of the Girl Child, recognizing the

1990 (*cont.*) detrimental attitudes of many parents toward their daughters.

1990 The Permanent Working Group on the Situation of Women in the UN High Commissioner on Refugees (UNHCR) suggests that more women professionals should be hired at UNHCR. Because the majority of refugees are women and children, the Working Group believes that more women on staff at local sites will encourage more refugee women to participate in activities designed to help them and their children.

1990 Women from Latin America and the Caribbean meet in San Bernardo, Argentina, to discuss relevant women's issues. Almost 3,000 participants come from a variety of fields and levels of activism and include ecologists, pacifists, union organizers, squatters, parliamentarians, political party militants, Christians, lesbians, indigenous women, and black women. The women form new women's networks and coordinate regional campaigns on issues such as abortion and representations of women in the media.

1990 In Riyadh, Saudi Arabia, 47 women drive cars to protest the law against women driving. They are briefly imprisoned, with religious leaders believing that they have tried to corrupt society by their behavior. They are fired from their jobs, some are threatened, and many of their families are also threatened. The government reinforces the ban on driving by women.

1990 In Algeria, Islamic fundamentalists increase their efforts to suppress women's rights and force women to follow strict Islamic practices.

1990 In Chile, the government creates the National Women's Service (SERNAM) to develop and promote programs that focus on women.

1991 The Inter-American Development Bank (IDB) develops an action plan for changing its approach to

1991 (*cont.*) women in development (WID) activities. This plan changes the ways that the IDB participates in various country programs, project development, and project analysis. The plan calls on the IDB to treat women's participation as an integral part of all IDB activities and mandates that WID issues be addressed at the beginning of projects or during the planning process.

1991 In Kenya, over 300 schoolboys attack a girls' dormitory following the girls' refusal to join a protest against the headmaster. The boys kill 19 girls and rape 71. When questioned about the boys' behavior, a deputy principal claims that the "boys never meant any harm against the girls. They just wanted to rape."

1991 The Pakistani government adopts Islamic (Shari'a) law. Women's rights as witnesses, judges, and lawyers are limited.

1991 According to a report by the United Nations, the number of rural women in developing countries who are living in poverty has increased by 50 percent in the past 20 years. The number of rural men living in poverty is found to be much lower.

1992 An Expert Group Meeting on Population and Women is held in Botswana. Participants develop several recommendations concerning the promotion of responsible fatherhood. Recommendations encourage the participation of both parents in providing material and emotional support to their children. Governments are encouraged to support responsible parenting and to develop measures to facilitate this practice through educational activities, information services, employment legislation, and institutional support. The overall message is that family responsibilities should be equitably shared by both parents.

1992 At the annual meeting of the World Health Assembly, which consists of representatives of all members of the World Health Organization, a call is made to implement international policies that focus on

1992 (*cont.*) improving women's health. The group recognizes that although recommendations have been made over the years to improve the health of women throughout the world, little progress has actually been made.

1992 The UN Conference on Environment and Development is held in Rio de Janeiro. Participants focus attention on women as managers of natural resources and as the moving force behind sustainable development, as well as on the need for planners to recognize women's role in development when creating development projects. Experts at this meeting blame the growing population in Rwanda on husbands who refuse to let their wives use birth control pills because of the belief that pills weaken women, making them unable to work in the fields.

1992 In Kenya, 50 women, some over 70 years old, demonstrate for the release of political prisoners and are attacked by police with batons and tear gas. Four of them, including environmental activist Wangari Maathai, are knocked unconscious.

1992 Religious leaders in Nigeria blame a severe drought in the country on "indecent" women. Women who are wearing nontraditional dress are attacked and many women protest these attacks. The offices of the Association des Femmes Nigeriennes are burned.

1993 At the UN World Conference on Human Rights in Vienna, Austria, in June, the women's caucus demands that violations of female human rights be examined when UN Treaty Committees meet to monitor and enforce the provisions of their treaties. Women's rights are finally seen as an important component of international human rights. But at the meeting, many Muslim governments who had supported the Universal Declaration of Human Rights in 1948 withdraw their support, believing that universal human rights is a Western concept, that Muslim societies should not be judged in terms of these

1993 (*cont.*) Western concepts, and that Islam can provide the basic elements of a fair society, including women's basic rights.

1993 The Canadian government grants refugee status to a female Saudi national on the basis of gender-related persecution. The woman's advocates argue that her basic human rights to life, liberty, and security of the person are threatened because she does not accept the restrictions imposed on her by Saudi society. Her freedom to work, study, and dress as she wants is restricted, along with her freedom of movement into and out of the country. In addition, government policy, as well as public attitudes, led to her persecution, since she was subjected to violence whenever she walked down the street without covering her face.

1993 The UN General Assembly unanimously adopts the Declaration on the Elimination of Violence against Women. The Declaration defines violence against women as "any act of gender-based violence that results in, or is likely to result in physical, sexual or psychological harm or suffering to women, including threats of such acts, coercion or arbitrary deprivation of liberty, whether occurring in public or in private life." The declaration states that acts of violence against women include battering, sexual abuse of female children, dowry-related violence, marital rape, female genital mutilation, non-spousal violence, rape, sexual abuse, sexual harassment, intimidation at work and in schools, trafficking in women, and forced prostitution.

1993 The World Health Organization condemns the genital mutilation of women following lengthy and intense lobbying on the part of Ghanaian-British feminist Efua Dorkenoo.

1993 In Tehran, Iran, almost 800 women are arrested for violating Islamic dress codes requiring them to cover everything but their hands and faces when they are out in public. Some of the women arrested are sentenced to be flogged.

1993 Over 1,300 women in Latin America meet for their biannual *encuentro* (encounter) in Costa del Sol, El Salvador. They discuss human rights violations, women's rights, electoral quotas, and problems of discrimination they face within the women's movement. The organizers of the meeting receive death threats and consider moving subsequent gatherings to another country.

1994 The International Conference on Population and Development is held in Cairo, Egypt. Participants agree that population and development policies should focus on women's equality, empowerment, reproductive rights, and sexual health. Attendees state that women must be empowered and their status improved in order for them to realize their full potential in the areas of economic, political, and social development. Empowering women is also an important goal in and of itself. As women achieve status, opportunities, and social, economic, and legal rights equal to men, human health and well-being will be enhanced. At the conference, the Muslim governments join forces with representatives from the Vatican to oppose human rights for women.

1994 The Inter-American Development Bank forms a Task Force on Women in response to requests by the Bank's Professional Women's Network. The task force analyzes gender differences in hiring practices, pay, assignments, advancement opportunities, work quality, and other areas of concern. Recommendations are made to improve the situation of women employees.

1994 The United Nations declares 1994 the International Year of the Family to promote policies that foster equality between women and men within the family and to bring about a fuller sharing of domestic responsibilities and employment opportunities.

1994 Vast numbers of Rwandan women are subjected to sexual violence during the genocide perpetrated by

1994 (*cont.*) Hutu militias. Over 20,000 children are born as a result and many of the women contract AIDS during this period.

1994 Women's World Banking (see Chapter 7) convenes the UN Expert Group on Women and Finance in preparation for the Fourth World Conference on Women to be held in Beijing. The group focuses on transforming financial systems to open access to low-income women entrepreneurs and producers. Delegates to the meeting include world leaders in banking with the poor as well as representatives from NGOs, financial institutions, research organizations, and funding sources.

1994 The UN Secretariat for the Fourth World Conference on Women convenes an Expert Group Meeting on Women and Economic Decision-Making. Women leaders from government organizations, the private sector, NGOs, and research organizations participate in this meeting.

1995 The Geneva-based Women's World Summit Foundation awards the 1995 Prize for Women's Creativity in Rural Life to ten rural women and women's groups from eight countries. The awards honor the women's courage and creativity and their innovative projects that enhance their quality of life and contribute to sustainable development. The women, who win cash awards, come from Africa, Asia, and Latin America, and include Domitila Barrios of Bolivia, an internationally known grassroots leader; Lia Junqiao of China, who built a village skills-training school; Lai Xiao, a Mongol herdswoman who developed a scientific strategy for breeding and raising sheep; Gawaher Saad El Sherbini Fadi of Egypt, a leader of land reclamation cooperatives; Joan Abgo of Ghana, who coordinates activities of rural women in farming and trading; Samuben Ujabhai Thakore and Ranbai Jemalji Rauma of India, who share one prize for leading a union of 14,000 rural women to secure employment programs from the government; Samake

1995 (*cont.*) Nekani and Sangare Aminata of Mali, who share a prize for being effective group leaders in their efforts to fight poverty, Huda Abdel-Elhameid of Sudan, who expanded her fishing abilities into a successful business; and the Coordinating Bureau for Women's Groups in Togo, led by Segou Tida, which trains women in poverty-stricken areas to earn and manage money and provides health care, food, housing, and clothing.

1995 President Alberto Fujimori of Peru, in his second-term inaugural speech, announces an aggressive government campaign to provide family planning services to low-income Peruvians. The Peruvian bishops' conference protests the campaign, arguing that contraception is not morally acceptable. Although Peru is 90 percent Roman Catholic, a poll suggests that many people support the president's position on family planning.

1995 The World Summit for Social Development is held in Copenhagen. Women's issues are on the agenda, but at this meeting women also help set the agenda. Women's empowerment is a major issue, and it is also accepted as a necessary element in all strategies that seek to solve social, economic, and environmental problems. Participants recognize the importance of empowering women politically, socially, and economically in order to eliminate poverty, unemployment, and other social problems.

1995 The Fourth World Conference of Women is held in Beijing, China, in September. The key points established in the Platform for Action note the importance of women's rights as human rights superseding cultural restrictions on women's rights, a guarantee of reproductive and sexual rights, a call for review of laws that mandate punishment of women who have abortions, recognition of adolescent rights, and finally, the importance of women's right to control their sexuality. Prior to this meeting, five regional conferences are held in Indonesia, Argentina, Austria, Senegal,

1995 (*cont.*) and Jordan to focus on specific regional priorities. These meetings helped each region offer concrete suggestions for the meetings in Beijing.

1995 Over 30,000 participants attend the NGO Forum on Women in Huairou, China. It is the largest international gathering on women to date.

1995 The First International Conference on Dowry and Bride-Burning convenes at Harvard Law School. The conference organizers focus attention on the practice of dowry-related violence toward women in India. The National Crimes Bureau of India reports that there were 5,817 dowry deaths in 1993 and 5,199 deaths in 1994, although the Supreme Court of India estimates that up to 15,000 women die each year from dowry disputes. These deaths occur despite the fact that in 1961, the Indian government enacted the Dowry Prohibition Act. The conference suggests practical ways that dowry and bride-burning can be eliminated, such as providing residential training centers and apartment complexes for abused women.

1995 An International Symposium on Women and the Media: Access to Expression and Decision-Making is organized by UNESCO and held in Toronto. As one of UNESCO's contributions to the Fourth World Conference on Women, the symposium brings together 200 media experts, journalists, researchers, and representatives from international organizations and NGOs. Participants examine women's success stories, women's access to expression and decision-making in and through the media, and ways to encourage more female representation in the media.

1996 The city of Khartoum, Sudan, issues a public law that orders the separation of the sexes in public in order to conform to fundamentalist Muslim law. The law requires that barriers must be erected between men and women at social events, weddings, parties, picnics, and all other social gatherings. Buses must display a verse from the Koran that reminds people

1996 (*cont.*) that they are prohibited from looking at members of the opposite sex. Male students are to be separated from female students.

1996 Forty Kuwaiti women—lawyers, scientists, and teachers—protest outside the Kuwaiti legislature to demand the vote and the right to run for parliament. Many of the women were members of the civilian resistance during Iraq's occupation from 1990 to 1991; during the occupation, Sheik Jaber al-Ahmad al-Sabah had said that he would consider giving women the vote because of their bravery during the resistance to Iraqi rule. In Kuwait, women occupy top positions in the civil service, oil industry, and education; they are allowed to drive and to wear Western-style clothes. However, they do not have political rights and equality with men on social issues.

1996 In Afghanistan, the Taliban outlaws the examination of women and girls by male physicians and bans female physicians and nurses from providing any type of health care.

1997 The Office of Special Advisor to the Secretary-General on Gender Issues and Advancement of Women is created within the United Nations.

1997 The Secretary General of the United Nations encourages all UN entities to mainstream human rights into their programs and activities.

2000 The progress of the Beijing Platform for Action is reviewed at the 23rd Special Session of the UN General Assembly, Women 2000: Gender Equality, Development and Peace for the 21st Century.

2000 Eight Millennium Development Goals are adopted by the UN General Assembly. One of the goals is to "promote gender equality and empower women."

2000 Women in Zimbabwe begin to organize to demand their human rights following forced evictions from

2000 (*cont.*) their homes and market spaces among other abuses by the government.

2000 The first UN Security Council resolution (Resolution 1325) recognizing that the experiences of women in war and conflict are different from men's experiences is adopted.

2000 The UN Protocol to Prevent, Suppress, and Punish Trafficking in Persons is signed by 80 countries.

2001 The UN Children's Fund issues a report examining the continuing practice of forced marriages of underage girls.

2002 The government of Peru adopts a health care plan that will provide health care to pregnant women, new mothers, and children under four years old, but many women, especially in rural areas, do not have access to it.

2004 Louise Arbour becomes the UN High Commissioner for Human Rights.

2004 The Third Session of the Permanent Forum on Indigenous Issues focuses on the situation of indigenous women. Over 150 million indigenous women throughout the world are marginalized and face discrimination in their daily lives.

2005 A World Summit is convened by the United Nations to determine the progress made toward meeting the Millennium Development Goals adopted in 2000.

2005 The Kuwaiti Parliament approves women's right to vote and allows them to run for political office.

2005 The Pakistani government rejects a bill that would have strengthened the law against honor killings.

2005 The Jordanian Parliament rejects a bill that would have imposed a more stringent penalty on individuals convicted of honor killings.

2005 The World Health Organization issues the *WHO Multi-Country Study on Women's Health and Domestic Violence against Women: Initial Results on Prevalence, Health Outcomes and Women's Responses*, the first global study on domestic violence.

2005 India amends the Hindu Succession Act of 1956, providing for equality in property rights. Females are now able to inherit ancestral property on an equal basis with men.

2006 The Nicaraguan National Assembly votes to ban all therapeutic abortions, including those performed to save a woman's life and in cases of rape and incest.

2006 The Million Signatures Campaign is organized by Iranian women in an attempt to end discriminatory laws concerning divorce, custody rights, and inheritance.

2007 The Global Campaign to Stop Violence against Women in the name of culture is organized to prevent the misuse of religion and culture as justification for killing women.

2008 Fourteen activists from the Women of Zimbabwe Arise (WOZA) (see Chapter 7) are arrested in Harare following a peaceful protest.

2008 In Somalia, Ausha Ibrahim Duhulow, a 13-year-old girl, claims she was raped, but Islamic extremists accuse her of adultery and stone her to death.

2008 The annual meeting of the Female Supreme Court Justices of the Spanish-Speaking Americas and Spain draws 74 female judges from Latin America to discuss state obligations required by CEDAW.

2008 Police raid the wedding of a 5-year-old girl and 7-year-old boy in Pakistan. Even though marriage under the age of 18 is illegal in Pakistan, a Pakistani court fails to censure the parents.

2009 Musawah, a worldwide effort to encourage equality and justice in the Muslim family, is launched in Malaysia. Over 250 Muslim scholars and activists representing 47 countries come together to share research, experiences, and strategies for achieving this goal.

2009 Wajeha al-Huwauder, a women's rights activist, tries to cross the border into Bahrain but is stopped by Saudi border guards because she does not have her guardian's permission to leave the country.

2009 The UN General Assembly unanimously votes to create a new UN agency for women.

2009 The Magna Carta of Women Act (the Republic Act No. 9710) is enacted in the Philippines. A comprehensive human rights law, it relies heavily on CEDAW to provide a variety of protections for women.

2009 A well-known Egyptian cleric, Sheik Mohammed Tantawi, claims he will issue a fatwa against any Muslim woman who wears the niqab (a veil covering her face) in school. Tantawi believes that Islam does not require a woman to wear the niqab and that this practice only encourages religious extremism.

2009 The Taliban assassinates Sitara Achekzai, well-known human rights activist and a secretary in the Kandahar Provincial Council.

2009 All of Mexico's 32 states adopt the Mexican General Law on Women's Access to a Life Free from Violence.

2010 At a global summit on the Millennium Development Goals, UN Secretary-General Ban Ki-moon announces the formation of the Global Strategy for Women's and Children's Health, a concerted worldwide collaborative attempt to save the lives of 16 million women and children. Over $40 million is pledged to assist in this effort.

2010 The National Action Plan on Women, Peace and Security is launched in the Philippines.

2010 Dilma Rousseff is elected president of Brazil.

2010 In Iran, Sajjad Qaderzadeh, the son of Sakineh Mohammadi Ashtiani, demands that his mother's death sentence (by stoning) for adultery be commuted. A final decision concerning her fate has not been made by the courts or the government.

2011 The new UN agency for women, UN Women, is created. Michelle Bachelet, former president of Chile, is named its first executive director.

2011 France's ban on the wearing of burqas and other Islamic face coverings in public places goes into effect.

References

Europa Publications. 2009. *International Who's Who of Women 2010.* New York: Routledge.

Europa Publications. 2010. *Who's Who in International Affairs 2011.* New York: Routledge.

Smith, Bonnie G., ed. 2005. *Women's History in Global Perspective,* vol. 2. Urbana: University of Illinois Press.

5

Biographical Sketches

Throughout history, women have played major roles in politics, social activism, health care, education, and other areas that contribute to their local communities and nations, as well as to the international community. Thousands of women have participated in major UN conferences and have contributed to the movement to improve women's status and the fight for equal rights around the world. This chapter provides short biographical sketches of individuals who are playing or have played a key role in one or more of the above-mentioned areas. But the women included here are only a few of the many who are actively involved in working to improve women's lives.

Aminah Al-Said (1914–1995)

Born in Cairo, Egypt, Aminah Al-Said was a writer and advocate for women's rights. Her father, a doctor, believed that girls should be educated along with boys. Karimah Al-Said, her sister, was a teacher who in 1965 became the first female minister of education in the Egyptian government. In 1935, Aminah Al-Said was among the first group of women to attend and graduate from Cairo University.

She founded and was the editor of *Hawaa-Eve*, Egypt's first women's magazine, which developed the largest foreign circulation of all Arabic papers. The first woman elected to the Egyptian Press Syndicate Executive Board, Al-Said was a member of the Supreme Board of Journalism, president of Dar al Hilal Publishing House, Secretary-General of the Pan-Arab League Women's

Union, and a well-respected participant in international conferences. She spoke frequently on the status and lives of Arab women and helped audiences throughout the world understand the differences between Arab women and Western women.

Aduke Alakija (b. 1921)

A well-known Nigerian lawyer, Aduke Alakija attended primary and secondary school in Lagos, Nigeria, and continued her secondary education in the United Kingdom. After studying medicine at Glasgow University, she changed her major to social science and attended the London School of Economics. While attending Cambridge, she founded the West African Students' Union. She returned to Nigeria to work as a welfare officer but when she realized she needed to be better prepared to fight for women's rights, she returned to England to study law. She joined the Nigerian delegation to the United Nations in 1961 and spent five years as a delegate. She has been a trustee of the Federal Nigeria Society for the Blind and the International Women's Society; she was also an adviser to the International Academy of Trial Lawyers, the first black African female director of Mobil Oil, and a president of the International Federation of Women Lawyers. She received an honorary Doctor of Laws degree from Columbia University in 1964.

Corazon Aquino (1933–2009)

Corazon Aquino was president of the Philippines from 1986 to 1992. She was born in Luzon to one of the important landowning families. Her family was active politically: her father was a congressman and both of her grandfathers were senators. Aquino was educated at Catholic schools in Manila and the United States. She received her B.A. from Mount St. Vincent College in New York City and then returned to the Philippines to attend law school at Far Eastern University.

In 1954 she married Benigno Aquino, Jr. When Ferdinand Marcos came to power in the Philippines in 1965 and declared martial law in 1972, many politicians and activists were arrested, including Benigno Aquino. During the seven years that her husband spent in prison, Corazon became an activist.

In 1984 Marcos allowed elections and Benigno returned to the Philippines from the United States, where he and his family had settled. Moments after his plane touched down he was assassinated. Corazon flew home, buried her husband, and began her political career working for anti-Marcos candidates. By 1985, many Filipinos had realized that Corazon was an effective leader. She was asked to run for president and was elected in 1986.

Aquino believed she should continue her husband's fight for democracy. She called for a new constitution that would set additional limits on presidential power. The military made many attempts to gain control; seven of these attempts led to the deaths of over 150 people. Aquino continued to fight for what she believed would most benefit her country's citizens: freedom and democracy. She initiated military reform, appointed many women to high government positions, and appointed three women to the Philippine Supreme Court. She also focused attention on helping NGOs and cooperatives organize.

Aung San Suu Kyi (b. 1945)

Aung San Suu Kyi is known throughout the world for her work in human rights and her fight for democracy in Burma (now referred to as Myanmar by its military leaders). Her father, Bogyoke Aung San, was a legendary Burmese hero. Her education focused on politics, philosophy, and economics at St. Hugh's College, Oxford University.

In 1972 she married Michael Aris, a scholar of Tibetan civilization, and they moved to Bhutan. She worked in the foreign ministry as a researcher on UN affairs. In 1973, she and Aris returned to England and for the next several years she cared for their two sons while her husband taught at Oxford University. She became increasingly interested in learning more about her father, whom she never really knew because he was assassinated in 1947. Suu Kyi went to Japan as Visiting Scholar at the Centre for Southeast Asian Studies at the University of Kyoto and continued her research on her father while there. She moved again in 1986, to Simla, India, where she joined her husband and became a researcher for the Indian Institute of Advanced Study.

Returning to Burma in 1988, she became involved in prodemocracy demonstrations and entered politics, quickly becoming the symbol of the fight for democracy. The opposition hurried to silence her by disqualifying her candidacy, claiming that she could not run because she had married a foreigner. The authorities placed her under house arrest in 1989. Prior to her house arrest, Suu Kyi traveled throughout the country, urging her people to be courageous and support democratic reform. Despite the absence of her name from the ballot her party, the National League for Democracy, won in a landslide victory, but the ruling army council refused to honor the election results.

In 1991 she won the Nobel Peace Prize for her work in human rights and the European Parliament's Andrei Sakharov Human Rights Prize. The Nobel Prize committee recognized her as "the leader of a democratic opposition that employs nonviolent means to resist a regime characterized by brutality" (Schlessinger and Schlessinger 1996, 173). She was released from house arrest in 1995 but continued to be harassed by government forces. In 2003 she was again placed under house arrest, and she spent seven years confined to her home until her release in 2010. Suu Kyi continues to be a symbol of freedom and democracy for her country.

Sirimavo Bandaranaike (1916–2000)

As president of the Sri Lanka Freedom Party since 1960 and prime minister of Sri Lanka, Sirimavo Bandaranaike participated extensively in politics. She was prime minister and minister of defense and external affairs from 1965 through 1970; a member of the Senate until 1965; leader of the opposition party from 1965 through 1970; and prime minister, minister of defense, and minister of foreign affairs, planning, economic affairs and plan implementation from 1970 to 1977. Her husband was prime minister of Ceylon from 1956 through 1959.

She was born into a wealthy family that was actively involved in politics. Sent to a Catholic school in Colombo, and after her graduation she married Solomon Bandaranaike, an Oxford-educated lawyer and politician. He was elected to the House of Representatives, served as minister of health and local government, and became prime minister in 1956. Following much unrest in the country as a result of proposals to replace English with Sinhalese as the national language and to make Buddhism the national religion, he was assassinated in 1959. When the Sri Lanka Freedom Party asked Sirimavo to campaign on their behalf, the party won 75 out of 151 seats in the House of Representatives, and as party leader she was appointed prime minister, becoming the first woman in the world to become a prime minister. During her second term, Ceylon became the Socialist Republic of Sri Lanka and cut off all political ties to Great Britain. She ran an unsuccessful campaign for president in 1988. In 1989 she won a seat in the National Assembly and led the opposition party. In 1994 her daughter Chandrika Bandaranaike Kumaratunga (see separate entry) became the new prime minister of the country.

Ela Bhatt (b. 1933)

Ela Bhatt is a well-known politician and women's organization executive in India and a founding member and chairperson of the executive committee and board of directors of Women's World Banking (see Chapter 7). She also founded the Self- Employed Women's Association (SEWA), one of the most successful organizations for economic empowerment of self-employed women in India. In 1989 she became the first woman appointed to the Planning Commission in India. Prior to this Bhatt was a member of the Indian Parliament, a member of the Union Planning Committee, chairwoman of the Global Video Network, and a member of the National Committee on Self-Employed Women and the advisory committee of the All-India Weavers' Foundation. Bhatt's many awards include the Right Livelihood Award and the Ramon Magsaysay Award for Community Leadership.

She understands the importance of helping women organize: today SEWA has approximately 700,000 members. SEWA has organized individual cooperatives, including groups of artisans, dairy workers, traders, and vendors. A wide variety of support services are provided by SEWA, including the SEWA Bank (founded in 1974), health care, legal aid, housing assistance, child care, and affiliations with international labor groups. She was awarded the Niwano Peace Prize in 2010 for her work in uplifting poor women in India.

Benazir Bhutto (1953–2007)

Born in Karachi, Pakistan, to her father's second wife, Benazir Bhutto was raised as a Sunni Muslim. Her parents were progressive thinkers and allowed her more freedom than most girls in Pakistan.

She graduated from Radcliffe College in 1973 and completed a second B.A. in philosophy, politics, and economics at Oxford University. Staying on another year to study international law and diplomacy, she was elected president of the Oxford Union in 1976, becoming the first Asian woman to serve as president. Following her graduation in 1977, she returned to Pakistan to work for her father, Zulfikar Ali Bhutto, the prime minister of Pakistan.

Her father was overthrown in a coup in July 1977 by General Zia and kept under house arrest for several weeks. Later charged with conspiracy to murder at least one of his political opponents, her father was found guilty along with four codefendants and sentenced to death by hanging; the sentence was carried out in 1979. Following the 1977 coup, Benazir traveled throughout the country to encourage support for the Pakistan People's Party. She was arrested along with her mother several times while her father was in prison.

Moving to London to escape the wrath of General Zia, Benazir continued to lead the Pakistan People's Party in opposition to Zia and his policies. Over the next several years she traveled back to Pakistan several times and was arrested, confined to her home, and otherwise harassed by the Zia government. When General Zia was killed in a plane crash in August 1988, Pakistani president Ishaw Khan asked Benazir to become prime minister and form a new government. In 1988 she became the first woman to lead a modern Muslim nation as well as the youngest head of state in the world.

She promised to deal with the serious drug problem throughout the country, the growing ethnic violence, poverty, other social problems, as well as conflict between India and Pakistan. She established women-only police stations in response to widespread rape and torture of women prisoners. She was, however, unable to overturn the repressive Hudood Ordinance which specifies punishment for adultery, rape, fornication, and prostitution; under this law, rape may be considered as adultery or fornication if there are not four male witnesses to testify that the woman was raped. Women are not allowed to testify.

In 1993 Bhutto was re-elected prime minister and vowed to fight corruption and modernize Pakistan. Until her dismissal from office by Pakistan's president in 1996, she was able to bring electricity to many rural areas and made progress in fighting hunger, building housing, and providing health care to many Pakistanis.

She left Pakistan for London with her children in 1998 following the imprisonment of her husband but continued to fight for democracy in her native country. In 2007 she returned to Pakistan to run for prime minister but was assassinated before the January 2008 elections.

Ester Boserup (1910–1999)

Ester Boserup was a noted Danish rural economist. She received her Ph.D. in economics from the University of Copenhagen and in 1970 she published what is now considered a classic text, *Women and Economic Development,* which caused most experts in the field of economic development to rethink their ideas concerning the roles women play in development activities. For this book Boserup gathered and analyzed data from official statistics and research. She provided clear and concise evidence that women play a crucial role in economic development, although their contributions had usually gone uncounted by measurements of national economic productivity. Boserup was one of the first experts in the field of development to believe that women's exclusion from capitalist development activities and programs widened an already wide gap between women's and men's economic power.

Boserup was a member of the UN Expert Committee for Development Planning, the Scandinavian Institute of Asian Studies, and the International Research and Training Institute for the Advancement of Women (INSTRAW). In 1972, Boserup prepared the working document for and attended the Meeting of Experts on the Integration of Women in Development, co-sponsored by the Commission on the Status of Women and the Commission on Social Development of the United Nations. This historic meeting provided advice to the United Nations and its member states concerning policy measures that should be followed in regard to women's role in economic and social development.

Elise Boulding (1920–2010)

Born in Oslo, Norway, Elise Boulding was a sociologist with a global view of the world and the role that women play in it. She received a B.A. in English from Douglass College, an M.S. in sociology from Iowa State University, and a Ph.D. in sociology from the

University of Michigan. She conducted numerous transnational and comparative cross-national studies on conflict and peace, development, and women in society. She committed herself to working for peace and world order as an activist as well as a scholar. She served as a member of the governing board of the UN University from 1980 to 1985, a member of the International Jury of the UN Educational, Scientific, and Cultural Organization (UNESCO) Prize for Peace Education, and a member of the U.S. Commission for UNESCO from 1981 to 1987.

Boulding taught in the Department of Sociology and Institute of Behavioral Science at the University of Colorado at Boulder from 1967 through 1977. She was a professor and chair of the department of sociology at Dartmouth College from 1978 to 1985. From 1988 to 1991 she was secretary general of the International Peace Research Association.

She was a member of the Commission on Proposals for a National Academy of Peace and Conflict Resolution, which recommended that Congress establish a U.S. Institute of Peace. She served as editor of the *International Peace Research Newsletter* from 1963 to 1968 and from 1983 to 1987. Her many books focus on women's roles in history and their social status, as well as on the peace movement.

Angie Brooks-Randolph (1928–2007)

Angie Brooks-Randolph was a well-known Liberian lawyer and diplomat. She worked her way through high school as a typist and stenographer in the justice department of the Liberian government. She was the first woman to become a legal apprentice in Liberia; people laughed at her during her first court appearance because they had never before seen a woman in a position of authority in court. Brooks-Randolph later received a grant to attend school in North Carolina and received her degree from the University of Wisconsin. She studied at University College, London, and then returned to Liberia to practice law. Becoming assistant attorney general in 1953, Brooks-Randolph also taught law. From 1958 until 1978 she was assistant secretary of state, and for three years (1964–1967) she was president of the International Federation of Women Lawyers.

She became the second woman to preside over a session of the UN General Assembly, serving from 1969 through 1970. She represented Liberia at the UN Plenary Session from 1970 to 1973 and was also the Liberian ambassador to Cuba. She was a strong advocate for women's rights, especially for professional opportunities and broader educational opportunities. During her life she provided care for 47 foster children. She participated in many international conferences and committees, served on advisory panels, was awarded many honors, and received 18 honorary degrees from universities in the United States.

Charlotte Bunch (b. 1944)

As a well-known feminist author, teacher, organizer, and activist, Charlotte Bunch has played a leading role in the women's movement for over 35 years. She was the first female resident fellow at the Institute for Policy Studies in Washington, D.C., and founded DC Women's Liberation and *Quest: A Feminist Quarterly*, which she edited during the 1970s. She has edited several anthologies, including *Learning Our Way: Essays in Feminist Education, Women Remembered: Biographies of Women in History,* and *International Feminism: Networking against Female Sexual Slavery.*

In 1979 she participated in an international workshop, "Feminist Ideology and Structures in the First Half of the Decade for Women," which was sponsored by the UN Asian and Pacific Center for Women and Development in Bangkok, Thailand. Bunch helped organize a worldwide conference on the topic of traffic in women and female sexual slavery that was held in Rotterdam, the Netherlands, in 1983. In a 1989 speech to Amnesty International she urged the organization to recognize and address gender-specific issues in the field of human rights. She continued to urge organizations to examine gender-specific issues in various forums, including through presentations at the World Conference on Human Rights in Vienna in 1993 and the 1995 UN Conference on Human Rights in Beijing.

Currently she is the director of the Center for Global Issues and Women's Leadership at Rutgers University, where she continues to advocate for women's rights.

Violeta Barrios de Chamorro (b. 1929)

Born in Rivas, Nicaragua, Violeta Chamorro was educated at Catholic schools in the United States and Nicaragua, and for one year at Blackstone College in Virginia. In 1950 she married Pedro Chamorro Cardenal, the publisher of the newspaper *La Prensa,* which openly criticized the government of General Somoza. Throughout the 1950s, her husband was repeatedly arrested and jailed by the Somoza regime. He was banished in 1957 and he and his family escaped to Costa Rica, where they remained for several years. The family returned to Nicaragua during a period of amnesty in 1960 and Pedro Chamorro continued his vocal opposition to the government of Somoza's sons, Luis Somoza Debayle and Anastasio Somoza Debayle. Chamorro was assassinated in 1978; most people believed his murder was ordered by the government. His murder ignited the final rebellion against the Somoza regime.

When Violeta Chamorro took over the task of publishing *La Prensa* after her husband's death she endured bomb threats. She contributed money to the Sandinista National Liberation Front, which focused on overthrowing the corrupt Somoza regime. Following the downfall of General Somoza in 1979, she became a member of the civilian junta that held the executive powers of the Government of National Reconstruction. She resigned her membership in 1980 after she became disillusioned with the Marxist leanings and excessive militarism of the new Sandinista government.

Thereafter she often wrote articles denouncing the Sandinistas and the newspaper was frequently closed down by the government; a 1986 shutdown lasted for 15 months. Chamorro became a target of the leftist regime, which continued to harass her even after the paper reopened. She became leader of the opposition party, the Unión Nacional Opositora (UNO), in September 1989 and was elected president of Nicaragua in February 1990, becoming Central America's first female president. Voters looked to her to bring peace and outside aid to the country's battered economy. During her presidency she ended the draft and greatly reduced the size of the Sandinista army, privatized many state-owned industries, and worked to unite the various political factions. Barred from running for a second term, Chamorro retired from politics in 1997.

Eugenia Charles (1919–2005)

Eugenia Charles was the prime minister of the Commonwealth of Dominica from 1980 until 1995. She attended Catholic schools in Dominica and Grenada and received a bachelor's degree in law from the University College of the University of Toronto in 1946. She was called to the English bar in 1947 and enrolled at the London School of Economics for additional study. When she returned to Dominica she became the only woman to practice law on the island. As a co-founder and the first leader of the Dominica Freedom Party, she was a member of Parliament from 1975 to 1980. Dominica achieved independence from Great Britain in 1979 amid concerns that the country was not ready economically or socially for independence. Charles was a strong anticommunist leader and received millions of dollars from the United States during the 1980s to strengthen the country's weak infrastructure. She focused on structural adjustment programs that encouraged the development of infrastructure over social welfare programs.

Gaositwe Keagakwa Tibe Chiepe (b. 1926)

Born in Serowe, Botswana, Gaositwe Keagakwa Tibe Chiepe attended Fort Hare University in South Africa from 1944 to 1947 and Bristol University from 1955 to 1957. Returning to Botswana, she worked as an education officer and became director of education in 1968. By 1970 she had been appointed high commissioner to the United Kingdom and to Nigeria and held ambassadorial positions in Europe and Scandinavia. She became Botswana's first female minister of commerce in 1974, minister of mineral resources and water affairs in 1977, and minister of external affairs in 1984. She played a major role in the development of the educational system and potable water systems in Botswana.

Jeanne Martin Cissé (b. 1926)

Jeanne Martin Cissé started her career as a teacher in 1945 and became a well-known Guinean diplomat. She was director of a school until she decided to move into politics in 1958. She became a member of the Democratic Party in 1959 and worked in the federal office of the Kinda region of Guinea, focusing on activities to improve the lives and status of women. She served on the National and Regional Women's Committees of the National Assembly and eventually became secretary-general of the Conference of African Women in 1962. She remained in this role for ten years and at the same time was a member of the UN

Committee on the Status of Women. As her country's permanent representative to the United Nations from 1972 to 1976, she was the first woman appointed as a delegate and the first to preside over the UN Security Council. She was awarded the Lenin Peace Prize in 1975. In 1976, she returned to Guinea to become minister of social affairs and remained in that post until her retirement in 1984. More recently, she has been the coordinator of an NGO that focuses on the education of girls who would otherwise have little chance of an education.

Shirin Ebadi (b. 1947)

Born in northern Iran, Shirin Ebadi attended law school at Tehran University and became the first Iranian woman to serve as a judge in the Iranian judicial system. Following the Islamic Revolution in Iran in 1979 she and other female judges were removed from their positions and placed in clerical positions, based on the belief that Islam forbids women to be judges. She filed an application to practice law with the Justice Department but was denied, so she "retired" from the law and spent her time writing books and articles until 1992, when she was able to practice law again. She takes many civil rights cases, often on a pro bono basis. Ebadi was awarded the Nobel Peace Prize in 2003 for her work in defending women and children's rights in Iran and for encouraging a view of Islam compatible with democracy and human rights.

Dr. Ebadi joined other female Nobel Peace Prize winners, including Jody Williams, Wangari Maathai, Rigoberta Menchu Tum, Betty Williams, and Mairead Corrigan Maguire, to establish the Nobel Women's Institute. These women believe that by combining their efforts, they can more effectively work toward peace, justice, and equality for women by promoting and encouraging the work of women's rights activists, researchers, and organizations worldwide.

Nawal El Saadawi (b. 1931)

A well-known Egyptian doctor, novelist, and militant writer, Nawal El Saadawi was born in a small village on the banks of the Nile. She graduated from Cairo University in 1955. She refused to accept the subservient role that Egyptian society offered women. After studying medicine at Columbia University in New York she returned to Egypt and joined the staff of Cairo University Hospital as a doctor practicing in rural areas. She later became a psychiatrist; her book *Women and Sex* (1972) caused a great deal of controversy because it openly discussed chastity and the taboos that women faced in Arab society. She called for radical changes in the position of women within the family and as wage earners. She had been Egypt's director of public health but lost this position following the publication of her radical views when highly placed political and religious authorities called for her dismissal.

To date she has written twenty-seven books, including *The Hidden Face of Eve: Women in the Arab World* (1979), which describes her horrifying personal experience with female genital circumcision and examines the price that Arab women pay for being second-class citizens and the property of their husbands. In 1981 she was imprisoned at the notorious Qanatir prison with several other women on the order of President Anwar Sadat because she was publishing a feminist magazine (*Confrontation*) and stirring up protest among women. She was released in 1982 but her life continued to be threatened by Islamic fundamentalists and others who opposed her viewpoints. She founded the Arab Women's Solidarity Association in 1981 (see Chapter 7 for a description of program activities). She continues to write, speak, and advocate for women's rights.

Ana Figuero (1908–1970)

Chilean feminist Ana Figuero was born in Santiago and graduated from the University of Chile. She taught school until the start of World War II when she traveled to the United States to study at Columbia University and Colorado State College. An active advocate for women, she was president of the committee to gain the vote in Chile. She directed the national secondary school system from 1947 to 1949 and then became the head of the Women's Bureau in the Ministry of Foreign Affairs in the Chilean government. In 1951 she was her country's special envoy to the United Nations. As chair of the Social, Humanitarian, and Cultural Committee, Figuero was the first woman to head a UN committee of the General Assembly. She became the first woman on the Security Committee in 1952 and the first female assistant director general of the International Labour Organization (ILO). In 1967, she retired from the ILO.

Indira Gandhi (1917–1984)

Indira Gandhi was the daughter of Jawaharlal Nehru, the first prime minister of India following independence from Great Britain, and the granddaughter of Motilal Nehru, who played a prominent role in India's struggle against British colonial rule. She grew up an only child; her father and grandfather were frequently absent, having been arrested for their freedom activities. She attended school in Switzerland and England and married journalist Feroze Gandhi in 1942. Upon their return to India in 1942 Gandhi and her husband were imprisoned for 13 months because they supported the independence movement.

When India gained independence in 1947, Gandhi and her two sons moved home to help her father during his years as prime minister. Her marriage to Feroze effectively ended (although they were never divorced) about the time she moved into her father's home. She became her father's hostess and confidant, meeting many world leaders and traveling with her father to many foreign countries. Following his death in 1964 she was elected to fill his seat in Parliament. The same year she was appointed minister of information and broadcasting by Lal Shastri, who had succeeded her father as prime minister. After Shastri's death in 1966, Gandhi was elected leader of the Congress Party and became prime minister of India.

Her years as prime minister were often stormy. Congress Party members split over opposition to her policies and Gandhi called for a general election in 1971. She traveled throughout the country campaigning for public support and won an overwhelming majority of votes. The country experienced economic difficulties in 1974 and she declared an emergency rule following demonstrations throughout India. She imprisoned political adversaries and censored the press, outraging many Indians. Although she released many prisoners from jail and lifted the press censorship before elections were held in 1977, voters removed her from office. By October 1977 she had been charged with official corruption and jailed briefly.

In 1978 she ran for office in a rural district in South India after forming her own party, Congress-I Party (I for Indira), and was elected to Parliament. During national elections in 1980 she was swept back into power, with her party gaining two-thirds of the seats in Parliament. Many Indians forgave Gandhi for her excesses while in office, believing that she was the best the country had to offer. She became a forceful speaker and advocate for developing countries though trouble again mounted at home. During 1983 and 1984 she sent troops to stop disturbances in the Punjab, and these troops destroyed the large Sikh temple there. Two of her Sikh bodyguards assassinated her in New Delhi in June 1984 in retaliation for the destruction of the temple. Her son Rajiv followed in her footsteps and was sworn in as prime minister of India in October 1984.

Lydia Gueiler Tejada (b. 1921)

A well-known accountant, politician, and diplomat from Bolivia, Lydia Gueiler Tejada played an active role in the Bolivian revolution of 1952. She received a B.A. in accounting from the Institute Americano in Cochabamba, Bolivia. She was the Bolivian ambassador to Colombia from 1983 to 1986 and spent some time in charge of Bolivian business affairs in Germany. She was also political director and secretary general of the Partido Revolucionario de Izquierda. After serving as president of the National Congress from August through November 1979, Gueiler Tejada became president of Bolivia in November 1979. However, she was overthrown in a coup in July 1980 and lived in exile in Paris until the dictatorship ended in 1982.

Before being exiled, Gueiler Tejada was undersecretary of farmers' affairs in the Bolivian government, served six years as a national deputy, and represented Bolivian women at the Comision Interamerica de Mujeres. She authored several laws to help Bolivian women gain their rights. The author of *La Mujer y la Revolución* (Women and Revolution) in 1959, she received Bolivia's highest decoration, Condor de los Andes Gran Cruz, in 1979. At the United Nations in 1979, along with Margaret Thatcher and Indira Gandhi, Gueiler Tejada received the UN Woman of the Year award. She continued to serve as an ambassador to several countries, including Colombia, West Germany, and Venezuela, until her retirement in the mid-1990s.

Asha Hagi (b. 1962)

Born in Somalia, Hagi has worked tirelessly to bring peace to her country. She received a B.A. in economics from Somalia National University and an M.B.A. from the US International University in

Africa. In 1992 she co-founded Save Somali Women and Children (SSWC), an NGO promoting a safe and sustainable Somalia through programs to help women overcome discrimination, violence, and poverty.

In 2000, Hagi and several other women formed the Sixth Clan, a women's clan, to complement the traditional five Somali Clans, which are all male-dominated. The Sixth Clan participated in the Arta peace talks that year, the first time that women were included in the peace process.

In December 2006 Ethiopian forces overran Mogadishu and within four months, over 350,000 people fled from the city, including Hagi. Because she had spoken out against the Ethiopian takeover of the city, she moved to Nairobi, where she continues to work toward peace in Somalia.

Asma Jahangir (b. 1952)

As a well-known Pakistani lawyer, Asma Jahangir has fought legal inequities and human rights violations and continues to fight to end discrimination against women. Her father was a well-known liberal politician and she was active in student politics while in college. After graduation, she married a very successful businessman. She moved in with her husband's family, had children, and acted "appropriately" for her position as a woman. Finally, disgusted with herself, she asked her family to allow her to study law. She studied at home, attending college only when she was required to take exams. After graduation, her husband would not allow her to work in a "man's law office"; therefore, in 1980, she and three other women started their own law firm, the first woman's legal practice in Pakistan. Today, about 70 percent of their cases are pro bono. In 1983 she was beaten, tear-gassed, and arrested by police after protesting the Proposed Law of Evidence, in which a woman's testimony in court is valued at half a man's testimony.

Jahangir was the UN Special Rapporteur on Extrajudicial, Arbitrary, and Summary Executions, and since 2004 has been the UN Special Rapporteur on Freedom of Religion or Belief. When Pakistani President Pervez Musharraf declared a state of emergency in 2007, she was placed under house arrest for 90 days. She has also served on the Human Rights Commission of Pakistan.

Annie Ruth Baeta Jiagge (1918–1996)

Annie Ruth Baeta Jiagge, a prominent jurist and human rights activist in Ghana, received a teacher's certificate from Achimota College in 1937 and an LL.B. from the London School of Economics and Political Science in 1949. She was a teacher and headmistress and operated her own legal practice from 1951 to 1956. Jiagge had broad experience in the legal profession as a senior magistrate, a circuit court judge, a high court judge, a judge in the Court of Appeal, and president of the Court of Appeal. She was chairperson of the Commission on Investigation of Assets of Senior Public Servants and Named Political Leaders. She was the author of the draft of the 1968 UN Declaration on Elimination of Discrimination against Women and has written many articles in various journals. She was president of the World Council of Churches (1975–1983), moderator of the WCC Programme to Combat Racism (1984–1991), a member of the UN Commission on the Status of Women (1962–1974) and its president in 1968, as well as chairperson of the Ghana National Council on Women and Development (1975–1982). She also served as vice president of the YWCA at the international level, Ghana YWCA president, and chairperson of the Committee of the Churches Participation in Development, Christian Council of Ghana.

Fatima Jinnah (1893–1967)

Born in Karachi, Pakistan, Fatima Jinnah was sent to live with her brother in Bombay when she was eight years old, following the death of her father. She attended a mission school and later studied dentistry. She and her brother attended a Round Table Conference in London in 1929 and then remained in England for four years. Returning to Pakistan in 1934, she joined the Muslim League, which opposed the conservative orthodox attitudes of Pakistani society toward women; this was the start of her active participation in the fight for the emancipation of women. She led the All-India Muslim Women's Committee in 1938. She traveled throughout India, founding branches of the committee and student federations and inspiring the establishment of industrial schools, collectives, and other associations. She also founded the Fatima Jinnah Women's Medical College in Lahore.

When her brother Ali Jinnah became the first governor-general of Pakistan in 1947, she lived with him and served as his hostess; he died in 1948 and Fatima Jinnah retired from all public activity. In 1954 she re-entered the public eye, campaigning for the Muslim League and becoming an outspoken critic of the totalitarian government in East Pakistan. Persuaded to run against Ayub Khan in presidential elections as the representative of the combined opposition parties, she gained many staunch supporters. Although she lost the election, she continued to maintain a strong base of support. Known as the "mother of the country," she was a popular public figure; riots broke out during her funeral in Karachi in 1967 as an overwhelming number of her supporters crowded into the site of her funeral to mourn her death.

Ellen Johnson-Sirleaf (b. 1938)

Ellen Johnson-Sirleaf, born in Monrovia, Liberia, was educated at the College of West Africa in Liberia and at Harvard, where she earned a master's degree in public administration. She returned to Liberia and served as Finance Minister in William Tolbert's government from 1972 to 1973. Following the 1980 coup d'état, Samuel Doe took over the government. Doe named Johnson-Sirleaf president of the Liberian Bank for Development and Investment but she left that post after speaking out against many of Doe's advisers. She was briefly arrested but was released and fled the country for the United States, where she worked for Citibank, the World Bank, and the United Nations. Doe was assassinated in 1997 and Johnson-Sirleaf returned to Liberia to run for president, coming in second to Charles Taylor. Following Taylor's exile in 2005, she ran successfully for president.

Following her inauguration in January 2006, she set to work to solve Liberia's many problems; the country had little infrastructure, electricity and safe drinking water were in short supply, and schools and hospitals had limited staff and very little equipment. Her government identified four key development goals: peace and security, economic revitalization, governance and the rule of law, and basic infrastructure and services. She received the Presidential Medal of Freedom in 2007 from George W. Bush and has served on many advisory boards and commissions, including the International Crisis Group, Women's World Banking, Women Waging Peace, and the Center for Africa's International Relations.

Begum Liaquat Ali Khan (1905–1990)

Born into an aristocratic Muslim family in India, Begum Liaquat Ali Khan received her education at the universities of Lucknow and Calcutta. At age 26 she moved to New Delhi, where she taught economics at Indraprastha College for Women. In 1941 she submitted a carefully thought-out plan to develop a women's association as her master's thesis. Eighteen years later she finally founded such an organization, the All Pakistan Women's Association, which consisted of over two million women who were nurses, teachers, and administrators. Her husband, Liaquat Ali Khan, became prime minister of Pakistan in 1947; he was assassinated four years later in Rawalpindi.

In 1952 the All Pakistan Women's Association became a major force in the Pakistani women's movement, encouraging women to become involved in politics and social causes. The organization founded schools, hospitals, and craft industries. Continuing her involvement in politics, Ali Khan became the first Muslim woman ambassador from Pakistan; she served as ambassador to Belgium and the Netherlands in 1954 and later as ambassador to Italy and Tunisia. She participated on committees of the United Nations and in studies for the International Labour Organization. She became the first woman to become governor of a province in Pakistan (Sind). She was also the chancellor of the University of Karachi. In 1978, she was awarded the UN's Human Rights Award.

Gwendoline Konie (1938–2009)

Gwendoline Konie was born in Lusaka, Zambia, and received her early education from local schools; she later attended the University College in Cardiff, Wales, and American University in Washington, D.C. Following her return to Zambia, she found a job in the ministry of local government and social welfare. In 1963 Konie became a member of the Legislative Council and joined the ministry of foreign affairs the following year.

In 1972 she joined the staff of the presidential office and was the Zambian ambassador to Sweden, Norway, Denmark, and Finland from 1974 to 1877. In 1977 she represented Zambia at the United Nations, leading the UN Council for Namibia. Since

1979 she has been a permanent secretary in the Zambian Civil Service, acted as an adviser and consultant to many organizations, and served as a member of executive boards of several organizations that focus on adult education and family planning. In 2001 she contested the results of the presidential election that saw President Levy Mwanawasa elected.

Chandrika Bandaranaike Kumaratunga (b. 1946)

Following in her mother's footsteps, Chandrika Bandaranaike Kumaratunga served as president of Sri Lanka from 1994 to 2005. Kumaratunga's father, Solomon Bandaranaike, was the nation's prime minister until his assassination in 1959. Her brother Sirimavo Bandaranaike served two terms, from 1960 to 1965 and from 1970 to 1977.

She received a degree in political science from the Sorbonne in Paris in 1985. Although she has held teaching positions in England and India, she has focused primarily on political activities. During her mother's second term, she headed the land reform office. With her husband, a politician and film star, she formed the People's Alliance, a coalition to the right of her mother's Freedom Party and to the left of the United National Party. Following her husband's assassination in 1988, Kumaratunga assumed leadership of the alliance. She was named prime minister in 1994 following her party's narrow win in Parliament.

During her time in office, she has pledged to end the 12-year-old civil war between the government and the Liberation Tigers of Tamil Eelam. Women, especially in rural areas, have been vulnerable to rape, kidnapping, and torture, according to human rights groups, and Kumaratunga has fought to protect these women. She has advocated and won progressive revisions to the country's rape laws that increase penalties for this crime.

Bertha Lutz (1894–1976)

Bertha Lutz was a well-known Brazilian feminist who founded the Brazil Federation for the Advancement of Women in 1922 and was the federation's president until her death in 1976. At the same time, she was a permanent delegate to the Inter-American Commission of Women from Brazil. She studied biology at the Sorbonne in Paris and returned to Rio de Janeiro to become the first woman to enter government service at the National Museum. She organized and led the fight for women's suffrage, which was won in 1932. In 1936 she developed a government department to deal with the specific problems that women face in society, and she represented her country at many international conferences. She participated in the campaign to organize the UN Commission on the Status of Women. Lutz also taught zoology at the University of Rio de Janeiro.

Wangari Maathai (b. 1940)

Known around the world for her environmental and human rights activities, Wangari Maathai was born in Nyeri, Kenya, and raised in a farming community. Her parents were subsistence farmers from the Kikuyu tribe. After winning one of the many scholarships awarded to Kenyans by the Kennedy administration, Maathai attended Mount St. Scholastica College in Kansas, where she received a B.A. in biology in 1964. She earned her M.S. from the University of Pittsburgh, the first woman in all of eastern and central Africa to earn an advanced degree. In 1971 she earned a Ph.D. in biology from the University of Nairobi. She later became the first woman to hold an associate professorship at the University of Nairobi and was the first woman invited to chair a department there.

During her husband's campaign for a seat in Parliament she realized the problems that people in the lower economic class face in finding a job and supporting their families. Following her husband's election she started an employment agency to help people find work either cleaning the homes of wealthy people or planting trees and shrubs. She believed that planting trees would help stop desertification and soil erosion and support beautification. Even though her agency was not successful, she continually searched for ways to involve Kenyans in preserving the environment.

In 1977 Maathai succeeded in persuading the National Council of Women of Kenya to support her cause. First known as the Save the Land Harambee, the group soon became known as the Green Belt Movement (GBM). On World-Environment Day in 1977 her group planted seven trees in a small Nairobi park and gained the public's attention; it eventually grew into a large, influential organization. The group has the support of the United Nations, several European governments, and hundreds of individual donors throughout the world. Maathai has written several books about GBM, including *The Green Belt Movement* (1985) and *The Green Belt Movement: Sharing the Approach and the Experience* (1988). She and the GBM were awarded the Nobel Peace Prize in 2004.

Maathai continues to play an active role in politics. In 2002 she was elected to the Kenyan Parliament. She is a member of the Forum for the Restoration of Democracy and the founder of the Tribal Clashes Resettlement Volunteer Service to encourage the government to stop inciting tribal violence. She has won many awards, including the Woman of the Year Award in 1983, the Right Livelihood Award in 1984, the Better World Society Award for the Protection of the Global Environment in 1986, the Windstar Award for the Environment in 1988, the Woman of the World Award in 1989, the Africa Prize for Leadership for the Sustainable End to Hunger in 1991, the Petra Kelly Prize for Environment in 2004, the Conservation Scientist Award in 2004, and the Disney Conservation Award in 2006. She continues to fight for the environment and for human rights.

Rigoberta Menchu Tum (b. 1959)

Rigoberta Menchu is an internationally known civil rights activist who works for the rights of the Mayan and Aztec people of Guatemala. Born in Chimel, Guatemala, she witnessed the brutality of government forces toward her people, the Quiche Mayan Indians. She has tirelessly traveled throughout the world to bring attention to the plight of Guatemala's indigenous people, who have been persecuted by the landowning class and the military. Human rights organizations estimate that the number of indigenous people killed during the 33-year civil war has exceeded 15,000. Menchu traveled the country with her father, activist Vincente Menchu, a founding member of the Peasant Unity Committee (CUC), until he was tortured and killed by the Guatemalan security forces. Her mother and younger brother were also tortured and killed. In 1981 she escaped to Mexico and then traveled to France.

Menchu won the Nobel Peace Prize in 1992 for her work in human rights. The Nobel Prize Committee cited Menchu as a "vivid symbol of peace and reconciliation across ethnic, cultural, and social dividing lines." The committee noted that "by maintaining a disarming humanity in a brutal world, Rigoberta Menchu appeals to the best in us. She stands as a uniquely potent symbol of a just struggle" (Schlessinger and Schlessinger 1996, 174). She is the youngest person and the first indigenous person to win the Nobel Peace Prize. In a book about her life, *I, Rigoberta Menchu: An Indian Woman in Guatemala,* she describes many of her civil and human rights activities.

In 1999 several aspects of her autobiography were called into question by David Stoll, an anthropologist, in his book *Rigoberta Menchu and the Story of All Poor Guatemalans.* The reaction was swift: some accused Stoll of being a tool of the right wing in attacking Menchu while others attacked her, asking that the Nobel Committee revoke her Peace Prize. Menchu did admit to some inaccuracies but survived the controversy.

In 2007, she was one of 14 candidates running for president of Guatemala; she received only three percent of the vote and failed to qualify for the next round of elections. She was a member of the UN International Indian Treaty Council and served as the goodwill ambassador to the United Nations in 1993 for the Year of the Indigenous Peoples.

Fatima Mernissi (b. 1940)

Fatima Mernissi is a well-known Moroccan sociologist and feminist and the author of several publications; she is best known for her classic *Beyond the Veil: Male-Female Dynamic in Modern Muslim Society* (1975, revised edition 1987). This book vividly describes the status and lives of women and their interaction with men in Muslim society. Mernissi has also reinterpreted classical Islamic texts from a feminist perspective and supervised the publication of a series of books on the legal status of women in Morocco, Algeria, and Tunisia.

In 1992 she wrote *Islam and Democracy: Fear of the Modern World,* in which she argued that the Islamic faith has been used and compromised by Arab leaders to control their countries and prevent democratic reforms. According to Mernissi, these rulers have distorted Islamic beliefs to fit their needs and have abused human rights by suppressing democratic reforms. In 1994 she wrote *Dreams of Trespass: Tales of a Harem Girlhood* (published in

England as *The Harem Within: Tales of a Moroccan Girlhood*), which recounts her childhood growing up in a harem. Life was repressive and boring; Mernissi and the other women and girls in the harem were restricted in what they could do and where they could go. Her latest publication is *Dreams of Trespass* (1994), a collection of interviews she conducted during the mid-1970s. This collection provides incredible insight into the lives of Moroccan women. Formerly a professor of sociology at Mohammed V University in Rabat, Morocco, Mernissi is recognized around the world for her analyses of sexual ideology, gender identity, and the status of women in Islam.

Shushila Nayar (1914–2001)

Born in Gujarat, Pakistan, Dr. Shushila Nayar received her education at Lahore College for Women, Lady Hardinge Medical College in Delhi, and Johns Hopkins University in Baltimore, Maryland. As medical attendant to Mahatma Gandhi, she supported the Indian struggle for independence and was arrested and imprisoned from 1942 to 1944. Following India's independence from Britain, she worked as senior medical officer. She became minister of health, rehabilitation, and transport in Delhi State and was Speaker of the Delhi Legislative Assembly from 1952 to 1956. She was elected to the Lok Sabha (lower house of Parliament) in 1957. Appointed minister of health from 1962 through 1967, Nayar lost her seat in Parliament in 1971 but remained a highly influential figure. In 1969 she was named director of the Mahatma Gandhi Institute of Medical Sciences, where she was professor of preventive and social medicine. During this time she also served as secretary of the Leprosy Board of the Mahatma Gandhi Memorial Trust.

Teurai Ropa Nhongo (b. 1955)

Born to peasant parents, Nhongo ran away from her family and village to join the boys who were fighting in the bush for the creation of Zimbabwe. By the time she was 18 years old she was a member of the Zimbabwe African National Liberation Army's (ZANLA) general staff, and she was only 21 years old when she was named camp commander of Chimoio, the largest guerrilla and refugee camp in Mozambique. She married Rex Nhongo, deputy head of the ZANLA forces. During her time fighting with the guerrilla forces, she became one of the most famous guerrillas in Robert Mugabe's forces. She was hunted by the Rhodesian security forces but never captured. Following the creation of Zimbabwe, Nhongo was named the minister of youth, sport, and recreation in 1980 and became minister of community development and women's affairs in 1981.

Isabel Peron (b. 1931)

Not as well known as Eva Peron, Juan Peron's second wife, Isabel Peron was the third wife of Juan Peron, president of Argentina, and the first woman to serve as president of a nation. She gave up a career as a dancer to become Peron's secretary and then his wife. In 1955, they were exiled from Argentina during his second term as president because of his suppression of free speech and the faltering economy. Following many years of political ups and downs, Juan and Isabel Peron were allowed back into the country in 1973. Encouraged to run for the presidency, Juan Peron chose his wife to be his running mate. They won in a landslide victory in September 1973. As vice president, Isabel championed the cause of women's rights. With her husband's health failing, Isabel assumed the duties of head of state. She presided over the cabinet, traveled to Paraguay, traveled to Geneva to address the International Labour Organization, and went on to Madrid and Rome, where she met with Pope Paul VI. The day following her return to Argentina, Juan turned over full presidential power to her; he died on 1 July 1974.

She had a troublesome presidency, with many factions fighting for power, and was ousted in a coup in March 1976 by the military junta. She was held under house arrest in a remote government resort and later arrested and charged with corruption. She was released in 1981 and went into exile to Spain. In 1997 she was questioned about decrees she had issued in 1975 that allegedly allowed the military to eliminate subversive individuals. She denied allowing or encouraging any abuses during her presidency. In 2007 she was again detained by Spanish police but was released after a Spanish court rejected an Argentinian court's request to extradite her. Argentina continues to investigate alleged crimes committed during her presidency.

Fumilayo Ransome-Kuti (1900–1978)

An active feminist from Nigeria, Fumilayo Ransome-Kuti received her education from Anglican primary and secondary schools and then studied domestic science at Wincham Hall College in England. She returned to Nigeria and took a teaching job; she also became involved in advocating for women's rights, including women's suffrage. In the 1940s the British instituted tax policies that had serious negative effects on women and their economic independence. Ransome-Kuti organized strikes, demonstrations, and other acts of civil disobedience; these actions were instrumental in abolishing the heavy taxation of market women in Egbaland. She fought against sexism and racism and participated in the fight for independence from Great Britain. She was honored with an honorary law degree in 1968 from the University of Ibadan. She was elected to the Native House of Chiefs, was a member of the National Council of Nigeria and the Cameroons, was leader of the Commoners People's Party and the Nigeria Women's Union, and was a winner of the Lenin Peace Prize.

Aisha Ráteb (b. 1928)

Aisha Ráteb received her law degree from the Faculty of Law in Cairo and rose to become the first professor of international law at Cairo University. She became the minister of social affairs in the Egyptian government in 1971, the first woman to hold a ministerial position. She remained in this position until 1977, when she went on to become the minister of insurance. Ráteb became chair of the Legislative Affairs Committee in 1973 and the Egyptian minister of foreign affairs in 1978. She was the Egyptian ambassador to Denmark in 1979 and to Germany in 1981. Her efforts to reform the judiciary led to the appointment of Tahani al-Gebali, the first woman to serve on the Supreme Constitutional Court.

Dhanvanthi Rama Rau (1893–1987)

Dhanvanthi Rama Rau was a well-known social worker from India who was born into an aristocratic family and educated at the University of Madras in southern India. She was one of the first Indian women to attend college. She was a lecturer in English at Queen

Mary's College in Madras from 1917 to 1921 when she married Sir Bengal Rama Rau, a leading Indian diplomat. Following her marriage she began to work for social reform. She became the secretary of the All-India Child Marriage Abolition League in 1927, a member of the International Alliance for Suffrage and Equal Citizenship in 1932, and president of the All-India Women's Conference in 1946. She became interested in family planning, and from 1949 to 1963 she worked for the Family Planning Association of India. In 1963 she became the president of the International Planned Parenthood Association, a position she held until 1971.

Nibuya Sabalsajaray (1951–1974)

Nibuya Sabalsajaray, born into a poor family in Uruguay, was an active unionist. She studied in local schools and qualified as a teacher. She soon became a union organizer and leader, and in 1974 she participated in a major demonstration against the Uruguayan dictatorship. She was arrested and tortured and died two days after her arrest, at the age of 23 years. She is now revered as one of the martyrs of the country's repressive policy toward the unions during the 1970s.

Gita Sen (b. 1948)

Gita Sen is a leading researcher on women's issues as they relate to development, health and population, and the environment. She is a professor of Economics at the Indian Institute of Management in Bangalore, India, and an adjunct professor in the Department of Global Health and Population at Harvard University. A founding member of DAWN (Development Alternatives with Women for a New Era), Sen received her M.A. from the Delhi School of Economics and her Ph.D. in economics from Stanford University. She has taught at the New School for Social Research in New York, Radcliffe College, Vassar College, and the Center for Population and Development Studies at Harvard University.

Her publications include *Women and the New World Economy: Feminist Perspectives on Alternative Economic Frameworks; Development, Crisis, and Alternative Visions: Third World Women's Perspectives* (with Caren Grown); *Population Policies Reconsidered: Health, Empowerment, and Rights* (with Adrienne Germain and Lincoln C. Chen);

and *Power and Decision: The Social Control of Reproduction* (with Rachel Snow).

Huda Shaarawi (1879–1947)

A well-known Egyptian women's rights advocate, Huda Shaarawi was born into a wealthy family in Minia and educated in Turkish and French, the language of the wealthy. She taught herself Arabic. She started a school for girls in 1910, teaching general educational courses instead of courses such as midwifery that women were usually taught in vocational classes.

Shaarawi organized hundreds of women to demonstrate against the British during the nationalist movement. She helped organize and became head of the first women's association in Egypt in 1920. Three years later she traveled to Rome as the Egyptian representative to the International Conference of Women. In 1924 she organized the Women's Feminist Union. She and Saiza Nabarawi started the open feminist movement in Egypt by taking off their veils at the Cairo train station as they returned from an international feminist conference. Shaarawi and the union advocated for women's rights and the integration of urban women into public life. They wanted changes in the personal status laws, equal access to secondary and university education, expanded professional opportunities in business, and support systems for working mothers to provide child care; they also advocated for an end to legalized prostitution. Union members lobbied the government for these and other changes.

Shaarawi founded *Egyptian Women,* a journal published in both Arabic and French that described the goals of the Women's Union to its readers. In 1935 and 1939, Shaarawi attended the international women's conferences. In 1944, she helped organize the All Arab Federation of Women. In 1945, she advocated for the abolition of all atomic weapons.

Leticia Ramos Shahani (b. 1929)

Leticia Shahani has been involved in a variety of political and advocacy activities. Born in Lingayen, Pangasinan, the Philippines, she received a B.A. in English literature in 1951 from Wellesley College, an M.A. in comparative literature in 1954 from Columbia

University, and a Ph.D. in comparative literature and sociology in 1961 from the University of Paris (France). She has been on the faculty at the University of the Philippines, the New School for Social Research in New York, and the International Study and Research Institute in New York. Other positions include dean of the graduate school at the Lyceum of the Philippines and president of the national YMCA of the Philippines.

She was a senator in the Congress of the Philippines and has had a varied and active career in politics. At the international level, she has participated in many UN activities, including representative to the UN Commission on the Status of Women (1970–1974), member of the Philippine delegation to the UN General Assembly (1974–1979), member of the Philippine delegation to the UN World Conference during International Women's Year (1975), Philippine representative to the Preparatory Committee for the UN Conference on the Mid-Decade for Women (1978–1980), chairwoman of the Philippine delegation to the World Conference on the UN Mid-Decade for Women (1980), UN assistant secretary general for Social Development and Humanitarian Affairs (1981–1986), and secretary general of the World Conference to Review and Appraise the Achievements of the UN Decade for Women (1985).

Helvi Sipilä (1915–2009)

After receiving her education at the University of Helsinki, Helvi Sipilä became an acting judge in the rural district courts in Finland. Between 1941 and 1951 she held various legal posts on the Supreme Court and the Supreme Administrative Court. She was a member of various Finnish government committees on matrimonial legislation, protection of children, social benefits for children, citizenship education, and international development. She was a member of the Council of the Human Rights Institute in Strasbourg, France, beginning in 1969.

As an attorney, she founded and operated her own law office in Finland from 1943 to 1972; at the same time she was actively involved in UN activities. Sipilä retired from her post of assistant secretary general of the UN's Centre for Social Development and Humanitarian Affairs (CSDHA) in 1980. In this position she had played a major role in planning the 1975 International Women's Year (IWY) Conference in Mexico City. CSDHA administered the

IWY Trust Fund, and its Branch for the Advancement of Women acted as the secretariat for the Commission on the Status of Women. Before taking the post at CSDHA, Sipilä served as international president of Zonta International (see Chapter 7).

During International Women's Year, Sipilä appealed to governments to set aside prejudices of race, sex, language, and religion in order to confront problems affecting everyone. She traveled extensively to government capitals around the world to build understanding and interest in International Women's Year. In 1981 she founded the Finnish National Committee on UNIFEM, which consisted of 400 individual and 30 organizational members. She also represented Finland as a delegate to the UN Commission on the Status of Women (CSW). The Helvi Sipilä Seminar was established at the 50th Session of the CSW to honor her contributions in the field of human rights and the status of women.

Margaret Snyder (b. 1929)

Margaret Snyder has been involved in women's development activities for many years and is the founding director of the UN Development Fund for Women. She received her Ph.D. from the University of Dar es Salaam and was honored at Makerere University in 1993 for her valuable contributions to the advancement of women in agriculture and education. She has been a Visiting Fellow in International Studies at Princeton University.

Snyder has long been involved in development policies and women's issues in Africa. As a regional adviser for the UN Economic Commission for Africa, she initiated their Women's Programme, led the Voluntary Agencies Bureau, and cofounded the African Training and Research Centre for Women. She is also a cofounder of Women's World Banking, an organization that provides loans and other business services to women through a network of affiliate organizations (see Chapter 7). Her publications include *Farmers and Merchants: Some Observations on Women and the State in Africa; Politics, Poverty and Participation: A History of Women's Leadership in Development;* and *Women: The Key to Ending Hunger.*

She was the founder and first director of the UN Development Fund for Women (UNIFEM). In writing *Transforming Development: Women, Poverty and Politics,* Snyder traveled to 15 countries to examine projects that UNIFEM had supported and interviewed women and men who were helped by these projects.

Mu Sochua (b. 1954)

Mu Sochua fled Phnom Penh in 1972 as the Vietnam War spread into Cambodia. Her parents disappeared, victims of the Khmer Rouge. Sochua spent 18 years in exile in France, the United States, and Italy, during which time she earned a B.A. in psychology from San Francisco State University and an M.S.W. from the University of California at Berkeley. She also worked in refugee camps along the border between Thailand and Cambodia.

Sochua returned to Cambodia in 1989, becoming an activist on women's and children's issues. She created Khemara, the first Cambodian organization to focus on women's issues. In 1998 she won a national assembly seat and became the first female minister for women's and veterans' affairs. Her advocacy for women's rights led her to launch a national campaign for gender equality. In 2004, however, she resigned her government position, citing her frustration with governmental and outside corruption that hindered her work. She received the Vital Voices Human Rights Global Leadership Award from then-Senator Hillary Clinton for her efforts to stop human trafficking. She is currently a member of parliament for the opposition party, fighting for women's rights and participatory government.

Mary Tadesse (b. 1932)

As a former vice minister for education and culture as well as an assistant minister of education in Addis Ababa, Ethiopia, Mary Tadesse has worked extensively with policy development and programs concerning women and development. These activities include developing and advancing policies and strategies for the advancement of women in developing countries on a regional as well as a global level. She has worked with organizations such as the Council of African Advisers to the World Bank, the Board of Trustees of the International Research and Training Institute for the Advancement of Women (INSTRAW), the Federation of African Women Entrepreneurs, and the Africa Regional Coordinating Committee for the Integration of Women in Development. She has participated in many academic and governmental conferences. With Margaret Snyder, Tadesse published *African Women and Development: A History* in 1995. She is a board member of the Fistula Foundation.

Sakena Yacoobi

Born in Herat, Afghanistan, Sakena Yacoobi traveled to the United States for her education, earning a B.S. in biological sciences from the University of the Pacific and a M.P.H. from Loma Linda University. She spent several years in the United States as a health consultant and professor of biology, mathematics, and psychology at D'Etre University in Michigan.

She began working with Afghan refugees in Pakistan in 1992, joining the International Rescue Committee in Peshawar first as manager, then coordinator, of their Female Education and Teacher Training Program; she expanded the number of Afghan girls enrolled in school, and girls' and women's access to education. In 1995, she formed the Afghan Institute of Learning (ALI) to provide teacher education to Afghan women, encourage education for all children, and offer health education to women and children. During Taliban control in the 1990s, ALI supported 80 underground schools for girls throughout the country. Yacoobi and ALI received the 2004 Women's Rights Prize from the Peter Gruber Foundation, and the 2005 Democracy Award of the National Endowment for Democracy.

Yacoobi is also a co-founder and vice president of Creating Hope International, an NGO that works to improve the lives of individuals dealing with natural disasters, world strife, and other devastating conditions. She is on the board of directors of the Global Fund for Women, and was a 2000 delegate to the United Nations Millennium Forum for NGOs and a 2001 delegate to the Roundtable on Women's Leadership in Rebuilding Afghanistan.

Begum Khaleda Zia (b. 1945)

Begum Khaleda Zia was the prime minister of Bangladesh from 1991 to 1996 and from 2001 to 2006—She also served as the minister for establishment, information, and mineral resources, and was a leader of the Bangladesh Nationalist Party. She attended primary and secondary school and then married Zia-ur Rahman when she was 16 years old. He was the country's president from 1977 until 1981, when he was assassinated. At that point Hossain Mohammad Ershad came to power and martial law was declared and political parties officially abolished. The Bangladesh Nationalist

Party continued to exist unofficially, however, and Khaleda Zia led her party as chairwoman in 1984. Zia was at the center of the fight to end martial law and restore free elections, participating in strikes, street protests, and mass demonstrations. During this period she was placed under house arrest several times. Ershad resigned his position in 1990, elections were held in 1991, and Khaleda Zia became prime minister. She focused her attention on population control, mass literacy, compulsory primary education, fighting poverty, and extending electricity to rural areas.

She won a second term as prime minister in elections held in February 1996, but the other major parties refused to accept the results. A caretaker government was appointed. Her party lost in June 1996. Winning again in the 2001 elections, she was named prime minister; she spent most of her five years in office fighting religious militancy, continuing charges of corruption, and growing attacks on minority groups

Zia has been criticized by many women for her silence on women's issues, especially the conditions of women working in the garment industry. Over two million women work in appalling conditions in Bangladeshi sweatshops. She has also been criticized for her unwillingness to fight the growing Islamic fundamentalist movement in her country. In January 2006, her Bangladesh National Party was defeated in the general election, winning only 29 out of a possible 300 seats.

References

Europa Publications. 2009. *International Who's Who of Women 2010*. New York: Routledge.

Europa Publications. 2010. *Who's Who in International Affairs 2011*. New York: Routledge.

Schlessinger, Bernard S., and June S. Schlessinger, eds. 1996. *The Who's Who of Nobel Prize Winners, 1901–1995*. Third ed. Phoenix: Oryx Press.

6

Facts and Data

The World Bank estimates that over 80 percent of the world's population live in developing countries and earn individual incomes under $2.00 per day (World Bank 2008). Poverty is a major concern for many residents of developing countries and limited access to education, health services, and employment opportunities mean that it is very difficult to escape. While a significant number of developing countries have enacted laws to protect women, discrimination and violence remain a daily fact of life for many. Countries may have laws providing for compulsory education but access to education is limited, especially in rural areas. Health care resources may be minimal or nonexistent. Employment opportunities are often scarce, especially in rural areas, and without adequate education these opportunities may be out of reach for many women.

This chapter provides comparative statistics on the status of women in developing countries, including access and enrollment levels in primary and secondary school, maternal mortality rates and access to health care, rates of female genital mutilation, labor participation, political participation, domestic violence, and other human rights issues. The chapter begins with a summary of the major human rights instruments that were designed to promote women's rights and eliminate and prohibit discrimination against women.

International Conventions and Protocols

The Charter of the United Nations and the International Bill of Rights are two instruments that provide a forceful statement on women's rights in the international arena. The International Bill of Rights includes the Universal Declaration of Human Rights, the International Covenant on Civil and Political Rights, and the International Covenant on Economic, Social, and Cultural Rights. The UN Charter is the first international document to specifically mention equal rights of women and men.

The Charter of the United Nations

The UN Charter, adopted in 1945, established the United Nations as an international body to encourage peace and tolerance, unite the countries of the world in maintaining international peace and security, ensure that armed forces would not be used except for the common interest, and promote economic and social advancement of all people. Article 1 describes the purposes of the United Nations, including "to achieve international cooperation in solving international problems of an economic, social, cultural, or humanitarian character, and in promoting and encouraging respect for human rights and for fundamental freedoms for all without distinction as to race, sex, language, or religion" (Art.1[3]).

Commission on the Status of Women

The Commission of the Status of Women was created in 1946 by the UN General Assembly to ensure women's equality and promote women's rights. Close working relationships were built with NGOs, human rights treaty bodies, the Commission on Human Rights, and other UN agencies. Members assisted in drafting the Universal Declaration of Human Rights and conducted in-depth country-specific analyses of the legal status of women as well as their access to education, work opportunities, and other measures of their experiences. During the 1960s and 1970s the Commission focused on the role of women in development and suggested that the United Nations expand its technical assistance activities to help women in developing countries. Members urged the United Nations to declare 1975 the International Women's Year; the General Assembly agreed and included the recognition of women's role in the peace process in its agenda. The First World Conference on Women was part of the International Women's Year and subsequent conferences were organized. During the UN Decade for Women, the Commission drafted the Convention on the Elimination of All Forms of Discrimination against Women (CEDAW), which was adopted by the General Assembly in 1979. The Commission continues its work on behalf of women's rights and advancement, currently focusing its attention on implementing the Beijing Platform for Action.

Universal Declaration of Human Rights

Recognizing that member states have "reaffirmed their faith in fundamental human rights, in the dignity and worth of the human person and in the equal rights of men and women," the Universal Declaration of Human Rights was adopted in 1948. It proclaims that all persons are "born free and equal in dignity and rights" (Art. 1), and that every person is "entitled to all the rights and freedoms set forth in this Declaration, without distinction of any kind, such as race, colour, sex, language, religion, political or other opinion, national or social origin, property, birth or other status" (Art. 2), and that all are entitled to equal protection under the law (Art. 7).

Article 16 states that all men and women have the right to marry and create a family, and that they "are entitled to equal rights as to marriage, during marriage and at its dissolution." Both spouses are to enter into the marriage with "free and full consent." Article 25 focuses on the right to a standard of living that includes adequate food, clothing, housing, medical care, and social services, as well as social security in the event of unemployment, sickness, disability, widowhood, or old age. In addition, "[m]otherhood and childhood are entitled to special care and assistance." Article 26 proclaims the right of all individuals to education, stating that elementary education should be compulsory and free and that everyone should have equal access to higher education.

Convention on the Suppression of the Traffic in Persons and of the Exploitation of the Prostitution of Others

This convention, adopted in 1949 and entered into force in 1951, was written in response to many previous attempts to suppress activities related to prostitution. The General Assembly believed that prostitution and trafficking in persons for the purpose of prostitution were not compatible with human worth and dignity and endangered the welfare of individuals, families, and communities.

Each signatory agrees "to punish any person who, to gratify the passions of another (1) procures, entices or leads away, for purposes of prostitution, another person, even with the consent of that person; [and] (2) exploits the prostitution of another person, even with the consent of that person" (Art. 1). In addition, persons who keep, manage, or finance a brothel or rent a building to be used for the purpose of prostitution will be punished (Art. 2). If a national commits one of the above offenses in another country and returns to his or her home country, he or she can be extradited to the country where the offense was committed; if his or her home country does not permit extradition, then Article 9 provides that the offender be tried for the offense in his or her home country.

Article 14 requires that each signatory establish and maintain a service that coordinates results of the investigations into trafficking offenses and shares that information with other interested parties. Immigrants are protected by Article 17, which requires each party to adopt regulations to protect these individuals, to warn the public of the dangers of trafficking, to monitor public places such as train and bus stations and airports in order to prevent trafficking, and to warn the appropriate authorities of the arrival of persons who may be traffickers or victims of traffickers.

Equal Remuneration Convention

The Equal Remuneration Convention was adopted in 1951 and entered into force in 1953 by the General Conference of the International Labour Organization. Remuneration includes both "ordinary, basic or minimum wage or salary" and indirect or in kind payment. Recognizing the importance of equal pay for men and women, it calls on each member state to "promote and, in so far as is consistent with such methods, ensure the application to all workers of the principle of equal remuneration for men and women workers for work of equal value" (Art. 2[1]). This goal can be accomplished through national laws, legally established means for determining wages, collective agreements, or any combination of these methods (Art. 2[2]).

Convention on the Political Rights of Women

The Convention on the Political Rights of Women, adopted in 1952 and entered into force in 1954, provides a number of rights to women regarding voting and running for elections. It provides that women are "entitled to vote in all elections on equal terms with men" (Art. 1), that they can be elected "to all publicly elected bodies, established by national law, on equal terms with men" (Art. 2), and that they can hold public office, all without suffering discrimination.

Convention on the Nationality of Married Women

Adopted in 1957 and entered into force in 1958, the Convention on the Nationality of Married Women provides protection for a woman who marries someone outside of her country or nationality. The Contracting States agree that neither marriage nor the dissolution of marriage "between one of its nationals and an alien, nor the change of nationality by the husband during marriage, shall automatically affect the nationality of the wife" (Art. 1). It allows women to adopt the nationality of their husbands, if they so desire, but does not require it.

Discrimination (Employment and Occupation) Convention

Adopted in 1958 and entered into force in 1960 by the governing body of the International Labour Office, the Discrimination (Employment and Occupation) Convention follows the Declaration of Philadelphia, which "affirms that all human beings, irrespective of race, creed or sex, have the right to pursue both their material well-being and their spiritual development in conditions of freedom and dignity, of economic security and equal opportunity." It defines discrimination as "any distinction, exclusion or preference made on the basis of race, colour, sex, religion, political opinion, national extraction or social origin, which has the effect of nullifying or impairing equality of opportunity or treatment in employment or occupation" (Art. 1[a]).

Convention against Discrimination in Education

Adopted by the General Conference of the UN Educational, Scientific and Cultural Organization in 1960 and entered into force in 1962, the Convention against Discrimination in Education prohibits all discrimination, including that based on race, color, sex, language, religion, political or other opinion, national origin, economic condition or birth, in the provision of education. The term "education" includes "all types and levels of education, and includes access to education, the standard and quality of education, and the conditions under which it is given" (Art. 1). All Parties to this Convention agree to develop a national policy to promote equal opportunities to education, including free and compulsory primary education, generally accessible secondary and higher education, and equal standards in all public institutions, as well as to provide teacher training without discrimination (Art. 4). Article 5 specifies that education should strengthen "respect for human rights and fundamental freedoms; it shall promote understanding, tolerance and friendship among all nations, racial or religious groups," among other tenets.

International Covenant on Economic, Social, and Cultural Rights

Adopted in 1966 and entered into force in 1976, the International Covenant on Economic, Social and Cultural Rights recognizes that the "inherent dignity and . . . the equal and inalienable rights of all the members of the human family is the foundation of freedom, justice and peace in the world." It declares that "all peoples have the right of self-determination . . . they freely determine their political status and freely pursue their economic, social and cultural development" and they cannot be deprived of their own means of subsistence (Art. 1). Member states must work to "guarantee that the rights enunciated in the present Covenant will be exercised without discrimination of any kind as to race, colour, sex, language, religion, political or other opinion, national or social origin, property, birth or other status" (Art. 2). Member states are also required to "ensure the equal right of men and women to the enjoyment of all economic, social and cultural rights" set forth in this Covenant (Art. 3).

The right to work is also recognized, and it "includes the right of everyone to the opportunity to gain his living by work which he freely chooses or accepts, and will take appropriate steps to safeguard this right" (Art. 6[1]). Fair wages must also be provided without any distinctions, "in particular women being guaranteed conditions of work not inferior to those enjoyed by men, with equal pay for equal work" (Art. 7[1]).

Families also are considered in this covenant. It calls for the "widest possible protection and assistance" for the family, specifically while it is responsible for caring for and educating children (Art. 10). It also requires that marriage should be "entered into with the free consent of the intending spouses" (Art. 10[1]). Mothers must be protected before childbirth and once children are born, and if they are employed they should be given paid leave or leave with some type of adequate social security benefits (Art. 10[2]). Child labor should be prohibited (Art. 10[3]).

Article 11 focuses on the right to an adequate standard of living, including adequate food, clothing, and shelter. Article 12 recognizes the right to enjoyment of physical and mental health and calls for reduction of infant mortality and the number of stillbirths. The right of all persons to education is the focus of Article 13, including free primary education for all and accessible secondary and higher education.

International Covenant on Civil and Political Rights

The International Covenant on Civil and Political Rights recognizes that conditions must be created in which every human is able to enjoy his or her civil and political rights, and that member states are obliged to provide these rights to their citizens. Adopted in 1966 and entered into force in 1976, this convention provides for a variety of rights for the individual, including the right to life, liberty, and personal security, and freedom of thought and association. Article 3 requires that member states work to "ensure the equal right of men and women to the enjoyment of all civil and political rights set forth" in the convention. Men and women have the equal right to marry freely, with mutual consent, and have equal rights and responsibilities during a marriage and after its dissolution (Art. 23).

Declaration on the Elimination of Discrimination against Women

The UN General Assembly declared that although the Charter of the United Nations, the Universal Declaration of Human Rights, and other instruments of the United Nations affirmed the importance of human rights for all individuals, including women, women still faced a considerable amount of discrimination. As a result, in 1967 they adopted this Declaration, which stated that "discrimination against women, denying or limiting as it does their equality of rights with men, is fundamentally unjust and constitutes an offence against human dignity" (Art. 1). They called for member states to abolish all existing laws and practices that discriminate against women (Art. 2), provide legal protection for women (Art. 2), and give women the right to vote and to hold public office (Art. 4) as well as the right to "acquire, administer, enjoy, dispose of and inherit property, including property acquired during marriage" (Art. 6). Child marriage is also to be prohibited (Art. 6). Member governments agree to repeal discriminatory laws (Art. 7); curb trafficking and prostitution of women (Art. 8); and ensure women equal rights in education (Art. 9), economics, social life, and equal pay (Art. 10).

Declaration on the Protection of Women and Children in Emergency and Armed Conflict

The Declaration on the Protection of Women and Children in Emergency and Armed Conflict was adopted and entered into force in 1974. The Economic and Social Council of the United Nations recognized the need to protect civilian women and children during wars, civil unrest, and other emergency and armed conflicts because they are "often the victims of inhuman acts and consequently suffer serious harm." Understanding that women and children experience abuse as a result of "suppression, aggression, colonialism, racism, alien domination and foreign subjugation," this Declaration is intended to protect them and future generations from harm. Attacks on civilian populations and the use of chemical and bacterial weapons in warfare are prohibited and condemned. The Declaration further requires that all "necessary steps shall be taken to ensure the prohibition of measures such as persecution, torture, punitive measures, degrading treatment and violence," especially against women and children. All types of repression and cruel and inhuman treatment of women and children, including "imprisonment, torture, shooting, mass arrests, collective punishment, destruction of dwellings and forcible eviction," will be considered criminal acts. Shelter, medical care, food, and other inalienable rights must be provided to all women and children caught in emergency and other conflicts.

Convention on the Elimination of All Forms of Discrimination against Women (CEDAW)

Seen as an international bill of rights for women, CEDAW was adopted by the UN General Assembly in 1979 and came into force on 3 September 1981. Calling for a plan of action to eliminate sex-based discrimination, it requires all signatories to include gender equality in their domestic legislation; repeal all discriminatory provisions in their country's laws; enact new legislation to protect women from discrimination; establish public institutions to ensure protections for women against discrimination; and eliminate all types of discrimination that are currently practiced by individuals, organizations, and businesses. It has been ratified in all UN member countries except for eight, including the United States (see Chapter 3).

CEDAW was the first international instrument to specifically define discrimination against women as "any distinction, exclusion or restriction made on the basis of sex which has the effect or purpose of impairing or nullifying the recognition, enjoyment or exercise by women, irrespective of their marital status, on a basis of equality of men and women, of human rights and fundamental freedoms in the political, economic, social, cultural, civil or any other field" (Art. 1).

International Convention on the Protection of the Rights of All Migrant Workers and Members of Their Families

Adopted in 1990 and entered into force in 2003, this convention recognized the growing number of migrants and the importance of providing them with protection from discrimination, abuse, and trafficking. Protection is provided to all migrant workers regardless of their "sex, race, colour, language, religion or conviction, political or other opinion, national, ethnic or social origin, nationality, age economic position, property, marital status, birth or other status" (Art. 7). Member states are encouraged to prevent trafficking in migrant workers.

Fourth World Conference on Women Beijing Declaration

At the Fourth World Conference on Women, participating governments reaffirmed their commitment to equality, development, and peace for all women with this declaration. They reaffirmed their commitment to equal rights for women, the full implementation of the Nairobi Forward-Looking Strategies for the Advancement of Women, and the "empowerment and advancement of women." Participants declared that "women's rights are human rights"; that women have the right to "control all aspects of their health, in particular their own fertility"; that policies and programs that are gender-sensitive are essential to the empowerment of women; and that participation by women's groups, NGOs, and other community-based organizations are important factors in implementing the Platform for Action. Participants also vowed to ensure that women and girls enjoy all human rights and basic freedoms, eliminate all forms of discrimination against women, encourage men to participate in the process, promote the economic independence of women, prevent all violence against women, protect women's human rights, ensure women's equal access to education, respect international laws, promote women's access to economic resources, and ensure the success of the Platform for Action.

Home Work Convention

Adopted in 1996 and entered into force in 2000, this convention offers protections to individuals who work at home for pay, including equal treatment concerning occupational safety and health, remuneration, social security protection, access to training, minimum age of employment, and maternity protection.

It calls on members to adopt and implement a national policy regarding home work and calls for protection against discrimination in employment.

Protocol to Prevent, Suppress, and Punish Trafficking in Persons, Especially Women and Children, Supplementing the UN Convention against Transnational Organized Crime

Adopted in 2000 and entered into force in 2003, the Protocol to Prevent, Suppress and Punish Trafficking in Persons, Especially Women and Children, supplements the Convention against Transnational Organized Crime. The protocol's purposes include preventing and combating trafficking in persons, especially women and children; protecting and assisting victims of trafficking; and promoting cooperation within member states to meet these purposes. It requires that signatories enact legislative and other measures to establish trafficking as a criminal offense (Art. 5); provide a wide range of assistance to victims, including the provision of services to assist in the "physical, psychological and social recovery of victims" (Art. 6); and establish comprehensive policies and programs to prevent and combat trafficking (Art. 9).

UN Security Council Resolution 1325 on Women and Peace and Security

The Security Council observed that women and children often bear the brunt of armed conflict as refugees and internally displaced persons and are increasingly targets of combatants and other armed elements. The Council believed that women and girls need full protection using international humanitarian and human rights laws and recognized the "urgent need to mainstream a gender perspective into peacekeeping operations." Adopted in October 2000, this resolution calls for increased numbers of women at all decision-making levels of government and institutions and in conflict resolution and peace processes; a gender perspective in peacekeeping processes; additional support for gender-sensitive training efforts; and the development of "training guidelines and materials on the protection, rights and the particular needs of women" (¶6). All actors involved in negotiating and implementing peace agreements are asked to adopt a gender perspective during repatriation and resettlement activities; to support women's peace initiatives; to ensure human rights protection for women and girls; and to protect women and children from armed conflicts and gender-based violence, especially rape and other forms of sexual abuse.

Regional Conventions: Inter-American Conventions, Statutes, and Declarations

The Organization of American States (OAS) has adopted a number of conventions and statutes to protect the human rights of women and children and to prevent violence against them. Several of these are summarized below.

American Convention on Human Rights ("Pact of San Jose, Costa Rica")

The American Convention on Human Rights was adopted by member states of the OAS in 1969 and entered into force in 1978. The signatories agree to "respect the rights and freedoms recognized herein and to ensure to all persons subject to their jurisdiction the free and full exercise of those rights and freedoms, without any discrimination for reasons of race, color, sex, language, religion, political or other opinion, national of social origin, economic status, birth or any other social condition" (Art. 1). Among the rights protected are the right to life, the right to humane treatment, the right to freedom from slavery, the right to personal liberty, the right to a fair trial, the right to privacy, the right to freedom of conscience and religion, the right to freedom of thought and expression, the right to nationality, the right to property, the right to freedom of movement, the right to participate in government, and the right to judicial protection. Rights especially relevant to women are the right to equal protection and rights related to the family, including "the right of men and women of marriageable age to marry and raise a family" and the provision that "no marriage shall be entered into without the free and full consent of the intending spouses" (Art. 17).

Additional Protocol to the American Convention on Human Rights in the Area of Economic, Social, and Cultural Rights ("Protocol of San Salvador")

This protocol, adopted in 1988 and entered into force in 1999, provides for specific economic, social, and cultural rights for individuals. Signatories are obligated to enact legislation related to these rights and to provide them "without discrimination of any kind for reasons related to color, sex, language, religion, political or other opinions, national or social origin, economic status, birth or any other social condition" (Art. 3). Individuals are to be provided with just, equitable, and satisfactory conditions of work, including equal wages, adequate and fair pay for work, stability of employment, a safe work environment, and reasonable limits to daily and weekly hours of work (Art. 7). Workers are also to be provided with the right to organize trade unions (Art. 8). Article 10 provides for the "right to health, understood to mean the enjoyment of the highest level of physical, mental and social well-being," including primary health care, immunizations, disease prevention, health education, and health services for high risk groups and those living in poverty. Article 12 affirms the right to food. Education is also declared a right, including free and accessible primary education and generally available secondary education (Art. 13). Family rights encompass assistance to mothers before and after childbirth, adequate nutrition, and programs for family training (Art. 15). Other rights include protection of children, the elderly, and the handicapped.

Statute of the Inter-American Commission of Women

The statute creating the Inter-American Commission of Women was approved in 1960 by the Assembly of Delegates of the OAS. The Commission's purpose is to "promote and protect women's rights, and to support the member states in their efforts to ensure full exercise of civil, political, economic, social, and cultural rights that will make possible equal participation by women and men in all aspects of society" (Art. 2). The Commission is directed to identify areas in which women's participation must be increased;

to develop strategies to recognize the roles of women and men as having equal worth; to suggest means of removing barriers to equal rights; to encourage women to fully participate in all civil, political, economic, and cultural activities; to promote access to education and training; and to persuade governments to comply with the statute's provisions.

Inter-American Convention on the Granting of Civil Rights to Women

Adopted in 1948 and entered into force in 1949, the parties to this convention noted that the majority of American countries have granted civil rights to women and that Resolution XX of the Eighth International Conference of American States declared that women have the right to equality of civil status. They "agree to grant to women the same civil rights that men enjoy."

Inter-American Convention on the Granting of Political Rights to Women

Recognizing that the majority of member states have granted political rights to women, the Inter-American Convention on the Granting of Political Rights to Women encourages member nations to grant full voting rights to all women in addition to the right to run for political office. This convention was adopted in 1948 and entered into force in 1949.

Inter-American Convention on the Prevention, Punishment, and Eradication of Violence against Women ("Convention of Belem do Para")

Adopted in 1994 and entered into force in 1995, this convention builds on the Declaration on the Elimination of Violence against Women, adopted in 1993. Understanding that "violence against women pervades every sector of society regardless of class, race or ethnic group, income, culture, level of education, age or religion and strikes at its very foundations," this convention focuses on protecting the rights of women and eliminating violence perpetrated against them. Violence is defined as "any act or conduct, based on gender, which causes death or physical, sexual or psychological harm or suffering to women, whether in the public or the private sphere" (Art. 1).

Rights endowed by this convention include the right to respect of a woman's life; the integrity of her person and her physical, mental, and moral integrity; personal liberty; equal protection under the law; access to a competent court for protection from all violations of her rights; freedom of association and religion; and equal access to public services (Art. 4). Included within the right to freedom from violence are the rights to be free from all types of discrimination, to be valued, to be educated free from stereotypes of the roles of men and women, and to have access to services for abused women and training programs. Public awareness programs should be developed to educate the public on the dangers of and penalties for domestic violence and research should be conducted to gather relevant statistics on domestic violence and to implement effective preventive and treatment programs (Art. 8).

Inter-American Convention on Support Obligations

In Montevideo, Uruguay, in July 1989, member states of the OAS adopted the Inter-American Convention on Support Obligations to establish a legal instrument enforcing the obligations that spouses or former spouses have toward supporting their spouses and children.

Convention on the Nationality of Women

Signed in Montevideo, Uruguay, in December 1933, this Convention protects the nationality of women. Member states agreed that they would not make any distinction based on sex regarding the nationality of their citizens. Women are free to adopt the nationality of the husband if different from their own, but are no longer required to do so.

Regional Conventions: Africa

The Organization of African Unity and individual countries have created and adopted several conventions and charters that include rights of African women.

African (Banjul) Charter on Human and Peoples' Rights

This Charter was adopted by the members of the Organization of African Unity in 1981 and entered into force in 1986. Its aim was to promote human rights and freedoms in Africa. In addition to providing basic rights for all people, including the right to liberty, free association, assembly, freedom of movement, work, and education, this charter specifically identifies the family as the "natural unit and basis of society" (Art. 18). The elimination of all discrimination against women and protection of their rights is to be ensured by all members.

Protocol to the African Charter on Human and Peoples' Rights on the Rights of Women in Africa

This protocol, adopted in 2003 and entered into force in 2005, expands the human rights afforded to all people in the African Charter on Human and Peoples' Rights. Violence against women is defined as "all acts perpetrated against women which cause or could cause them physical, sexual, psychological, and economic harm, including the threat to take such acts; or to undertake the imposition of arbitrary restrictions on or deprivation of fundamental freedoms in private or public life in peace time and during situations of armed conflicts or of war" (Art. 1 [j]). All forms of discrimination are to be eliminated through the national constitutions and legislative initiatives of member states; through the development of a gender perspective in all government policies and programs; and through government support for all local, national, regional, and international conventions and initiatives (Art. 3).

Articles also promote every woman's right to dignity, to integrity, and security, and to to participation in the political and decision-making process, as well as to peace, education and training, health and reproductive rights, food security, adequate housing, a positive cultural context, a healthy environment, sustainable development, and inheritance. Female genital mutilation is to be eliminated through public awareness campaigns, legislative measures, and protection (Art. 5). Women and men are to be "regarded as equal partners in marriage," both partners must freely and fully consent to the marriage, women must be at least 18 years old before entering into a marriage, both spouses are to choose where they reside, the woman can choose to keep her maiden name and nationality, and the woman has the right to acquire and manage property (Art. 6). Women and men have equal rights in seeking divorce or annulment, in the custody of their children, and in sharing of property (Art. 7). International law is to be followed to protect all civilians in armed conflicts and States Parties are to "protect asylum seeking women, refugees, returnees and internally displaced persons, against all forms of violence, rape and other forms of sexual exploitation" (Art. 11). Widows are to be protected and have full rights to guardianship of their children as well as the right to remarry (Art. 20).

Condition of Women in Developing Countries

This section presents statistics, legislation, and other information regarding health, education, domestic violence and rape, prostitution and sex trafficking, voting and elections, labor and employment, and property rights as they relate to women in developing countries.

Health

Women in developing countries face many issues concerning their health, including access to health care providers and other services, availability of trained health care providers during pregnancy and delivery, high rates of maternal mortality, availability of contraceptives and other family planning services, and availability of abortion.

Reducing maternal mortality is part of Goal 5 of the Millennium Development Goals. The availability of effective reproductive health services is a critical component of meeting this goal. Many countries have begun to offer improved health services to women, but these improvements are not enough to meet the goal of reducing maternal mortality by 5.5 percent by 2015. Despite improvements, in 2008 over 350,000 women died because of complications related to pregnancy and childbirth (Wilmoth et al. 2010). Rates by region vary from 14 deaths per 100,000 live births in the industrialized nations to 640 in sub-Saharan Africa.

The presence of a trained health care professional with adequate equipment during pregnancy and childbirth generally has a positive effect on the lives of women and their babies. In 2008, 99 percent of births in developed regions were attended by skilled healthcare personnel, while only 63 percent of births in developing regions had skilled personnel in attendance. Rates ranged from 30 percent of births in southern Asia to 46 percent in sub-Saharan Africa and 98 percent in Eastern Asia (United Nations 2010b).

Access to and use of contraceptives helps prevent unwanted pregnancies and reduce the need for abortions. While the availability of contraceptives has increased from 52 percent of women in developing regions in 1990 to 62 percent in 2007, many women still do not have access to family planning. According to the United Nations (2010b), providing access to effective family planning could reduce the number of unintended pregnancies each year from 75 million to 22 million. Access to safe abortion services is also critical to reducing unintended pregnancies and maternal deaths. Table 6.1 provides information regarding maternal mortality, availability of skilled health personnel and contraceptives, and abortion policies by country (WHO 2010a, WHO 2010b). Data were taken from the UN Interagency Estimates (WHO 2010b).

Female Genital Mutilation or Cutting

Although the Protocol to the African Charter on Human and Peoples' Rights on the Rights of Women in Africa calls for all signatories to eliminate harmful practices, including female genital mutilation, many girls and young women continue to undergo this procedure in several African countries. The United Nations estimates that between 100 and 140 million girls and women have been victims of FGM and that an estimated 3 million girls are at risk each year (United Nations 2010a). Table 6.2 presents information concerning the existence and extent of FGM in Africa, the Middle East, and Indonesia.

Education

Over the past decade education has become more accessible to many children in developing nations. More girls have been provided with access to education and have enrolled in school. Throughout the world, the ratio of girls to boys in primary school has increased from 91 to 96, and it has increased from 88 to 95 in

TABLE 6.1
Maternal Mortality, Health Care Personnel, Family Planning Availability, and Government Abortion Policies

Country	Maternal Mortality Rate (Rate per 100,000 Live Births) 2008	Births Attended by Health Care Personnel (%)	Contraceptive Use (%) (2000–2008)	Government Abortion Policies
Africa				
Angola	610	47	6.2	Prohibited
Benin	410	78	17.0	To save the woman's life, to preserve physical health
Botswana	190	94	44.4	To save the woman's life, to preserve physical or mental health
Burkina Faso	560	54	17.4	To save the woman's life, to preserve physical health
Burundi	970	34	19.7	To save the woman's life, to preserve physical health
Cameroon	600	63	29.2	To save the woman's life, to preserve physical health
Cape Verde	94	78	61.3	No restriction except for gestational limits
Central African Republic	850	54	19.0	Prohibited
Chad	1,200	14	2.8	To save the woman's life, to preserve physical health
Comoros	340	62	25.7	To save the woman's life, to preserve physical health
Congo, Democratic Republic of	670	74	20.6	Prohibited
Cote d'Ivoire	470	57	12.9	To save the woman's life
Djibouti	300	93	17.8	To save the woman's life, to preserve physical health
Equatorial Guinea	280		10.1	To save the woman's life, to preserve physical health
Eritrea	280	28	8.0	To save the woman's life, to preserve physical or mental health
Ethiopia	470	6	14.7	To save the woman's life, to preserve physical health
Gabon	260	86	32.7	Prohibited
Gambia	400	57	17.5	To save the woman's life, to preserve physical or mental health

(continued)

TABLE 6.1 (CONTINUED)

Country	Maternal Mortality Rate (Rate per 100,000 Live Births) 2008	Births Attended by Health Care Personnel (%)	Contraceptive Use (%) (2000–2008)	Government Abortion Policies
Ghana	350	57	23.5	To save the woman's life, to preserve physical or mental health
Guinea	680	38	9.1	To save the woman's life, to preserve physical health
Guinea-Bissau	1,000	39	10.3	To save the life of the woman
Kenya	530	42	39.3	To save the woman's life
Lesotho	530	55	37.3	Prohibited
Liberia	990	46	11.4	To save the woman's life, to preserve physical or mental health
Madagascar	440	51	27.1	Prohibited
Malawi	510	54	41.0	To save the woman's life
Mali	830	49	8.2	To save the woman's life
Mauritania	550	61	9.3	Prohibited
Mauritius	36		75.8	Prohibited
Mozambique	550	48	16.5	To save the woman's life, to preserve physical health
Namibia	180	81	55.1	To save the woman's life, to preserve physical or mental health
Niger	820	18	11.2	To save the woman's life, to preserve physical health
Nigeria	840	39	14.7	To save the woman's life
Rwanda	1,300	52	36.4	To save the woman's life, to preserve physical health
Sao Tome and Principe	—	81	29.3	Prohibited
Senegal	410	52	11.8	Prohibited
Seychelles	—	—	—	To save the woman's life, to preserve physical or mental health
Sierra Leone	970	42	8.2	To save the woman's life, to preserve physical or mental health
Somalia	1,200	33	14.6	Prohibited
South Africa	410		60.3	To save the woman's life, to preserve physical or mental health, socioeconomic grounds
Sudan	750	49	7.6	To save the woman's life

Swaziland	420	74	50.6	To save the woman's life, to preserve physical or mental health
Tanzania	790	46	26.4	To save the woman's life
Togo	350	62	16.8	To save the woman's life, to preserve physical health
Uganda	430	42	23.7	To save the woman's life
Zambia	470	47	40.8	To save the woman's life, to preserve physical or mental health, socioeconomic grounds
Zimbabwe	790	69	60.2	To save the woman's life, to preserve physical health
East Asia and the Pacific				
Brunei Darussalam	21	99	—	To save the woman's life
Burma	240	57	17.4	To save the woman's life
Cambodia	290	44	40.0 (2004)	No restriction except for gestational limits
China	38	98	86.9	No restrictions
Fiji	26	99	43.1	To save the woman's life, to preserve physical or mental health, socioeconomic grounds
Indonesia	240	73	61.4	To save the woman's life
Kiribati	—	90	36.1	To save the woman's life
Korea, Democratic People's Republic	250	97	68.6	No restrictions except for gestational limits
Korea, Republic of	18	99	84.5	To save the woman's life, to preserve physical health
Laos	580	21	38.4	Prohibited
Malaysia	31	99	—	To save the woman's life, to preserve physical or mental health
Marshall Islands		95	44.6	To save the woman's life
Micronesia		88	23.0 (2004)	To save the woman's life
Nauru	—	97	35.6	To save the woman's life, to preserve physical or mental health
Palau		99	32.8	To save the woman's life
Papua New Guinea	250	39	32.4	To save the woman's life
Philippines	94	62	50.6	Prohibited
Samoa	—	99	—	To save the woman's life, to preserve physical or mental health

(continued)

TABLE 6.1 (CONTINUED)

Country	Maternal Mortality Rate (Rate per 100,000 Live Births) 2008	Births Attended by Health Care Personnel (%)	Contraceptive Use (%) (2000–2008)	Government Abortion Policies
Singapore	9	99	—	No restrictions except for gestational limits
Solomon Islands	100	43	27.0	To save the woman's life
Thailand	48	99	81.1	To save the woman's life, to preserve physical or mental health
Timor-Leste	370	19	19.8	Prohibited
Tonga	—	99	23.9	Prohibited
Tuvalu	—	99	—	To save the woman's life
Vanuatu	—	93	38.4	To save the woman's life, to preserve physical health
Vietnam	56	88	79.5	No restrictions except for gestational limits
South and Central Asia				
Afghanistan	1,400	14	18.6	To save the woman's life
Bangladesh	340	18	55.8	To save the woman's life
Bhutan	200	51	30.7	To save the woman's life
India	230	47	56.3	To save the woman's life, to preserve physical or mental health, socioeconomic grounds
Maldives	37	84	39.0	To save the woman's life, to preserve physical health
Nepal	380	19	48.0	No restrictions except for gestational limits
Pakistan	260	39	29.6	To save the woman's life, to preserve physical health
Sri Lanka	39	99	68.0	To save the woman's life
Near East and North Africa				
Algeria	120	95	61.4	To save the woman's life, to preserve physical or mental health
Bahrain	19	99	—	No restriction except for gestational limits
Egypt	82	79	60.3	Prohibited
Iran	30	97	73.3	To save the woman's life
Iraq	75	89	49.8	Prohibited
Jordan	59	99	57.1	To save the woman's life, to preserve physical health
Kuwait	9	99	—	To save the woman's life, to preserve physical health
Lebanon	26	98	58.0	To save the woman's life

Libya	64	99	—	To save the woman's life
Morocco	110	63	63.0	To save the woman's life, to preserve physical health
Oman	20	98	—	Prohibited
Qatar	8	99	—	To save the woman's life, to preserve physical health
Saudi Arabia	24	96	23.8	To save the woman's life, to preserve physical health
Syria	46	93	58.3	To save the woman's life
Tunisia	60	90	60.2	No restrictions except for gestational limits
United Arab Emirates	10	99	—	To save the woman's life
Yemen Arab Republic	210	36	27.7	To save the woman's life
Latin America and the Caribbean				
Antigua and Barbuda	—	99	—	To save the woman's life
Argentina	70	99	65.3	To save the woman's life, to preserve physical health
Barbados	64	99	—	To save the woman's life, to preserve physical health, socioeconomic grounds
Belize	94	96	34.3	To save the woman's life, to preserve physical or mental health, socioeconomic grounds
Bolivia	180	66	60.6	To save the woman's life, to preserve physical health
Brazil	58	97	80.6	To save the woman's life
Chile	26	99	64.2	Prohibited
Colombia	850	96	78.2 (2004)	To save the woman's life, to preserve physical or mental health
Costa Rica	44	94	80.0	To save the woman's life, to preserve physical health
Dominica	—	94	—	To save the woman's life
Dominican Republic	100	98	72.9	Prohibited
Ecuador	140	99	72.7 (2004)	To save the woman's life, to preserve physical health
El Salvador	110	84	72.5	Prohibited
Grenada	—	99	54.0	To save the woman's life, to preserve physical health
Guatemala	110	41	54.1	To save the woman's life
Guyana	270	83	42.5	No restriction except for gestational limits
Haiti	300	26	32.0	Prohibited

(*continued*)

TABLE 6.1 (CONTINUED)

Country	Maternal Mortality Rate (Rate per 100,000 Live Births) 2008	Births Attended by Health Care Personnel (%)	Contraceptive Use (%) (2000–2008)	Government Abortion Policies
Honduras	110	67	65.2	Prohibited
Jamaica	89	97	69.0	To save the woman's life, to preserve physical or mental health
Mexico	85	94	72.9	To save the woman's life, incest, fetal impairment
Nicaragua	100	74	72.4	Prohibited
Panama	71	91	—	To save the woman's life
Paraguay	95	77	79.4	To save the woman's life
Peru	98	73	73.2	To save the woman's life, to preserve physical health
St. Kitts and Nevis	—	99	54.0	To save the woman's life, to preserve physical or mental health
St. Lucia	—	98	—	To save the woman's life, to preserve physical or mental health
St. Vincent and the Grenadines	—	99	48.0	To save the woman's life, to preserve physical or mental health, socioeconomic grounds
Suriname	100	90	42.1	Prohibited
Trinidad and Tobago	55	98	42.5	To save the woman's life, to preserve physical or mental health
Uruguay	27	99	78.0 (2004)	To save the woman's life, to preserve physical health
Venezuela	68	95	—	To save the woman's life

secondary schools. However, access to education is still limited for children, especially girls, in many developing countries. In northern Africa, for example, two-thirds of children not attending school are female (United Nations 2010b). In countries that have made education compulsory, parents may enroll their children in school but not allow them to actually attend for a variety of reasons, including prohibitive cost; the need for the children to remain at home to help out with chores, farming, or care for younger children; and the lack of available schools or teachers, especially in rural areas.

TABLE 6.2
Extent of FGM and Statutes and Enforcement Status

Country	Percentage of Girls and Women Undergoing FGM	Statutes Addressing FGM and Enforcement
Benin	12.9	Prohibited by law; little law enforcement; difficult to prevent; NGOs run public awareness and education campaigns
Burkina Faso	72.5	Prohibited by law; widely practiced; some law enforcement (several practitioners arrested, charged, and sentenced to prison); Burkina Faso and Niger campaigned against taking children across borders to a country where it is legal or authorities do not enforce the law
Cameroon	1.4	Not prohibited by law; no one has been prosecuted for practicing it; the Minister of Women's Empowerment and the Family and the President have urged abandonment of the practice; several practitioners have agreed to discontinue it and have been provided equipment for new economic activity
Central African Republic	25.7	Prohibited by law; occurs primarily in rural areas; appears practice is declining
Chad	44.9	Prohibited by law; widespread
Congo, Democratic Republic of		Prohibited by law; occurs in some immigrant communities
Cote d'Ivoire	36.4	Prohibited by law; widespread
Djibouti	93.1	Serious problem; government-run campaigns against it
Egypt	91.1	Prohibited by law except for medical emergencies; public awareness campaigns appear to be successful in lowering the rate
Eritrea	88.7	Prohibited by law; widespread; government-run campaigns against it
Ethiopia	74.3	Prohibited by law; National Committee for Traditional Practices in Ethiopia working to discourage practice
Gabon	—	Prohibited by law; occurs among immigrant communities
Gambia	78.3	Not prohibited by law; widespread; less likely to be practiced among educated and urban populations; campaigns to prohibit it
Ghana	3.8	Prohibited by law; remains serious problem; several intervention programs
Guinea	95.6	Prohibited by law; widely practiced; increasing numbers of men and women opposed to it; government runs educational campaigns
Guinea-Bissau	44.5	Not prohibited by law; no government campaigns to prevent it
Indonesia	—	Government decree prohibits medical personnel from performing it; still practiced in many areas
Iraq	—	Not prohibited by law; commonly practiced
Kenya	27.1	Prohibited by law; practiced primarily in rural areas; public awareness campaigns against it
Liberia	58.2	Not prohibited by law; practiced primarily in rural areas; practitioners have been sentenced to life imprisonment after some girls died after undergoing the procedure
Libya	—	Not prohibited by law; no reported instances

(continued)

TABLE 6.2 (CONTINUED)

Country	Percentage of Girls and Women Undergoing FGM	Statutes Addressing FGM and Enforcement
Malawi	—	Not prohibited by law; public awareness campaigns against it
Mali	85.2	Not prohibited by law although government decree prohibits it in government health centers; widespread, occurring in most ethnic groups, not based on religious belief
Mauritania	72.2	Prohibited by law; practiced by all ethnic groups; active public awareness campaigns to eliminate it
Niger	2.2	Prohibited by law; government works with NGOs to eliminate it
Nigeria	29.6	Prohibited by law; primarily practiced by the Yoruba and Igbo; public awareness campaigns to educate public against it
Senegal	28.2	Prohibited by law; still widely practiced, although the Tostan program appears to be successful in educating the public regarding the practice (they report that 3,791 out of 5,000 communities have abandoned the practice)
Sierra Leone	94.0	Not prohibited by law; widely practiced
Somalia	97.9	Prohibited by law; laws not enforced; widespread; public awareness campaigns developed to educate the public
Sudan	90.0	Widespread, especially in northern Sudan
Tanzania	14.6	Prohibited by law; law enforcement not effective; continues to be practiced in some areas; coalition of NGOs and the Anti-Female Genital Mutilation Network are working to eliminate the practice
Togo	5.8	Prohibited by law; continues to be practiced, especially in rural areas; public awareness campaigns work to educate the public
Uganda	0.8	Prohibited by law; still practiced in some areas; public awareness campaigns to educate the public
Yemen	38.2	Prohibited by law; widely practiced, especially in coastal areas

Governments are becoming more aware of the importance of education to their citizens and to their national development and have begun to enact compulsory education requirements. In some countries, such as Burundi, school fees have been abolished and school enrollment has tripled since 1999. Table 6.3 provides information regarding the literacy rate for young women, the ratio of females to males in primary and secondary schools, and each government's requirements regarding education. The literacy rate is the percentage of people who are able to read, write, and comprehend a short, simple statement regarding their everyday lives. Data were taken from the UN Interagency Estimates (WHO 2010b) and the U.S. Department of State Country Reports.

TABLE 6.3
Literacy, School Enrollment, and Government Policies

Country	Literacy Rate (Women Ages 15–24)	Female Children Not Enrolled in Primary School	Ratio of Female to Male Primary School Enrollment	Ratio of Female to Male Secondary School Enrollment	Government Education Policy
Africa					
Angola	65.0	—	81		Free and compulsory to 6th grade
Benin	42	91,247	87	57	Free and compulsory for ages 6–11
Botswana	96	13,475	98	106	School fees can be waived, not compulsory
Burkina Faso	33	473,232	88	74	Free and compulsory to age 16
Burundi	75	67,091	95	71	Free primary, compulsory to age 12
Cameroon	84	254,582	86	80	Free primary, compulsory to age 14
Cape Verde	99	5,988	94	—	Free ages 6–12, compulsory to age 11
Central African Republic	56	148,184	71	57	Free tuition, compulsory to age 15
Chad	37.0	—	70	45	Free and compulsory from ages 6–12
Comoros	84	—	92	76	Compulsory to age 12, not free
Congo, Democratic Republic of	62.0	—	83	55	Neither free nor compulsory
Congo, Republic of	78.0	101,526	94	—	Free and compulsory to age 16 (parents pay for fees, books, and uniforms)
Cote d'Ivoire	60.0	—	79	—	Primary tuition free, not compulsory
Djibouti	—	33,820	88	70	Primary free and compulsory
Equatorial Guinea	980	—	95	—	Free and compulsory to age 13
Eritrea	84.0	186,710	82	71	Tuition free and compulsory to grade 7
Ethiopia	39.0	1,551,929	89	72	Primary tuition free and compulsory
Gabon	96.0	—	—	—	Compulsory to age 16
Gambia	58.0	33,174	106	94	Free and compulsory for ages 6–12 (primary)

(continued)

TABLE 6.3 (CONTINUED)

Country	Literacy Rate (Women Ages 15–24)	Female Children Not Enrolled in Primary School	Ratio of Female to Male Primary School Enrollment	Ratio of Female to Male Secondary School Enrollment	Government Education Policy
Ghana	78.0	377,761	99	89	Free tuition and compulsory through junior secondary
Guinea	51.0	244,946	85	59	Free tuition and compulsory primary
Guinea-Bissau	62.0	—	—	—	Free through high school, compulsory through grade 6
Kenya	93.0	524,454	98	92	Tuition free primary and secondary
Lesotho	98.0	46,969	99	132	Free tuition grades 1–7, not compulsory
Liberia	80.0	—	90	75	Free and compulsory primary
Madagascar	68.0	2,971	97	94	Free tuition, primary compulsory to age 14
Malawi	85.0	79,773	103	85	Free primary, not compulsory
Mali	31.0	315,748	83	64	Free and compulsory
Mauritania	63.0	47,588	107	89	Free through university, compulsory primary
Mauritius	97.0	3,808	99	101	Free and compulsory primary
Mozambique	62.0	485,601	88	75	Free and compulsory through age 12
Namibia	95.0	12,092	99	117	Free and compulsory to age 16 (grades 1–10), numerous fees
Niger	23.0	636,080	80	60	Free and compulsory primary
Nigeria	65.0	4,626,218	88	77	Free and compulsory to age 12, numerous fees
Rwanda	77.0	21,679	101	90	Free and compulsory through primary, parents required to pay unofficial fees
Sao Tome and Principe	96.0	—	101	112	Free tuition and compulsory to age 15 or grade 6
Senegal	45.0	232,611	102	81	Free and compulsory for ages 6–16
Seychelles	99.0	—	99	119	Compulsory through grade 10, free to age 18
Sierra Leone	46.0	—	88	66	Primary tuition free, secondary tuition free for girls in the north
Somalia	—	—	55	46	Neither free nor compulsory, few schools operating in 2009 (many were traditional Koranic schools)

South Africa	98.0	219,409	96	105	Fee-based and compulsory from ages 7–15
Sudan	82.0	—	90	88	Free tuition to grade 8, lack of schools in the south, girls denied equal access in the south
Swaziland	95.0	17,509	93	90	Primary free tuition and compulsory, many fees, government required to pay all fees and costs in grades 1–2
Tanzania	76.0	178,786	99	—	Primary free and compulsory through age 15
Togo	80.0	98,956	86	53	Compulsory to age 15, free primary tuition
Uganda	86.0	49,053	101	85	Free and compulsory for grades 1–7 and free high school for disadvantaged students
Zambia	68.0	31,806	98	83	Free through grade 7, not compulsory
Zimbabwe	99.0	102,804	99	92	Neither free nor compulsory
East Asia and the Pacific					
Brunei Darussalam	100	543	100	102	Free primary education
Burma	95.0	—	99	101	Free and compulsory through 4th standard (age 10)
Cambodia	86.0	131,368	94	82	Free, not compulsory through grade 9
China	99.0	—	104	105	Compulsory for 9 years, tuition free but many miscellaneous fees
Fiji	—	5,730	99	107	Compulsory to age 15, many fees limit attendance
Indonesia	96.0	—	97	99	Free and compulsory through 3 years of junior high school, many additional fees limit attendance
Kiribati	—	—	102	120	Free and compulsory to age 13
Korea, Democratic People's Republic of	100	—	—	—	11 years of free and compulsory education
Korea, Republic of	—	30,665	98	96	Free and compulsory

(*continued*)

TABLE 6.3 (CONTINUED)

Country	Literacy Rate (Women Ages 15–24)	Female Children Not Enrolled in Primary School	Ratio of Female to Male Primary School Enrollment	Ratio of Female to Male Secondary School Enrollment	Government Education Policy
Laos	79.0	76,419	91	81	Free and compulsory through grade 5, high additional fees limit attendance
Malaysia	99.0	62,722	100	107	Compulsory primary, lack of enforcement
Marshall Islands	—	1,446	97	102	Free tuition and compulsory to age 18, high registration fees and lack of schools in rural areas limit attendance
Micronesia, Federated States of	—	—	101	107	Compulsory to age 14 or grade 8, teacher shortage
Nauru	—	—	—	—	Free and compulsory to age 15, 4 years of secondary school compulsory, final two optional
Palau	—	—	102	97	Well-funded public education
Papua New Guinea	69.0	—	84	—	Neither free nor compulsory, limited attendance
Philippines	96.0	406,556	98	109	Free and compulsory through age 11, poor quality
Samoa	100	35	99	112	Not free, compulsory through age 14, law not enforced
Singapore	100	—	—	—	Free and compulsory primary
Solomon Islands	—	12,167	97	84	Not compulsory, high school fees limit attendance
Thailand	98.0	329,688	98	109	Free and compulsory primary
Timor-Leste	—	22,445	94	100	Free and compulsory primary, no system to ensure existence of schools where needed
Tonga	100	—	97	103	Free and compulsory to age 14
Tuvalu	—	—	99	—	Free and compulsory primary
Vanuatu	94.0	483	96	—	Free, not compulsory, shortage of schools and teachers after grade 6
Vietnam	96.0	—	—	—	Free and compulsory through age 14; law not enforced

South and Central Asia					
Afghanistan	—	—	66	38	Free to college level, compulsory to secondary level
Bangladesh	76.0	914,530	106	105	Free and compulsory primary; high fees limit attendance
Bhutan	68.0	5,099	100	99	Free for 11 years, not compulsory, some fees
India	74.0	3,781,495	97	86	Free and compulsory for ages 6–14
Maldives	99.0	1,012	94	105	Free primary, not compulsory
Nepal	75.0	—	—	89	Free primary to age 12, not compulsory
Pakistan	59.0	4,201,000	83	76	Neither free nor compulsory; secondary schools not widely available in rural areas
Sri Lanka	99.0	1,371	100	—	Free through university; compulsory to age 14
Near East and North Africa					
Algeria	89.0	87,562	94	108	Free through high school, compulsory to age 16
Bahrain	100	445	98	104	Free through grade 12, compulsory through age 14
Egypt	82.0	323,950	95	—	Compulsory through grade 8
Iran	96.0	—	140	98	Free and compulsory to age 11
Iraq	80.0	409,534	84	67	Free for all levels, compulsory for 6 years
Jordan	99.0	23,176	101	104	Free through age 18, compulsory through age 16, no legislation to enforce law
Kuwait	99.0	8,010	98	104	Free through university for citizens, compulsory through secondary
Lebanon	99.0	24,937	97	111	Free through secondary, compulsory to age 11
Libya	100	—	95	117	Subsidized through university, compulsory through grade 9
Morocco	68.0	217,386	91	86	Free and compulsory to age 15
Oman	98.0	48,036	101	97	Free primary, not compulsory
Qatar	99.0	—	99	146	Free and compulsory through age 18
Saudi Arabia	96.0	259,390	96	85	All levels free for citizens
Syria	93.0	—	96	98	Free through university for citizens, compulsory to age 12

(continued)

TABLE 6.3 (CONTINUED)

Country	Literacy Rate (Women Ages 15–24)	Female Children Not Enrolled in Primary School	Ratio of Female to Male Primary School Enrollment	Ratio of Female to Male Secondary School Enrollment	Government Education Policy
Tunisia	96.0	251	98	108	Free through university, compulsory to age 16
United Arab Emirates	97.0	1,380	100	102	Free primary to citizens, compulsory through grade 9, law not enforced
Yemen	70.0	641,425	80	49	Free and compulsory to age 15, law not enforced
South and Central America					
Antigua and Barbuda	99.0	772	92	93	Free and compulsory to age 16
Argentina	99.0	—	99	113	Free to university, compulsory to age 16
Barbados	—	—	—	—	Free to university, compulsory to age 16
Belize	—	25	97	108	Free and compulsory to age 14, some school fees
Bolivia	99.0	31,822	100	97	Not free, compulsory through age 14
Brazil	99.0	392,879	93	111	Free and compulsory to age 14
Chile	99.0	45,709	95	103	Free and compulsory through secondary
Colombia	98.0	138,088	99	110	Free and compulsory primary, rural areas lack teachers
Costa Rica	99.0	—	99	106	Free and compulsory through grade 9
Dominica	—	969	106	93	Free and compulsory to age 15
Dominican Republic	97.0	102,993	93	119	Free and compulsory through grade 9
Ecuador	96.0	—	100	101	Compulsory to age 16, shortage of schools
El Salvador	96.0	14,834	97	102	Free primary, compulsory through grade 9
Grenada	—	65	95	92	Free and compulsory through grade 9
Guatemala	84.0	55,105	94	93	Free and compulsory to grade 9, low completion rates in rural areas
Guyana	—	723	99	101	Free and compulsory to age 16

Haiti	—	—	—	—	Free and compulsory through primary
Honduras	95.0	9,390	100	127	Free and compulsory to age 13
Jamaica	98.0	34,842	97	104	Free and compulsory through grade 6
Mexico	98.0	22,621	98	106	Free and compulsory through age 15
Nicaragua	89.0	24,341	98	113	Free and compulsory through grade 6
Panama	96.0	2,952	97	108	Free and compulsory through secondary
Paraguay	99.0	38,289	97	104	Free and compulsory through grade 9
Peru	97.0	43,272	100	99	Free primary and secondary, fees and costs lead to low attendance for low-income families
Saint Kitts and Nevis	—	54	106	98	Free and compulsory through grade 12
Saint Lucia	—	725	97	104	Free and compulsory through age 15
Saint Vincent and the Grenadines	—	231	92	111	Neither free nor compulsory
Suriname	95.0	3,141	95	128	Free and compulsory to age 12
Trinidad and Tobago	100	3,088	97	107	Free and compulsory to age 16
Uruguay	99.0	3,285	97	99	Free and compulsory to age 14
Venezuela	99.0	122,684	97	110	Free through university, compulsory to age 15

Domestic Violence and Rape

Laws vary from country to country regarding domestic violence and rape, and cultural norms often prevent women from reporting domestic abuse and rape even when laws prohibit this type of violence. Women also may fear reprisals from family members or may be concerned that their husbands will abandon them if they report the abuse, leaving them shunned by their families and unable to support themselves and their children. Table 6.4 provides summary information regarding domestic violence and rape for developing countries by region. Data were taken from the U.S. Department of State Country Reports.

TABLE 6.4
Domestic Violence and Rape Status and Extent

Country	Domestic Violence	Rape	Marital Rape
Africa			
Angola	Not prohibited by law; common	Prohibited by law; few prosecutions	Prohibited by law
Benin	Prohibited by law; common	Prohibited by law; little enforcement	Not distinguished by law
Botswana	Not prohibited by law; serious problem	Prohibited by law; effective enforcement	Not recognized as a crime
Burkina Faso	Not prohibited by law; common	Prohibited by law; not enforced	Not specifically prohibited
Burundi	Prohibited by law; common	Prohibited by law; laws not enforced; victim sometimes forced to marry rapist	Prohibited by law; laws not enforced
Cameroon	Not specifically prohibited by law; can be prosecuted under assault statutes	Prohibited by law; little law enforcement or prosecution	Not prohibited by law
Cape Verde	Prohibited by law; widespread	Prohibited by law; laws not effectively enforced	Prohibited by law; laws not effectively enforced
Central African Republic	Not specifically prohibited by law (violence against any person prohibited); common	Prohibited by law; laws not effectively enforced	Not specifically prohibited by law; common
Chad	Prohibited but common	Prohibited; punished by hard labor	Not addressed by law
Congo, Democratic Republic of	Assault considered a crime but law does not address spousal abuse	Prohibited by law but laws not enforced	Unknown
Congo, Republic of	Assault illegal but law does not address spousal abuse	Prohibited by law; laws not enforced; widespread	Prohibited by law; laws not enforced
Cote d'Ivoire	Not specifically prohibited by law; widespread	Prohibited by law; laws not enforced; widespread	Not specifically prohibited by law
Djibouti	Law only prohibits "torture and barbaric acts" against one's spouse; police rarely involved	Prohibited by law with punishment up to 20 years' imprisonment	Not specifically prohibited by law

Equatorial Guinea	Prohibited by law; laws not enforced	Prohibited by law	Not specifically prohibited by law
Eritrea	Prohibited by law; laws rarely enforced; no legal penalties	Prohibited by law; punishment up to 10 years' imprisonment	Unclear whether prohibited by law or not
Ethiopia	Prohibited by law; widespread	Prohibited by law; laws not enforced	Not specifically prohibited by law
Gabon	Prohibited by law; widespread	Prohibited by law; punishment 5–10 years' imprisonment	Not specifically prohibited by law
Gambia	Not prohibited by law; can be prosecuted under rape laws; widespread	Prohibited by law; laws effectively enforced; punishment can be up to life in prison	Prohibited by law; widespread; underreported
Ghana	Prohibited by law; laws not effectively enforced	Prohibited by law	Not specifically prohibited by law
Guinea	Assault considered a crime but law does not address spousal abuse	Prohibited by law; rarely prosecuted	Not regarded as criminal offense
Guinea-Bissau	Not prohibited by law; accepted as a means of settling marital disputes	Prohibited by law; limited law enforcement	Prohibited by law
Kenya	Assault considered a crime but law does not address spousal abuse; often considered a family matter	Prohibited by law; limited law enforcement	Not specifically prohibited by law
Lesotho	Assault considered a crime and domestic abuse is prosecuted under assault laws	Prohibited by law; widespread	Prohibited by law
Liberia	Prohibited by law; widespread	Prohibited by law; laws not effectively enforced; widespread	Not specifically prohibited by law
Madagascar	Prohibited by law; widespread	Prohibited by law; widespread	Not specifically prohibited by law
Malawi	Prohibited by law; maximum sentence is life in prison; not often reported by women	Prohibited by law; laws effectively enforced	Not specifically prohibited by law but can be prosecuted under rape laws
Mali	Not specifically prohibited by law, although spousal abuse is prohibited by law; police reluctant to enforce laws; women reluctant to report	Prohibited by law; laws not effectively enforced	Not specifically prohibited by law but can be prosecuted under rape laws

(*continued*)

TABLE 6.4 (CONTINUED)

Country	Domestic Violence	Rape	Marital Rape
Mauritania	Prohibited by law; laws not effectively enforced; no specific penalties	Prohibited by law; laws not effectively enforced; widespread; victims can be held responsible for the rape (based on belief that sexual relations outside of marriage are sinful)	Prohibited by law
Mauritius	Prohibited by law; laws not effectively enforced	Prohibited by law; laws generally enforced; penalty can be up to 20 years' imprisonment; widespread but not frequently reported	Prohibited by law
Mozambique	Prohibited by law; penalty can be up to 12 years' imprisonment; widespread; cultural practices discourage many women from reporting violence	Prohibited by law; laws not effectively enforced; no prosecution of rape cases in 2009	Prohibited by law; laws not effectively enforced
Namibia	Prohibited by law; widespread	Prohibited by law; laws generally enforced	Prohibited by law
Niger	Not specifically prohibited by law; widespread; women often afraid to report based on customary practices and fear of social stigma	Prohibited by law; punishable by up to 30 years' imprisonment	Not specifically prohibited by law but apparently rape laws cover spousal rape in practice
Nigeria	Not prohibited by law; penal code permits a husband to use physical force to "chastise" wife provided it does not cause "grievous harm"	Prohibited by law; punishable by up to life imprisonment; limited reporting and enforcement	Prohibited by law; laws not effectively enforced; no cases prosecuted in 2009
Rwanda	Prohibited by law; widespread	Prohibited by law; punishable by 10 years' to life imprisonment; enforcement generally good	Prohibited by law; punishable by 6 months' to 2 years' imprisonment
Sao Tome and Principe	Prohibited by law; many women are reluctant to complain or file charges	Prohibited by law; punishable by 2 to 12 years' imprisonment; enforcement level unknown	Prohibited by law; punishable by 2 to 12 years' imprisonment; enforcement level unknown

Senegal	Prohibited by law; laws not enforced; punishable by 1 to 10 years' imprisonment; widespread	Prohibited by law; laws rarely enforced; punishable by 5 to 10 years' imprisonment	Not specifically prohibited by law
Seychelles	Prohibited by law; punishable by up to 20 years' imprisonment; police rarely intervene	Prohibited by law; punishable by up to 20 years' imprisonment; often unreported	Prohibited by law; punishable by up to 20 years' imprisonment
Sierra Leone	Prohibited by law; widespread; not frequently reported	Prohibited by law; punishable by up to 14 years' imprisonment; commonplace; not frequently reported	Not specifically prohibited by law
Somalia	Not prohibited by law; believed to be widespread although statistics are unavailable; honor killings occur	Prohibited by law; laws not effectively enforced; no reported rape cases prosecuted during 2009	Not specifically prohibited by law
South Africa	Prohibited by law; not frequently reported	Prohibited by law; widespread	Prohibited by law; widespread
Sudan	Not prohibited by law; widespread; police unlikely to intervene in domestic disputes	Prohibited by law; laws not effectively enforced; punishment ranges from 100 lashes to 10 years' imprisonment; widespread	Not specifically prohibited by law
Swaziland	Not prohibited by law; assault considered a crime but law does not address spousal abuse; often considered a family matter; common	Prohibited by law; laws not always effectively enforced; widespread	Prohibited by law; laws not always effectively enforced
Tanzania	Not prohibited by law although domestic violence is recognized by courts as grounds for divorce; remains widespread; not frequently reported due to cultural norms and family pressures	Prohibited by law; laws not effectively enforced; not frequently reported; widespread	Prohibited by law; laws not effectively enforced; not frequently reported; widespread
Togo	Not specifically prohibited by law; widespread; police often reluctant to intervene in "family affairs"	Prohibited by law; punishable by 5 to 10 years' imprisonment; widespread; victims reluctant to report due to cultural norms and family pressures	Not specifically prohibited by law
Uganda	Widespread; most people regard it as a family matter	Prohibited by law; laws not consistently enforced; widespread	Unknown

(*continued*)

TABLE 6.4 (CONTINUED)

Country	Domestic Violence	Rape	Marital Rape
Zambia	Not prohibited by law; assault considered a crime but law does not address spousal abuse; widespread	Prohibited by law; laws not effectively enforced; punishable by up to life in prison; widespread	Not specifically prohibited by law; laws for rape not enforceable in these cases
Zimbabwe	Not prohibited by law; widespread; not frequently reported due to cultural and family norms	Prohibited by law; widespread; not widely reported	Prohibited by law; many women unaware that spousal rape is a crime; not widely reported
East Asia and the Pacific			
Brunei Darussalam	Not specifically prohibited by law; laws generally enforced effectively; Islamic courts recognize assault as grounds for divorce	Prohibited by law; laws not widely enforced; punishable by up to 30 years' imprisonment and caning	Laws provide that a man's sexual intercourse with his wife is not rape
Burma	Not specifically prohibited by law; victims can apply laws against committing bodily harm; widespread	Prohibited by law; laws not effectively enforced especially when the crimes are committed by soldiers	Not specifically prohibited by law unless the wife is under the age of 14 years
Cambodia	Prohibited by law; penalties are not specified; widespread	Prohibited by law; punishable by up to 5 years' imprisonment; widespread	Not specifically prohibited by law; may be included under domestic abuse laws
China	Not specifically prohibited by law (other laws stipulate that domestic violence is prohibited, although they are vague); domestic violence is a growing problem	Prohibited by law; convicted rapists may be executed; occurrence is unknown	Not specifically recognized or prohibited by law
Fiji	Not specifically prohibited by law; prosecuted under statutes regarding assault	Prohibited by law; punishable by up to life imprisonment thoughpunishment is uncommon; widespread	Not specifically prohibited by law although there have been some prosecutions under the general rape law
Indonesia	Prohibited by law; believed to be widespread, but reliable statistics are unavailable	Prohibited by law but definition is narrow; punishment is light although it can range between 4 and 14 years' imprisonment; reliable statistics are unavailable	Not prohibited by law

Kiribati	Not specially prohibited by law but prosecuted under general assault statutes; widespread; not always reported due to cultural and family norms	Prohibited by law; punishable by up to life imprisonment but sentences usually much lighter; widespread	Prohibited by law; widespread
Korea, Democratic People's Republic of	Statutes unknown; widespread	May be prohibited by law but details of statutes are unavailable	Unknown
Korea, Republic of	Prohibited by law; punishable by up to 5 years' imprisonment and fines; police are required to respond immediately and generally are quick to do so	Prohibited by law; punishable by up to three years' imprisonment; widespread	Not specifically prohibited by law but often prosecuted under general rape statutes
Laos	Prohibited by law; apparently not widespread	Prohibited by law; punishable by 3 to 5 years' imprisonment and can include capital punishment; reportedly rare	Prohibited by law; apparently not widespread
Malaysia	The Domestic Violence Act prohibits domestic abuse; frequent but not always reported; Muslim women generally prohibited from disobeying their husbands according to Shari'a law	Prohibited by law; laws effectively enforced; punishable by up to 30 years' imprisonment, caning and a fine	Prohibited by law
Marshall Islands	Prohibited by law; laws enforced when incidents are reported to officials	Prohibited by law; laws effectively enforced although not many cases prosecuted	Prohibited by law; laws effectively enforced
Micronesia, Federated States of	Not prohibited by law but can be prosecuted under assault charges; generally seen as a traditional family unit issue	Prohibited by law; rarely reported or prosecuted	Not specifically prohibited by law
Nauru	No reliable statistics available; believed to be sporadic	Prohibited by law; punishable by up to life imprisonment; no reliable statistics available	Not specifically prohibited by law; no reliable statistics available
Palau	Not prohibited by law but can be prosecuted under assault statutes; only 39 cases reported October 2008–September 2009	Prohibited by law; punishable by up to 25 years' imprisonment; no reported cases of rape in 2009	Prohibited by law; punishable by up to 25 years' imprisonment

(continued)

TABLE 6.4 (CONTINUED)

Country	Domestic Violence	Rape	Marital Rape
Papua New Guinea	Prohibited by law although most frequently perceived as private family matter	Prohibited by law; apprehension of rapists is limited; rape, especially gang rape, is widespread	Prohibited by law
Philippines	Prohibited by law; widespread; women sometimes required to pay fees to file complaint	Prohibited by law; law enforcement and prosecution are ineffective	Prohibited by law; law enforcement and prosecution are ineffective
Samoa	Prohibited by law; tolerated under traditional family practices and cultural norms	Prohibited by law; often unreported as result of cultural norms and social stigma	Not specifically prohibited by law
Singapore	Prohibited by law; punishable by mandatory caning and at least 2 years' imprisonment for any act that results in the victim's fear of injury or death	Prohibited by law; laws generally enforced effectively; punishable by up to 20 years' imprisonment and caning	Not prohibited by law unless husband and wife are separated; a husband's sexual relations with his wife are not considered a crime
Solomon Islands	Not prohibited by law but can be prosecuted under assault statutes; believed to be common	Prohibited by law; punishable by up to life imprisonment; widespread; limited reporting due to cultural norms and family pressures	Not specifically prohibited by law
Thailand	Prohibited by law; widespread; police frequently reluctant to investigate and victims often afraid to report it due to family pressures and cultural norms	Prohibited by law; laws not enforced effectively; penalties can range from four years' to life imprisonment; believed to be serious problem	Prohibited by law
Timor-Leste	Authorities often reluctant to respond aggressively to charges of domestic violence; some see this as a family matter	Prohibited by law; police often reluctant to investigate reports or prosecute perpetrators; sometimes dealt with through traditional laws	Not specifically prohibited by law but rape statute may be broad enough to include spousal rape
Tonga	Not specifically prohibited by law but can be prosecuted under assault statutes; "no drop" policy provides for instances when women change their minds after making a complaint (the case proceeds to prosecution even if woman requests that the charges be dropped)	Prohibited by law; punishable by up to 15 years' imprisonment; incidence appears low	Not specifically prohibited by law

Tuvalu	Not specifically prohibited by law but can be prosecuted under assault statutes; police may deal with it through traditional practices	Prohibited by law; punishable by a minimum of 5 years' imprisonment	Not specifically prohibited by law
Vanuatu	Prohibited by law; most cases are believed to be unreported; police have "no drop" policy	Prohibited by law; punishable by up to life imprisonment	Not specifically prohibited by law; police reluctant to investigate as many believe it is a family matter
Vietnam	Prohibited by law; police and legal authorities not equipped to handle domestic violence cases; government is working to train all involved	Prohibited by law	Not specifically prohibited by law but may be included in law prohibiting violence or tricking someone into having sexual intercourse without consent
South and Central Asia			
Afghanistan	Not specifically prohibited by law but prosecuted under the assault statutes; widespread; often not reported due to family or cultural traditions or social stigma	Prohibited by law; punishable by 6 months' to life imprisonment	Not specifically prohibited by law
Bangladesh	Not prohibited by law; widespread; 2000 study by the UN Population Fund found at least 50 percent of female respondents had experienced domestic violence	Prohibited by law; prosecution inconsistent; not frequently reported due to social stigma	Not specifically prohibited by law
Bhutan	Prohibited by law	Prohibited by law; punishable by up to life imprisonment	Prohibited by law
India	Prohibited by law; widespread; underreporting likely due to cultural practices or family pressure	Prohibited by law	Prohibited by law; punishable by up to one year's imprisonment

(continued)

TABLE 6.4 (CONTINUED)

Country	Domestic Violence	Rape	Marital Rape
Maldives	Not prohibited by law; most cases unreported due to variety of reasons including social stigma, fear of reprisals, or fear of losing economic support	Prohibited by law; very few convictions due to difficulty of proving rape	Not specifically prohibited by law
Nepal	Prohibited by law; widespread	Prohibited by law; punishable by up to 20 years' imprisonment; good police response; most rapes not reported	Prohibited by law; punishable by 3 to 6 months' imprisonment
Pakistan	Prohibited by law; widespread; violence against women increased in 2009 from previous year; dowry disputes often result in woman's death	Prohibited by law; punishable by 10 to 25 years' imprisonment; widespread; seriously underreported; prosecution is rare	Not specifically prohibited by law
Sri Lanka	Prohibited by law; laws not enforced effectively	Prohibited by law; laws not enforced effectively; not frequently reported; few services provided to victims	Prohibited by law only when husband and wife are legally separated
Near East and North Africa			
Algeria	Domestic violence more prevalent in rural areas where social stigma and cultural traditions limit the victim's willingness to report it	Prohibited by law; reaction to reports by law enforcement is improving; increasing number of reports	Not specifically prohibited by law
Bahrain	Not specifically prohibited by law; widespread; rarely reported	Prohibited by law; does not appear to be a widespread problem	Not specifically prohibited by law
Egypt	Not prohibited by law; can be prosecuted under assault statutes although victim must produce multiple eyewitnesses	Prohibited by law; punishable by 15 to 25 years' imprisonment (life sentence if rape includes armed abduction); not often reported	Not prohibited by law
Iran	Not prohibited by law; not widely reported because it is usually seen as a private family matter; "One Million Signatures for the Repeal of Discriminatory Laws" and other programs are working to change the law	Prohibited by law but victim must provide 4 male or 3 male and 2 female witnesses in order to convict perpetrator; widespread; not widely report due to family pressures, social stigma, and fear of punishment for being raped	Not prohibited by law

Iraq	Prohibited by the constitution; often unreported due to social stigma and belief that it should be considered a family matter	Prohibited by law; prevalence unknown	Not prohibited by law
Jordan	Prohibited by law but seen as private family matter; considered grounds for divorce but religious authority does allow husbands to strike their wives	Prohibited by law; punishable by at least 10 years' imprisonment; widespread	Not prohibited by law
Kuwait	Not specifically prohibited by law but can be prosecuted under assault statutes; perpetrators rarely arrested; rarely reported; woman must provide 2 male or 1 male and 2 female witnesses	Prohibited by law; laws not always enforced effectively; can be punishable by death; widespread; underreported	Not prohibited by law
Lebanon	Not specifically prohibited by law; religious law may require a victim to return to her husband; complaints often ignored by the government	Prohibited by law; laws effectively enforced; punishable by 5 or more years' imprisonment; family of victim allowed to offer the rapist marriage to the victim to preserve family honor	Not prohibited by law
Libya	Prohibited by law; prevalence unknown	Prohibited by law; punishment can be up to 25 years' imprisonment or marriage to the victim if she agrees	Rape and spousal rape not distinguished by the law
Morocco	Not specifically prohibited by law; general provisions of criminal code do address it; underreported	Prohibited by law; punishable by 5 to 10 years' imprisonment; often unreported; victim's family may offer marriage to victim to preserve family honor	Not prohibited by law
Oman	Not specifically prohibited by law but can be prosecuted under assault, battery, and aggravated assault statutes; laws generally enforced when reported	Prohibited by law; laws generally enforced by authorities; punishable by up to 15 years' imprisonment; underreported due to family pressures, social stigma, and cultural traditions	Not prohibited by law

(*continued*)

TABLE 6.4 (CONTINUED)

Country	Domestic Violence	Rape	Marital Rape
Qatar	Prohibited by law; underreported due to social stigma and cultural tradition	Prohibited by law; punishable by 10 years' imprisonment (14 if the victim is under 16 years old); underreported due to social stigma and cultural traditions	Not specifically prohibited by law
Saudi Arabia	Not prohibited by law; no clear definitions provided by the government	Prohibited under Shari'a law; laws generally enforced; punishment ranges from flogging to execution; both victim and perpetrator punished; underreported	Not prohibited by law
Syria	Not specifically prohibited by law; underreported due to social stigma, cultural traditions, and family pressures	Prohibited by law; punishable by a minimum of 15 years' imprisonment; if perpetrator agrees to marry the victim he receives no punishment	Not prohibited by law
Tunisia	Prohibited by law; law enforcement rare; widespread	Prohibited by law; laws effectively enforced; punishable by life imprisonment or execution if a weapon was involved; underreported due to social stigma and cultural tradition	Prohibited by law
United Arab Emirates	Statutes allow men to physically "control" their female family members; occasionally cases may be filed under assault statutes; complaints may be filed with police but are generally ineffective; underreported due to family pressures, social stigma, and cultural traditions	Prohibited under Shari'a law; high burden of proof required results in few convictions; underreported	Not specifically prohibited by law
Yemen	Prohibited by law; laws rarely enforced; considered a family matter	Prohibited by law; laws not enforced effectively; punishable by up to 15 years' imprisonment; underreported due to fear of shaming the family and retaliation; if perpetrator does not admit the crime the victim must provide 2 male or 4 female witnesses	Not prohibited by law as a woman is not allowed to refuse sexual relations with her husband

South and Central America			
Antigua and Barbuda	Prohibited by law; women often reluctant to testify against abusers	Prohibited by law; punishable by 10 years' to life imprisonment	Prohibited by law
Argentina	Prohibited by law; punishable as a misdemeanor in civil court; widespread	Prohibited by law; punishable by up to 20 years' imprisonment	Prohibited by law
Barbados	Prohibited by law; widespread; reliable data unavailable	Prohibited by law	Prohibited by law
Belize	Prohibited by law; significant problem	Prohibited by law; effectively enforced but few convictions (possibly due to reluctance of victim to testify in court)	Prohibited by law
Bolivia	Prohibited by law; laws not enforced effectively; widespread	Prohibited by law; underreported	Not prohibited by law
Brazil	Prohibited by law; widespread; underreported	Prohibited by law; punishable by 8 to 10 years' imprisonment; few convictions	Prohibited by law
Chile	Prohibited by law; widespread	Prohibited by law; laws effectively enforced; punishable by 5 to 15 years' imprisonment; underreported	Prohibited by law
Colombia	Prohibited by law; laws not effectively enforced; widespread	Prohibited by law; punishable by 8 to 15 years' imprisonment; underreported	Prohibited by law; punishable by 6 months' to 2 years' imprisonment
Costa Rica	Prohibited by law; protection measures are defined by law	Prohibited by law; laws effectively enforced; punishable by 10 to 18 years' imprisonment	Prohibited by law; few convictions due to difficulty providing proof
Dominica	Not specifically prohibited by law but can be prosecuted under assault and battery statutes; underreported	Prohibited by law; laws effectively enforced	Not specifically prohibited by law
Dominican Republic	Prohibited by law	Prohibited by law; punishable by 10 to 15 years' imprisonment; widespread; underreported due to social stigma	Unknown
Ecuador	Prohibited by law; widespread	Prohibited by law; punishable by up to 25 years' imprisonment; widespread	Not prohibited by law although family law treats marital rape as a type of violence

(continued)

TABLE 6.4 (CONTINUED)

Country	Domestic Violence	Rape	Marital Rape
El Salvador	Prohibited by law; widespread; underreported; considered socially acceptable by many individuals	Prohibited by law; laws not enforced effectively; punishable by 6 to 10 years' imprisonment; widespread	Not specifically prohibited by law
Grenada	Prohibited by law; widespread	Prohibited by law; punishable by flogging or up to 15 years' imprisonment	Prohibited by law; punishable by flogging or up to 15 years' imprisonment
Guatemala	Prohibited by law; authorities have little training; widespread	Prohibited by law; punishable by 5 to 15 years' imprisonment; authorities have little training; widespread	Prohibited by law; punishable by 5 to 15 years' imprisonment
Guyana	Prohibited by law; laws not frequently enforced; widespread	Prohibited by law; not frequently prosecuted; underreported	Not prohibited by law
Haiti	Prohibited by law; laws not enforced effectively; underreported; widespread	Prohibited by law; widespread; underreported due to social stigma, limited number of successful convictions, cultural tradition	Not prohibited, not recognized as crime
Honduras	Prohibited by law; punishable by 2 to 4 years' imprisonment;	Prohibited by law; perpetrator can be prosecuted even if victim does not testify	Prohibited by law
Jamaica	Prohibited by law; not enforced effectively; widespread	Prohibited by law; punishable by up to 25 years' imprisonment; underreported	Prohibited by law
Mexico	Prohibited by law; not enforced effectively; widespread; underreported	Prohibited by law; punishable by up to 20 years' imprisonment; underreported due to fear of publicity, social stigma, or unlikely chance of prosecution	Prohibited by law
Nicaragua	Prohibited by law; punishable by up to 6 years' imprisonment; widespread; underreported	Prohibited by law; underreported	Prohibited by law
Panama	Prohibited by law; widespread; underreported	Prohibited by law; punishable by 5 to 10 years' imprisonment; in some cases perpetrator may avoid prosecution by marrying the victim	Prohibited by law

Paraguay	Prohibited by law; widespread; underreported due to family pressure or lack of prosecution	Prohibited by law; punishable by up to 10 years' imprisonment; widespread; underreported	Prohibited by law
Peru	Prohibited by law; laws not enforced effectively; widespread; underreported	Prohibited by law; laws not enforced effectively	Prohibited by law
Saint Kitts and Nevis	Prohibited by law; laws not enforced effectively; underreported	Prohibited by law	Not specifically prohibited by law
Saint Lucia	Prohibited by law; effective law enforcement; underreported due to victims' reluctance to press charges	Prohibited by law; underreported; limited prosecution due to victims' reluctance to press charges	Not specifically prohibited by law
Saint Vincent and the Grenadines	Not specifically prohibited by law although victims are protected; authorities may be reluctant to investigate due to victims' reluctance to press charges	Prohibited by law; effective enforcement	Prohibited by law
Suriname	Prohibited by law; widespread	Prohibited by law; laws enforced effectively	Prohibited by law
Trinidad and Tobago	Prohibited by law; reliable statistics unavailable	Prohibited by law; punishable by up to life imprisonment; underreported due to social stigma and perception that police will not investigate effectively	Prohibited by law
Uruguay	Prohibited by law	Prohibited by law	Prohibited by law; underreported due to social stigma and ignorance of the law
Venezuela	Prohibited by law; widespread	Prohibited by law; underreported; perpetrator may avoid punishment by marrying the victim; reliable data unavailable	Prohibited by law

Prostitution and Sex Trafficking

Many countries have enacted laws prohibiting prostitution and trafficking; however, these laws are often ineffectively enforced. Statistics on these activities are often difficult to find and unreliable in many cases. Table 6.5 provides general information regarding individual country statutes and the existence of prostitution and sex trafficking in developing countries, by region.

Voting and Elections

Most countries have given women the right to vote, with the exception of Brunei Darussalum, Saudi Arabia, and the United Arab Emirates. Many countries have also enacted statutes that require a certain percentage of women be elected each year to their national congresses and parliaments. Table 6.6 provides information on the year that women were granted the vote in developing countries and the percentage of women elected to national congresses and parliaments. Data were taken from the Inter-Parliamentary Union (available at http://www.ipu.org/wmn-e/classif.htm).

Labor and Employment

Throughout the world the rate of women in paid employment outside of agriculture has slowly increased, and according to the Millennium Development Goals Report for 2010, it reached 41 percent in 2008. However, in certain regions the rate was lower; for example, only 20 percent of women in Southern Asia, Northern Africa, and Western Asia were employed in nonagricultural positions. Table 6.7 presents regional rates of employment, by industry, for 2008. Data were taken from *Global Employment Trends for Women* (2009). Table 6.8 presents rates of labor participation by females compared with males; these include both agricultural and nonagricultural employment. Data were taken from the UN Interagency Estimates (WHO 2010b).

TABLE 6.5

Status and Extent of Prostitution and Sex Trafficking

Country	Prostitution	Sex Trafficking
Africa		
Angola	Prohibited by law; law not enforced effectively	Slavery is prohibited but not trafficking; source and destination country for forced labor and sexual exploitation
Benin	Prostitution itself not prohibited by law but facilitating or profiting from prostitution is prohibited	Trafficking in children is prohibited by law but not adult trafficking; source, transit, and destination country for children only
Botswana	Prohibited by law; law enforcement not effective; widespread	Not prohibited by law although abduction, slave trafficking, and procuring women and girls for the purpose of prostitution is prohibited; source, transit, and destination country for forced labor and sexual exploitation
Burkina Faso	Not prohibited by law although soliciting and pimping are illegal	Prohibited by law; source, transit, and destination country for women and children for forced labor and sexual exploitation
Burundi	Prohibited by law; not significant problem	Prohibited by law; no reliable data on prevalence
Cameroon	Prohibited by law; laws not enforced effectively	Slavery and child trafficking are illegal; source, transit, and destination country; most trafficking in women is to other countries
Cape Verde	Legal for adults	Trafficking in adults not prohibited, only trafficking in children
Central African Republic	Not prohibited by law but facilitating or profiting from prostitution is illegal	Prohibited by law; believed to not be widespread although reliable data unavailable
Chad	Prohibited but widespread in certain areas	Not specifically prohibited by law
Comoros	Prohibited by law; not openly practiced	No reports of trafficking
Congo, Democratic Republic of	Forced prostitution prohibited by law; evidence of women and girls forced into prostitution by family members or security forces	Some forms prohibited by law including forced prostitution, sexual slavery, involuntary servitude; source and destination country for forced labor and sexual exploitation
Congo, Republic of	Prohibited by law; laws not effectively enforced; common	Prohibited by law; no evidence of trafficking of adults

(*continued*)

TABLE 6.5 (CONTINUED)

Country	Prostitution	Sex Trafficking
Cote d'Ivoire	Legal between consenting adults; soliciting prohibited	Not prohibited; problem; source and destination country for trafficking; internal trafficking for sexual exploitation and servitude
Djibouti	Prohibited by law; exists	Prohibited by law; reports of women and girls being trafficked for prostitution and domestic servitude
Equatorial Guinea	Prohibited by law; occurs in two major cities (Malabo and Bata)	Prohibited by law; some trafficking suspected
Eritrea	Prohibited by law but a serious problem	Prohibited by law
Ethiopia	Legal for individuals over 18 years; common, often because of poverty	Prohibited by law; source country for forced labor and some commercial sexual exploitation; internal trafficking of rural women
Gabon	Prohibited by law; not widespread	Prohibited by law; women and children trafficked into the country
Gambia	Prohibited by law but widespread, especially in tourist areas	Prohibited by law but widespread; source, transit, and destination country
Ghana	Prohibited by law; widespread in urban areas	Prohibited by law; source, transit, and destination country for women and children trafficked for sexual exploitation and forced labor
Guinea	Prohibited by law; widespread	Prohibited by law; source, transit, and destination country; girls trafficked for sexual exploitation and forced labor; National Action Plan to Combat Trafficking in Persons renewed but no funds available to implement
Guinea-Bissau	Not prohibited by law; widespread	Not prohibited by law; source, transit, and destination country, primarily for children trafficked for forced labor and some sexual exploitation
Kenya	Prohibited by law although soliciting is not a crime; widespread, especially in urban and tourist areas	Trafficking in children prohibited by law; trafficking of persons for sexual exploitation is prohibited; source, transit, and destination country for trafficking of women for forced labor and sexual exploitation; increasing cooperation of the government and NGOs to combat trafficking

Lesotho	Not prohibited by law; prevalence unknown	Not prohibited by law but slavery and forced labor are prohibited; source, transit, and destination country for women and children trafficked for forced labor and sexual exploitation; government working to draft anti-trafficking laws
Liberia	Prohibited by law; widespread	Prohibited by law; source, transit, and destination country; public awareness campaign by government and NGOs; National Anti-trafficking Task Force has no budget
Madagascar	Not prohibited by law; widespread, especially in tourist areas	Prohibited by law; girls and young women most frequent victims, trafficked for sexual exploitation and forced labor; government database established to track traffickers
Malawi	Not prohibited by law; law does prohibit owning a brothel, forcing a person into prostitution, and living off income earned through prostitution; widespread, especially in urban and tourist areas	Not prohibited by law; source, transit, and destination country for women and children trafficked for sexual exploitation, frequently to South Africa
Mali	Not prohibited by law; widespread, especially in urban areas	Trafficking in children prohibited by law, but not adult trafficking; trafficking of children and women for forced labor and sexual exploitation; government works with NGOs to repatriate victims
Mauritania	Prohibited by law; increasingly prevalent, especially in tourist areas	Prohibited by law; widespread; source, transit, and destination country; young girls trafficked to Gulf States for sexual exploitation or marriage
Mauritius	Prohibited by law; widespread; reports of school-age girls forced into prostitution by family members	Prohibited by law; not widespread
Mozambique	Not prohibited by law but indecency and immoral behavior are prohibited	Prohibited by law; source, transit, and destination country primarily for women and girls trafficked for forced labor and sexual exploitation
Namibia	Not prohibited by law; widespread	Prohibited by law; source, transit, and destination country
Niger	Prohibited by law; widespread, especially in urban areas	Not prohibited by law; source, transit, and destination country for women trafficked for domestic labor and sexual exploitation
Nigeria	Prohibited by law; widespread, especially in urban areas; women hired as employees by corporations to attract clients through prostitution	Prohibited by law; source, transit, and destination country; widespread; majority of victims are female, trafficked for domestic labor and sexual exploitation

(*continued*)

TABLE 6.5 (CONTINUED)

Country	Prostitution	Sex Trafficking
Rwanda	Prohibited by law; widespread	Not specifically prohibited by law but traffickers can be prosecuted using laws against slavery, kidnapping, rape, and defilement; source country, primarily for women and children trafficked for domestic labor and sexual exploitation
Sao Tome and Principe	Prohibited by law; increasingly prevalent	Prohibited by law; no reports of trafficking
Senegal	Legal if individuals are 21 years old or older; they must register with the police and test negative for any STDs	Prohibited by law; widespread; young girls trafficked within the country for domestic labor and sexual exploitation; source, transit, and destination country
Seychelles	Prohibited by law; widespread	Prohibited by law; no reports of trafficking
Sierra Leone	Not prohibited by law; widespread	Prohibited by law; women trafficked for domestic labor and sexual exploitation; source, transfer, and destination country; government works with NGOs to combat trafficking
Somalia	Prohibited by law; no reliable data	Not specifically prohibited by law; believed to be widespread but no reliable data; source, transit, and destination country
South Africa	Prohibited by law; widespread	Not specifically prohibited by law; source, transit, and destination country for women and children trafficked for domestic labor and sexual exploitation
Sudan	Prohibited by law; widespread	Not specifically prohibited by law but abduction, luring, and forced labor are prohibited; no reliable data regarding prevalence; women and girls trafficked for domestic labor and sexual exploitation
Swaziland	Prohibited by law; widespread	Prohibited by law; women and girls trafficked for domestic labor, forced labor, and sexual exploitation; source, transit, and destination country; anti-trafficking task force created; public awareness campaign by government
Tanzania	Prohibited by law; widespread	Prohibited by a law passed in 2009; women and girls trafficked for forced labor and sexual exploitation; girls considered to be burden on family and often trafficked

Togo	Prohibited by law; widespread in urban areas	Child trafficking prohibited by law; the law does not apply to adults; women and girls trafficked for domestic and other labor and sexual exploitation; source, transit, and destination country; government works with NGOs and other governments to reduce trafficking
Uganda	Prohibited by law; widespread	Prohibited by law; women and children trafficked within the country for forced labor and sexual exploitation; task force created to reduce trafficking
Zambia	Not specifically prohibited by law; widespread in urban areas	Prohibited by law; children, often girls, trafficked for domestic labor and sexual exploitation; government works with NGOs to provide services and support to victims; source, transit, and destination country
Zimbabwe	Prohibited by law; common in urban areas	Not prohibited by law; widespread; women and children trafficked for domestic labor and sexual exploitation; source, transit, and destination country
East Asia and Pacific		
Brunei Darussalam	Prohibited by law; not widespread	Prohibited by law but no prosecutions; destination country for women for forced labor and sexual exploitation; limited attempts by government to curb
Burma	Prohibited by law; increasingly widespread in urban areas; limited enforcement by police if bribes are paid	Prohibited by law; widespread; women and young girls trafficked for domestic and forced labor and sexual exploitation; government has established anti-trafficking task forces in 22 locations to curb trafficking
Cambodia	Prohibited by the constitution; widespread	Prohibited by law; women and children trafficked for forced labor and sexual exploitation; source, transit, and destination country
China	Prohibited by law; an estimated 1.7 to 6 million women are involved in prostitution	Prohibited by law; women and children trafficked for forced labor, forced marriage, and sexual exploitation; source, transit, and destination country
Fiji	Prohibited by law; prevalent in urban areas	Prohibited by law
Indonesia	Prohibited by law; widespread; generally tolerated by authorities	Prohibited by law; source and destination country; women and girls trafficked for domestic labor and sexual exploitation
Kiribati	Not prohibited by law although procuring sex and operating brothels are illegal	Prohibited by law; no reports of trafficking; some reports of young girls being trafficked within the country for sexual exploitation

(continued)

TABLE 6.5 (CONTINUED)

Country	Prostitution	Sex Trafficking
Korea, Democratic People's Republic of	Prohibited by law; prevalence unknown	Trafficking of women prohibited by law; trafficking of women and girls into China is widespread
Republic of Korea	Prohibited by law; widespread	Prohibited by law; women trafficked to the country for sexual exploitation and marriage to nationals; government works with international agencies and governments to curb trafficking
Laos	Prohibited by law; little law enforcement; widespread	Prohibited by law; women and children frequently trafficked for forced labor and prostitution; source, transit, and destination country; government runs public awareness campaign
Malaysia	Not prohibited by law; solicitation is prohibited; an estimated 50,000 to 150,000 women are involved in prostitution; Muslims involved in prostitution are punished under Shari'a law for sexual relations outside of marriage	Prohibited by law; widespread; women and girls trafficked for forced labor and sexual exploitation; source, transit, and destination country
Marshall Islands	Prohibited by law; uncommon	Not specifically prohibited by law; no reports of trafficking of any persons
Micronesia, Federated States of	Prohibited by law; uncommon	Not specifically prohibited by law; no victims of trafficking reported
Mongolia	Prohibited by law; prevalent in urban areas	Prohibited by law; source country for forced labor and sexual exploitation
Nauru	Prohibited by law; no reported incidences	Not specifically prohibited by law; no victims of trafficking reported
Palau	Prohibited by law; widespread	Prohibited by law; women trafficked to the country for domestic and forced labor and sexual exploitation
Papua New Guinea	Prohibited by law; laws not enforced; widespread	Trafficking of children for sexual exploitation or slavery; trafficking of adults not prohibited; women and girls trafficked for forced labor and sexual exploitation; no government programs to help victims
Philippines	Prohibited by law; laws not enforced; widespread	Prohibited by law; women and girls trafficked for forced labor and sexual exploitation; source, transit, and destination country
Samoa	Prohibited by law; not widespread	Not specifically prohibited by law; no victims of trafficking reported

Singapore	Not prohibited by law although public solicitation, operating brothels, and living on earnings from prostitution are prohibited; tolerated by authorities	Prohibited by law; women and girls trafficked for sexual exploitation
Solomon Islands	Prohibited by law; laws not enforced	Prohibited by law; no confirmed reports of trafficking
Taiwan	Prohibited by law; only prostitutes are prosecuted, not those patronizing prostitutes	Prohibited by law as of 2009; most frequently a destination country for women for forced labor and sexual exploitation
Thailand	Prohibited by law; little law enforcement; widespread	Prohibited by law as of 2008; trafficking of women and children for forced labor and sexual exploitation; source, transit, and destination country; several NGOs work with victims; government runs public awareness campaign
Timor-Leste	Not prohibited by law	Trafficking in persons for forced labor and sexual exploitation is prohibited; government works with NGOs to assist victims
Tonga	Not prohibited by law; some reports of women and girls participating in commercial sexual activities	Not specifically prohibited by law; no reports of trafficking
Tuvalu	Prohibited by law; uncommon	Not prohibited by law; no reports of trafficking
Vanuatu	Prohibited by law; not widespread although it appears to be increasing	Not prohibited by law; no reports of trafficking
Vietnam	Prohibited by law; not enforced; many women become prostitutes for financial reasons; occasionally parents force daughters into prostitution	Prohibited by law; widespread; women and girls trafficked for forced labor and sexual exploitation
South and Central Asia		
Afghanistan	Prohibited by law; exists, but is not widespread	Prohibited by law; women and girls trafficked for forced labor and sexual exploitation; source, transit, and destination country
Bangladesh	Male prostitution prohibited by law; female prostitution is legal	Prohibited by law; widespread; women and girls trafficked for forced labor and sexual exploitation
Bhutan	Limited, primarily occurs in border regions	Prohibited by law; little reliable data regarding prevalence but believed to be uncommon

(continued)

TABLE 6.5 (CONTINUED)

Country	Prostitution	Sex Trafficking
India	Prostitution itself not prohibited by law but selling, procuring, or exploiting a person for sex or profit is illegal	Some forms prohibited by law; widespread; source, transit, and destination county for women and children trafficked for forced labor and sexual exploitation; government established 297 anti-trafficking units around the country for training law enforcement officials
Maldives	Prohibited by law; limited in practice	Trafficking in persons not prohibited by law; few foreign women trafficked to the country for sexual exploitation; girls trafficked for domestic labor and sexual exploitation
Nepal	Not prohibited by law	Prohibited by law; widespread trafficking of women and children for sexual exploitation and domestic labor
Pakistan	Prohibited by law; little law enforcement	Prohibited by law; widespread; source, transit, and destination country; women and girls trafficked for domestic labor and sexual exploitation
Sri Lanka	Prohibited by law; widespread	Prohibited by law; source and destination country; women and girls trafficked for domestic labor and sexual exploitation
Near East and North Africa		
Algeria	Prohibited by law; increasingly prevalent	Prohibited by law as of 2009; transit and destination country
Bahrain	Prohibited by law; prostitutes and customers primarily non-nationals	Prohibited; widespread; some trafficking for sexual exploitation but primarily for construction and domestic labor
Egypt	Prohibited by law; common in urban areas	Not specifically prohibited by law; women and girls trafficked for domestic labor and sexual exploitation; source, transit, and destination country
Iran	Prohibited by law; widespread	Prohibited by law; widespread; women and girls trafficked for sexual exploitation and forced labor; source, transit, and destination country
Iraq	Prohibited by law; increasingly prevalent	Prohibited by law; women trafficked for forced labor and sexual exploitation
Jordan	Prohibited by law; exists in some urban areas	Prohibited by law as of 2009; source and destination country for women and girls for forced labor and sexual exploitation

Kuwait	Prohibited by law; several prostitution rings exist	Not specifically prohibited by law; widespread; women trafficked for domestic labor and sexual exploitation
Lebanon	Not prohibited by law; brothels required to be licensed but very few are	Not specifically prohibited by law; widespread; women trafficked for domestic labor and sexual exploitation
Libya	Prohibited by law; common in urban areas	Trafficking of women prohibited by law; believed to be common
Morocco	Prohibited by law; little law enforcement; increasingly prevalent, primarily in urban areas	Prohibited by law; women and girls primarily trafficked for forced labor and sexual exploitation
Oman	Prohibited by law; exists despite strict cultural norms	Prohibited by law; transit and destination country; government works effectively to curb trafficking
Qatar	Prohibited by law; increasingly prevalent	Not specifically prohibited by law; women trafficked for forced labor; some women and girls sexually exploited
Saudi Arabia	Prohibited by law; unknown prevalence	Prohibited by law as of 2009; widespread; women and children trafficked for forced and domestic labor and sexual exploitation
Syria	Prohibited by law; laws not strictly enforced	Trafficking considered a form of incarcerating or holding persons against their will; women trafficked for domestic labor and sexual exploitation; unknown prevalence
Tunisia	Prohibited by law; government sanctions brothels	Not specifically prohibited by law but statutes prohibiting forced labor, forced prostitution, or servitude can be applied; women and girls trafficked for domestic labor and sexual exploitation
United Arab Emirates	Prohibited by law; increasingly prevalent	Prohibited by law; widespread; women and girls trafficked for domestic labor and sexual exploitation
Yemen	Prohibited by law; little law enforcement; widespread	Not specifically prohibited by law but can be prosecuted under other statutes; some women and girls trafficked for sexual exploitation
Latin America and the Caribbean		
Antigua and Barbuda	Prohibited by law; common	Not specifically prohibited by law; destination country for women trafficked for sexual exploitation, also possibly domestic labor
Argentina	Prostitution itself is not prohibited by law but promoting, soliciting, or exploiting is prohibited	Prohibited by law; women and children trafficked primarily for sexual exploitation and forced labor

(*continued*)

TABLE 6.5 (CONTINUED)

Country	Prostitution	Sex Trafficking
Barbados	Prohibited by law; common, especially in urban and tourist areas	Not specifically prohibited by law but can be prosecuted using laws against forced labor and slavery
Belize	Carnal knowledge of a girl under the age of 18 years is prohibited by law	Prohibited by law; no reliable data regarding prevalence
Bolivia	Legal for persons 18 and older	Prohibited by law; women and girls trafficked for forced labor and sexual exploitation; NGOs run public awareness campaigns
Brazil	Legal, although operating a brothel is prohibited	Prohibited by law; widespread, primarily for sexual exploitation, also some forced labor; limited access to services for victims
Chile	Legal for persons 18 and older; brothels are prohibited; women can register with the National Health Services	All forms not specifically prohibited by law; many women trafficked for sexual exploitation; source and destination country; cross-border trafficking prohibited; government runs public awareness campaigns
Colombia	Legal for persons 18 and older but restricted to specified "tolerance zones;" widespread	Prohibited by law; trafficking for forced labor and sexual exploitation, primarily young women; source, transit, and destination country; government operates reporting hotline
Costa Rica	Legal for persons 18 and older; practiced openly, especially in urban and tourist areas	Transnational trafficking is prohibited by law; trafficking for forced labor and sexual exploitation
Dominica	Prohibited by law; little law enforcement	Prohibited by law; no reports of trafficking
Dominican Republic	Legal, although certain sexual relations with minors are prohibited; little law enforcement	Prohibited by law; unknown prevalence; young women at greatest risk for trafficking for sexual exploitation
Ecuador	Legal for persons 18 and older but they must register with the government	Prohibited by law; trafficking of women and children for forced labor and sexual exploitation; specialized anti-trafficking police unit along with prevention campaigns and networks; government assists victims
El Salvador	Legal for persons 18 and older; common	Prohibited by law; widespread, especially in urban and tourist areas and along the borders; women and girls trafficked for sexual exploitation; possible involvement by organized crime

Grenada	Prohibited by law; common	Not prohibited by law; no reports of trafficking
Guatemala	Legal, although forcing a person into prostitution is prohibited	Prohibited by law; widespread; women and girls trafficked for forced labor and sexual exploitation; source, transit, and destination country
Guyana	Prohibited by law; exists	Prohibited by law; no convictions
Haiti	Prohibited by law; little law enforcement; widespread	Not specifically prohibited by law; women and children trafficked for sexual exploitation; source, transit, and destination country
Honduras	Legal for persons 18 and older but promoting or facilitating is prohibited; widespread	Prohibited by law; women and girls trafficked primarily for sexual exploitation
Jamaica	Prohibited by law; widespread, especially in tourist areas	Prohibited by law; women trafficked for forced labor and sexual exploitation
Mexico	Legal for adults; widespread; sex tourism not prohibited by law	Prohibited by law; source, transit, and destination country
Nicaragua	Legal for persons 14 and older; common; sexual exploitation of young girls widespread	Prohibited by law; widespread; majority of victims are women and children trafficked for sexual exploitation
Panama	Legal, as long as prostitutes register with government (not many do)	Trafficking for sexual exploitation prohibited by law; other forms not specifically prohibited but prosecuted under other statutes; women and girls trafficked primarily for sexual exploitation
Paraguay	Legal for persons 18 and older; widespread	Most forms prohibited by law; most women and girls trafficked for sexual exploitation, also for domestic and forced labor
Peru	Legal for women 18 and older but they must register with the government and carry a health certificate	Prohibited by law; reliable data unavailable; primarily trafficking within the country of women and children for sexual exploitation and forced labor
Saint Kitts and Nevis	Prohibited by law; not common	Prohibited by law; no reports of trafficking
Saint Lucia	Prohibited by law; limited enforcement; no arrests in 2009	All forms not specifically prohibited by law; no reports of trafficking
Saint Vincent and the Grenadines	Prohibited by law; uncommon	Not prohibited by law; no reports of trafficking
Suriname	Prohibited by law; little law enforcement; common	Prohibited by law; source, transit, and destination country; extent unknown
Trinidad and Tobago	Prohibited by law; enforced by authorities	Not specifically prohibited by law but can be prosecuted under other statutes; not a major problem
Uruguay	Legal for persons 18 and older; found primarily in urban and tourist areas	Prohibited by law; women and girls trafficked for forced labor and sexual exploitation
Venezuela	Legal; unknown prevalence, but common in urban and tourist areas	Slavery, servitude, and transnational trafficking prohibited by law; source, transit, and destination country; women and children trafficked for sexual exploitation and forced labor

TABLE 6.6
Women's Suffrage and Elected Representatives

Country	Year Women Received the Vote	Percent of Women in National Parliaments (by Election Year)
Algeria	1962	7.7 Lower House (2007)
		5.1 Upper House/Senate (2009)
Angola	1975	38.6 (2008)
Benin	1956	10.8 (2003)
Botswana	1965	7.9 (2009)
Burkina Faso	1958	15.3 (2007)
Burundi	1961	32.1 Lower House (2010)
		46.3 Upper House (2010)
Cameroon	1946	13.9 (2007)
Cape Verde	1975	18.1 (2006)
Central African Republic	1986	9.6 (2005)
Chad	1958	5.2 (2002)
Comoros	1956	3.0 (2009)
Congo	1967	7.3 Lower House (2007)
		12.9 Upper House/Senate (2008)
Congo, Dem. Republic of	1963	8.4 Lower House (2006)
		4.6 Upper House/Senate (2007)
Cote d'Ivoire	1952	8.9 (2000)
Djibouti	1986	13.8 (2008)
Egypt	1956	1.8 Lower House (2005)
		6.8 Upper House/Senate (2007)
Equatorial Guinea	1963	—
Eritrea	1955	22.0 (1994)
Ethiopia	1955	27.8 Lower House (2010)
		16.3 Upper House/Senate (2010)
Gabon	1956	14.7 Lower House (2009)
		17.6 Upper House/Senate (2009)
Gambia	1960	7.5 (2002)
Ghana	1954	8.3 (2008)
Guinea	1958	10.0 (2008)
Guinea-Bissau	1977	10.0 (2008)
Kenya	1963	9.8 (2007)
Lesotho	1965	24.2 Lower House (2007)
		18.2 Upper House/Senate (2007)
Liberia	1946	12.5 Lower House (2005)
		16.7 Upper House/Senate (2005)
Libya	1964	7.7 (2009)
Madagascar	1959	12.5 Lower House (2010)
		11.1 Upper House/Senate (2010)
Malawi	1961	20.8 (2009)
Mali	1956	10.2 (2007)

Mauritania	1961	22.1 Lower House (2006) 14.3 Upper House/Senate (2009)
Mauritius	1956	18.6 (2008)
Morocco	1963	10.5 Lower House (2007) 2.2 Upper House/Senate (2009)
Mozambique	1975	39.2 (2009)
Namibia	1989	24.4 Lower House (2009) ? Upper House/Senate (2010)
Niger	1948	9.7
Nigeria	1958	7.0 Lower House (2007) 8.3 Upper House/Senate (2007)
Rwanda	1961	56.3% Lower House (2008) 34.6% Upper House/Senate (2003)
Sao Tome and Principe	1975	18.2 (2010)
Senegal	1945	22.7 Lower House (2007) 40.0 Upper House/Senate (2007)
Seychelles	1948	23.5 (2007)
Sierra Leone	1961	13.2 (2007)
Somalia	1956	6.8 (2004)
South Africa	1984 (Coloureds, Indians) 1994 (blacks)	44.5 Lower House (2009) 29.6 Upper House/Senate (2009)
Sudan	1964	25.6 Lower House (2010) 10.9 Upper House/Senate (2010)
Swaziland	1968	13.6 Lower House (2008) 40.0 Upper House/Senate (2008)
Tanzania	1959	30.7 (2005)
Togo	1945	11.1 (2007)
Tunisia	1959	27.6 Lower House (2009) 15.2 Upper House/Senate (2008)
Uganda	1962	31.5 (2006)
Zambia	1962	14.0 (2006)
Zimbabwe	1957	15.0 Lower House (2008) 24.2 Upper House/Senate (2008)
South and Central Asia		
Afghanistan	1965	27.7 Lower House (2010) 15.2 Upper House/Senate (2010)
Bangladesh	1972	18.6 (2008)
Bhutan	1953	8.5 Lower House (2008) 24.0 Upper House/Senate (2007)
India	1950	10.8 Lower House (2009) 9.0 Upper House/Senate (2008)
Maldives	1932	6.5 (2009)
Nepal	1951	33.2 (2008)
Pakistan	1947	22.2 Lower House (2008) 17.0 Upper House/Senate (2009)
Sri Lanka	1931	5.3 (2010)
Timor-Leste	—	29.2 (2007)

(continued)

TABLE 6.6 (CONTINUED)

Country	Year Women Received the Vote	Percent of Women in National Parliaments (by Election Year)
East Asia and the Pacific		
Brunei Darussalum	Not permitted	—
Burma	1946	—
Cambodia	1955	21.1 Lower House (2008) 14.8 Upper House/Senate (2006)
China	1949	21.3 (2008)
Fiji	1963	—
Indonesia	1945	18.0 (2009)
Kiribati	1967	4.3 (2007)
Korea, Democratic People's Republic of	1946	15.6 (2009)
Korea, Republic of	1948	14.7 (2008)
Laos	1958	25.2 (2006)
Malaysia	1957	9.9 Lower House (2008) 28.1 Upper House/Senate (?)
Marshall Islands	1979	3.0 (2007)
Micronesia, Federated States of	1979	0.0 (2009)
Nauru	1968	0.0 (2010)
Palau	1979	0.0 Lower House (2008) 15.4 Upper House/Senate (2008)
Papua New Guinea	1964	0.9 (2007)
Philippines	1937	21.4 Lower House (2010) 13.0 Upper House/Senate (2010)
Samoa	1990	8.2 (2006)
Singapore	1947	23.4 (2006)
Solomon Islands	1974	0.0 (2010)
Thailand	1932	13.3 Lower House (2007) 16.0 Upper House/Senate (2008)
Tonga	1960	0.0 (2010)
Tuvalu	1967	0.0 (2010)
Vanuatu	1975	3.8 (2008)
Vietnam	1946	25.8 (2007)
Near East and North Africa		
Bahrain	1973	2.5 Lower House (2010) 27.5 Upper House/Senate (2010)
Iran	1963	2.8 (2008)
Iraq	1980	25.2 (2010)
Jordan	1974	10.8 Lower House (2010) 15.0 Upper House/Senate (2010)
Kuwait	2005	7.7 (2009)
Lebanon	1952	3.1 (2009)
Oman	2003	0.0 Lower House (2007) 19.4 Upper House/Senate (2007)

Qatar	1997	0.0 (2010)
Saudi Arabia	Not permitted	0.0 (2009)
Syria	1949	12.4 (2007)
United Arab Emirates	Not permitted	22.5 (2006)
Yemen	1970	0.3 Lower House (2003)
		1.8 Upper House (2001)
South and Central America		
Antigua and Barbuda	1951	10.5 Lower House 2009)
		29.4 Upper House/Senate (2009)
Argentina	1947	38.5 Lower House (2009)
		35.2 Upper House/Senate (2009)
Barbados	1950	10.0 Lower House (2008)
		33.3 Upper House/Senate (2008)
Belize	1954	0.0 Lower House (2008)
		38.5 Upper House/Senate (2008)
Bolivia	1952	25.4 Lower House (2009)
		47.2 Upper House/Senate (2009)
Brazil	1932	8.6 Lower House (2010)
		16.0 Upper House/Senate (2010)
Chile	1949	14.2 Lower House (2009)
		13.2 Upper House/Senate (2009)
Colombia	1954	8.4 Lower House (2006)
		11.8 Upper House/Senate (2006)
Costa Rica	1949	38.6 (2010)
Dominica	1951	19.2 (2009)
Dominican Republic	1942	20.8 Lower House (2010)
		9.4 Upper House/Senate (2010)
Ecuador	1967	32.3 (2009)
El Salvador	1939	19.0 (2009)
Grenada	1951	13.3 Lower House (2008)
		30.8 Upper House/Senate (2008)
Guatemala	1946	12.0 (2007)
Guyana	1953	30.0 (2006)
Haiti	1950	4.1 Lower House (2006)
		6.9 Upper House/Senate (2009)
Honduras	1955	18.0 (2009)
Jamaica	1944	13.3 Lower House (2007)
		14.3 (2007)
Mexico	1947	26.2 Lower House (2009)
		19.5 Upper House/Senate (2006)
Nicaragua	1955	20.7 (2006)
Panama	1946	8.5 (2009)

(*continued*)

TABLE 6.6 (CONTINUED)

Country	Year Women Received the Vote	Percent of Women in National Parliaments (by Election Year)
Paraguay	1961	12.5 Lower House (2008) 15.6 Upper House/Senate (2008)
Peru	1955	27.5 (2006)
Saint Lucia	1924	11.1 Lower House (2006) 36.4 Upper House/Senate (2007)
St. Kitts and Nevis	1951	6.7 (2010)
Saint Vincent and Grenadines	1951	21.7 (2005)
Suriname	1948	9.8 (2010)
Trinidad and Tobago	1946	28.6 Lower House (2010) 25.8 Upper House/Senate (2010)
Uruguay	1932	15.2 Lower House (2009) 12.9 Upper House/Senate (2009)
Venezuela	1946	17.5 (2005)

TABLE 6.7
Regional Share in Employment, by Sector

	Agriculture		Industry		Services	
Region	**Males**	**Females**	**Males**	**Females**	**Males**	**Females**
East Asia	34.7	38.9	28.5	27.9	36.9	33.2
Southeast Asia and the Pacific	45.2	43.0	21.0	16.8	33.8	40.2
South Asia	39.9	64.5	24.8	17.3	35.3	18.2
Latin America and the Caribbean	21.1	9.2	28.9	14.1	50.0	76.7
Middle East	12.4	32.0	26.9	17.6	60.7	50.4
North Africa	30.3	38.1	25.8	16.6	43.6	45.3
Sub-Saharan Africa	59.5	64.3	13.2	6.6	27.3	29.0

TABLE 6.8
Labor Participation Rates

Country	Labor Participation Rate, Female (%)	Labor Participation Rate, Male (%)
Africa		
Angola	74	89
Benin	67	79
Botswana	72	81
Burkina Faso	78	91
Burundi	91	88
Cameroon	53	81
Central African Republic	71	87
Chad	63	79
Comoros	73	86
Congo, Democratic Republic of	56	85
Congo, Republic of	63	83
Cote d'Ivoire	51	82
Djibouti	61	79
Equatorial Guinea	38	92
Eritrea	60	83
Ethiopia	78	90
Gabon	69	81
Gambia	71	85
Ghana	74	75
Guinea	79	89
Guinea-Bissau	60	84
Kenya	76	88
Lesotho	70	78
Liberia	67	76
Madagascar	84	89
Malawi	75	79
Mali	37	68
Mauritania	59	81
Mauritius	42	76
Mozambique	85	87
Namibia	52	62
Niger	38	88
Nigeria	39	74
Rwanda	86	85
Sao Tome and Principe	44	76
Senegal	65	89
Seychelles	—	—
Sierra Leone	66	68
Somalia	57	85
South Africa	47	64
Sudan	31	74

(*continued*)

TABLE 6.8 (CONTINUED)

Country	Labor Participation Rate, Female (%)	Labor Participation Rate, Male (%)
Swaziland	53	75
Tanzania	86	91
Togo	63	86
Uganda	78	91
Zambia	60	79
Zimbabwe	60	74
East Asia and the Pacific		
Brunei Darussalam	60	75
Burma	64	85
Cambodia	73	84
China	68	80
Fiji	39	79
Indonesia	52	85
Kiribati	—	—
Korea, Democratic People's Republic of	55	77
Korea, Republic of	50	72
Laos	78	79
Malaysia	44	80
Marshall Islands	—	—
Micronesia, Federated States of	—	—
Mongolia	67	78
Nauru	—	—
Palau	—	—
Papua New Guinea	71	74
Philippines	49	79
Samoa	38	76
Singapore	54	76
Solomon Islands	24	49
Thailand	66	81
Timor-Leste	59	83
Tonga	53	75
Tuvalu	—	—
Vanuatu	79	88
Vietnam	68	76
South and Central Asia		
Afghanistan	33	85
Bangladesh	58	83
Bhutan	51	69
India	33	81
Maldives	56	75
Nepal	63	80
Pakistan	21	84
Sri Lanka	35	75
Near East and North Africa		

Algeria	37	80
Bahrain	32	85
Egypt	23	73
Iran	31	70
Iraq	13	69
Jordan	23	75
Kuwait	44	83
Lebanon	22	70
Libya	24	78
Morocco	27	80
Oman	25	77
Qatar	48	93
Saudi Arabia	21	80
Syria	21	80
Tunisia	26	71
United Arab Emirates	42	92
Yemen	20	73
South and Central America		
Antigua and Barbuda	—	—
Argentina	51	78
Barbados	66	78
Belize	46	81
Bolivia	62	82
Brazil	60	82
Chile	44	76
Colombia	41	78
Costa Rica	45	81
Dominica	—	—
Dominican Republic	51	80
Ecuador	47	78
El Salvador	47	77
Grenada	—	—
Guatemala	48	88
Guyana	46	82
Haiti	58	83
Honduras	42	83
Jamaica	57	75
Mexico	43	82
Nicaragua	46	80
Panama	49	84
Paraguay	56	88
Peru	57	76
Saint Kitts and Nevis	—	—
Saint Lucia	50	76
Saint Vincent and the Grenadines	56	79
Suriname	38	66
Trinidad and Tobago	54	77
Uruguay	53	76
Venezuela	51	80

References

United Nations. 2010a. *Facts & Figures on Women Worldwide.* New York: United Nations.

United Nations. 2010b. *The Millennium Development Goals Report 2010.* New York: United Nations.

U.S. Department of State. 2009. Country Reports. Available at http://www.state.gov/g/drl/rls/hrrpt/.

Wilmoth, John, Colin Mathers, Lale Say, and Samuel Mills. 2010. "Maternal Deaths Drop by One-third from 1990 to 2008: A United Nations Analysis," *Bull World Health Organ* 88: 718–718A.

World Health Organization. 2010a. *Trends in Maternal Mortality: 1990 to 2008: Estimates Developed by WHO, UNICEF, UNFPA and The World Bank.* Geneva: WHO.

World Health Organization. 2010b. *World Health Statistics 2010.* Geneva: WHO.

7

Directory of Organizations

This chapter describes government entities and private organizations that work with or provide services to women in developing countries. Government entities include UN agencies and councils. Private organizations, often referred to as nongovernmental organizations (NGOs), are independent agencies not affiliated with any government entity. They are typically focused on designing and implementing development-related projects that benefit women, on advocacy activities, or on providing direct services. In recent years, an increasing number of NGOs combine project design and implementation with advocacy activities and the provision of direct services. Some of these groups operate at the international or regional level and some are national in scope, while others provide services in local communities. Several governments have established women's bureaus to serve the particular needs of women in their countries. The organizations described here make up but a small part of the total number of organizations working on behalf of women in developing countries.

The information contained in this chapter focuses on international organizations, although it also includes several organizations that operate at the regional, national, and local levels. These organizations provide services in the areas of health, welfare, domestic violence, reproductive rights, AIDS, divorce, education, human rights, microfinance, and training. Many of these NGOs have been granted consultative status with the UN Economic and Social Council (ECOSOC), which means that they have met certain UN standards for participation and have received certain rights and privileges to work with ECOSOC and other UN entities.

Nongovernmental Organizations

Afghan Institute of Learning
Dearborn, MI, USA
Website: http://www.creatinghope.org/ail

Sakena Yacoobi founded the Afghan Institute of Learning in 1995 to provide education for poor Afghan women and children after the Taliban took control of the country and banned the education of girls. Since then the Institute has expanded its activities to include teacher training, preschool education, advanced classes, home school, women's learning activities, post-secondary education, and grassroots support programs. It offers human rights and leadership workshops that train women and men in ways to empower women through education, employment, and economic opportunities.

Africa Women's Development and Communications Network (FEMNET)
Nairobi, Kenya
Website: http://www.femnet.or.ke

A multinational organization founded in 1988, FEMNET shares information and strategies among NGOs focused on African women. The network works to strengthen the contributions made by NGOs in the areas of development, equality, and other human rights by serving as a conduit for information among the NGOs. The program focuses on advocacy, communications, and capacity building. It works with the UN Commission on the Status of Women to review progress on the implementation of the Beijing Declaration and Platform of Action.

Apne Aap
Bihar, India
Website: http://www.apneaap.org

Apne Aap (Hindi for "self help") focuses on empowering women and children from India's red light districts to help them escape sex trafficking. The program offers education, health care, and job skills training to women and children as a means of overcoming discrimination against them and improving their lives. Among its objectives are the support of community-based initiatives to help women and children escape the sex-slave industry, mitigate the circumstances that forced them into prostitution in the first place, develop leadership skills, prevent future generations from getting caught up in prostitution, develop connections between grassroots organizers and policy makers to work to eliminate prostitution and sex slavery, and create public awareness of discrimination against women.

Arab Women's Solidarity Association
Giza, Egypt
Website: http://www.awsa.net

Founded in 1982 by Egypt's Dr. Nawal el Saadawi, the Arab Women's Solidarity Association (AWSA) is a multinational organization that focuses on improving conditions for women in Arab countries. The association promotes the interests of Arab women and helps to empower them, coordinates activities, and disseminates information. AWSA organizes conferences that examine the status and needs of women throughout the Arab world. It organizes research and educational programs and produces materials by and for women in the fields of science, culture, art, and literature. AWSA also works to increase literacy rates throughout the region.

Asia Pacific Forum on Women, Law, and Development
Chiang, Thailand
Website: http://www.apwld.org

As a multinational network of organizations throughout the Asia Pacific region, the Asia Pacific Forum on Women, Law, and Development (APWLD) is composed of women's rights activists, lawyers, human rights activists, and other interested individuals and organizations. APWLD's major emphasis is on enabling women in the Asia Pacific region to use the law effectively in their struggles for justice and equality. Programs and activities include policy advocacy, education, and training on women's issues. The network has developed partnerships among women's groups, human rights groups, and development NGOs in the region to encourage the exchange of information. It also advocates for basic human rights and lobbies Asian-Pacific governments to ratify the UN Convention on the Elimination of All Forms of Discrimination against Women.

Asian-Pacific Resource and Research Centre for Women
Kuala Lumpur, Malaysia
Website: http://www.arrow.org.my

The Asian-Pacific Resource and Research Centre for Women (ARROW) researches and analyzes women's issues and provides advice to governmental and legislative organizations. The organization researches and evaluates media coverage of women's health issues and conducts programs to increase public awareness of population growth and reproductive health. It also provides counseling services on women's development. Staff members work to encourage and promote networking activities among women and women's organizations. They operate a database on women and health, conduct bibliographic searches, and provide other information and online services.

Asian Women's Human Rights Council
Manila, Philippines
Website: http://www.awhrc.org

Members of the Asian Women's Human Rights Council, a multinational organization, are female lawyers and feminist activists who are actively involved in promoting and defending basic human rights and women's rights. The council encourages the study of human rights and cooperation and solidarity between women's groups and individuals advocating human rights recognition. The staff compiles information on national policies throughout Asia that influence the provision of human rights for all citizens. The Council has a regional secretariat located in Bangalore, India.

Associated Country Women of the World
London, England
Website: http://www.acww.org.uk

As an organization with affiliates in over 70 countries throughout the world, the Associated Country Women of the World (ACWW) focuses its activities on rural areas and the problems that rural women face worldwide. Major objectives include raising the standard of living of rural women and their families, providing practical support to members including help in developing income-generating activities, and providing a voice for rural women in international forums. Staff members work to promote friendly relations among member organizations and provide assistance in the economic, social, and cultural development of the organization's members and their countries.

Association of African Women for Research and Development
Dakar, Senegal
Website: http://www.afard.org

The Association of African Women for Research and Development (AAWORD) was founded in 1977 as a multinational association to encourage the study of women and women's issues throughout Africa. AAWORD has 16 chapters, including 14 in Africa, one in Europe, and one for African women living in the Americas. Members work in the fields of sociology, anthropology, history, and natural sciences, and as advocates for including women in the fields of economics, education, political science, and communication. The association's goals are to transform gender relations in Africa, encourage women's participation in sustainable development and democracy, promote the ability of African women to conduct research, assist decision makers in the development of policies with a gender perspective, encourage the development of national organizations that focus on gender research at the local level, and create networks that allow African women researchers and organizations to exchange information on development issues. Several networks focusing on African women and development, including the Forum of African Women Educationalists (FAWE), have been created as a result of AAWORD's activities.

Averting Maternal Death and Disability Program
New York, NY, USA
Website: http://www.amddprogram.org

The Averting Maternal Death and Disability (AMDD) program conducts research, analyzes policies, and advocates for the reduction of maternal mortality in developing countries. Founded in 1999, the program works with developing countries and international agencies to increase the availability of quality emergency obstetric care for pregnant women and girls. Program partners collaborate to encourage the wider availability of mid-level health workers to women in developing countries in need of emergency obstetric care.

Bangladesh Women's Health Coalition
Dhaka, Bangladesh
Website: http://www.bwhc.org.bd

The Bangladesh Women's Health Coalition (BWHC) began in 1980 as a single-purpose clinic that offered a variety of health services to women and children. It currently provides reproductive health services and community education to underprivileged and marginalized women and children in Bangladesh. Major program areas include comprehensive reproductive and sexual health; integrated childhood disease management; adolescent health and reproductive health education; management and prevention of RTI, STI, and AIDS; community mobilization; and menstrual regulation training. Staff members collaborate with government and other relevant organizations to educate the local community about the importance of empowering women to participate in all sectors of society.

Bina Swadaya
Jakarta Pusat, Indonesia
Website: http://www.binaswadaya.org

A well-known NGO, Bina Swadaya was founded in 1967 to encourage communities to become self-reliant. The program helps microentrepreneurs gain access to available resources in order to build community self-reliance. Working in rural industries such as agriculture, forestry, and area development, Bina Swadaya focuses on integrated area development, education and training, capital development, book publication, agribusiness development, poverty alleviation, and alternative tourism. The organization promotes small enterprise development by providing training for female staff members of area NGOs, linking commercial banks and women's self-help groups to provide credit without collateral, promoting female leaders to operate microfinance institutions, and promoting social protection plans for women who are home-based workers.

BRAC Centre
Dhaka, Bangladesh
Website: http://www.brac.net

BRAC was initially formed in 1972 to assist refugees returning to Bangladesh following its liberation from Pakistan. It is one of the largest southern NGOs, employing over 100,000 people, most of whom are women, and has expanded its coverage to include Asia and Africa. Employing a holistic approach to alleviating poverty, the program provides economic and social development, health, education, and human rights and legal services to the people it serves. The core of BRAC's approach is village organizations composed of 30 to 40 women, which are established to distribute loans; collect repayments and contributions to savings; and raise awareness of the social, economic, legal, and personal issues affecting women in their everyday lives.

Campaign for Female Education
San Francisco, CA, USA
Website: http://www.camfed.org

The Campaign for Female Education (CAMFED) believes that one of the best ways to fight poverty and HIV/AIDS in Africa is to educate girls and empower women to become agents of change. It operates community-based programs throughout Africa that focus on helping girls and boys attend school by providing scholarships and working with the community to alleviate poverty. Its microfinance program helps women start small businesses; it also offers training programs for community health activists who advocate for better health care in rural areas.

CARE International
Chatelaine, Switzerland
Website: http://www.care.org

One of the leading organizations fighting poverty worldwide, CARE focuses on working with poor women in developing countries because research has shown that, given the proper resources, women are the ones most able to help entire families and communities. Its programs strengthen the ability of individuals and communities to become self-sufficient, provide economic opportunities, deliver emergency relief, work to influence policy at all levels of government, and address all forms of discrimination. CARE's program areas include agriculture and resources, cross-cutting initiatives, economic development, education, emergency relief, health, HIV/AIDS, nutrition, and water.

Center for Reproductive Rights
New York, NY, USA
Website: http://www.reproductiverights.org

The Center for Reproductive Rights is a legal advocacy organization that applies the law to advance reproductive freedom in countries around the world, believing that reproductive freedom is a fundamental human right. It partners with local lawyers and advocates to ensure that the strategies they use to advance reproductive rights in other countries are sensitive to the local cultural, economic, and political environment. They have brought cases before national courts, UN committees, and regional human rights bodies, resulting in expanded access to reproductive health care for many women. Staff members also work to document abuses, work with policy makers to create responsive legislation and policies, and encourage legal scholarship and teaching on reproductive health and human rights.

Center for Women's Global Leadership
New Brunswick, NJ, USA
Website: http://www.cwgl.rutgers.edu

The Center for Women's Global Leadership, part of a consortium of seven women's programs at Rutgers University, examines the ways in which gender affects leadership and power as well as the conduct of public policy throughout the world. The Center's two broad areas of focus are policy and advocacy and leadership development and education regarding women's human rights. Its programs encourage women to take leadership roles and promote a feminist approach to policy development at local, national, and international levels. Working with local organizations and governments, the Center holds governments accountable for ensuring the protection of women and their rights. It conducts two-week intensive leadership institutes each year for women at the grassroots and national levels to share experiences and work toward common goals. The Center also sponsors programs that bring women together to plan and coordinate specific strategies concerning women's rights. An annual global campaign, "16 Days of Activism against Gender Violence," highlights gender-based violence. It also holds global tribunals, hearings, and conferences on women's human rights.

Center for Women's Resources
Quezon City, Philippines
Website: http://cwr25.blogspot.com

Founded in 1982, the Center for Women's Resources is a research and training institute focused on encouraging Filipino women to become full participants in transforming Filipino society. In collaboration with institutions and community and volunteer groups, the center responds to the specific needs of women from different sectors of society. The Center coordinates the activities of a training school for women who work at the grassroots level, provides education modules and manuals, and conducts seminars on women's issues. It also maintains a library with a variety of resource materials on women's issues.

Central Asia Institute
Bozeman, MT, USA
Website: http://www.ikat.org

Founded in 1996 by Greg Mortenson, the Central Asia Institute focuses primarily on building schools and providing educational opportunities, especially for girls, in rural areas of Pakistan and Afghanistan. Each school built contains a large room used as a women's center, where women can gather to learn new skills, support their families, and work out problems. The Institute establishes teacher training programs, builds libraries, and provides scholarships to students who must travel out of their local villages to obtain higher education. It recently expanded its focus to encourage public health and environmental sustainability projects.

Centre for Development and Population Activities
Washington, D.C., USA
Website: http://www.cedpa.org

As an international nonprofit organization, the Centre for Development and Population Activities (CEDPA) works to improve the lives of women and girls, believing that women's participation in global development activities is critical to their success. Founded in 1975, CEDPA encourages positive change through partnership projects with local institutions as well as through training and advocacy. Its Global Women in Management training program, conducted in Mexico, Nigeria, and the United States, in multiple languages, strengthens participants' capabilities in project and financial management, leadership, fundraising strategic communication, and advocacy. Its website includes free downloads of a variety of publications concerning training, advocacy, capacity building, democracy, education, faith-based organizations, reproductive health, gender-based violence, HIV/AIDS, leadership development, male involvement, social mobilization, women's rights, and youth.

Committee for Asian Women
Bangkok, Thailand
Website: http://www.cawinfo.org

Through a regional network of 46 member groups in 14 Asian countries, the Committee for Asian Women (CAW) works to promote the interests of women workers throughout Asia and to protect the rights of women. It provides financial support to needy local women's organizations; it also organizes education, training, and workshops. It conducts research on the impact of industrial restructuring on women workers, and its publications include *Rising from the Waste: Organising Wastepickers in India, Thailand, and the Philippines* and *Domestic Workers are Workers: Decent Work for All.*

Development Alternatives with Women for a New Era
Loyola Heights, Philippines
Website: http://www.dawnnet.org

Development Alternatives with Women for a New Era (DAWN) is a network of researchers and activists from several developing nations that focuses on promoting economic and gender justice and sustainable development. The program works to reduce the negative impact of development activities on women and the environment; conducts research, training, and advocacy programs to eliminate inequalities of gender, class, and race; and encourages and promotes communication and networking among women's movements. Researchers focus on four areas: the political economy of globalization, sexual and reproductive health and rights, political restructuring and social transformation, and political ecology and sustainability.

Eastern African Sub-Regional Support Initiative for the Advancement of Women
Kampala, Uganda
Website: http://www.eassi.org

The mission of the Eastern African Sub-regional Support Initiative for the Advancement of Women (EASSI) is to enhance the advancement of women and social justice following the Beijing and African Platforms for Action in 1995. EASSI has prioritized 12 critical areas of concern in the Beijing and African Platforms and advocates for improvements in these areas. It advocates for effective sub-regional mechanisms for advancing gender equity, promotes transparency in the government's budgetary process for reproductive health and sexual rights, and works to increase the participation of women in challenges to the systemic causes of conflict and discrimination.

Engender Health
New York, NY, USA
Website: http://www.engenderhealth.org

Engender Health is an international organization focusing on improving the quality of health care in poor communities around the world. Partnering with governments, institutions, local communities, and health care professionals in 25 countries, the program helps people make informed choices about contraception, improves maternal health care, promotes gender equity, and advocates for improved policy development regarding reproductive health. Specific focus areas include family planning; maternal health; HIV, AIDS and sexually transmitted diseases; gender equity; youth; clinical quality; and advocacy.

Equality Now
New York, NY, USA
Website: http://www.equalitynow.org

Equality Now is an international human rights group founded in 1992 to protect and promote women's rights worldwide. By adapting the research, organizational, and action techniques of the mainstream international human rights community, Equality Now addresses human rights issues of rape, trafficking in women, domestic violence, female infanticide, genital mutilation, reproductive rights, gender discrimination, political representation, sexual harassment, and pornography. A network of activists gathers information concerning specific abuses and ongoing violations throughout the world; appropriate actions and strategies are established in collaboration with local experts and rapidly publicized and implemented through the network. Regional offices are located in Nairobi and London.

Family Care International
New York, NY, USA
Website: http://familycareintl.org

Family Care International (FCI) is a private, nonprofit organization dedicated to improving women's sexual and reproductive health in developing countries. Field offices are located in Kenya, Burkina Faso, Mali, Niger, Tanzania, Bolivia, and Ecuador. Working with governments and NGOs, FCI explores the many factors that lead to poor reproductive health and develops collaborative programs to improve health options. FCI provides assistance to local agencies in designing community-level programs based on women's needs and realities with an emphasis on comprehensive care, high-quality services and counseling, education to help women take action on improving their health, and women's participation in program development and implementation. FCI has worked directly with governments and local organizations in many countries to develop national plans, model programs, and essential tools to address reproductive health needs.

FINCA International
Washington, D.C., USA
Website: http://www.villagebanking.org

Founded in 1985, FINCA International is a nonprofit organization with a network of affiliated agencies in 21 countries. The program provides financial services to low-income entrepreneurs in order to create jobs, save money, and improve their standard of living. As of April 2009, program affiliates have provided services to over 740,000 clients. The organization's programs have become models for outreach and sound financial management. Its recently launched Village Banking Campaign uses microfinance to provide loans, microinsurance, and savings to 1,000,000 low-income families.

Fistula Foundation
Santa Clara, CA, USA
Website: http://www.fistulafoundation.org

Originally formed to support the work of the Fistula Hospital in Ethiopia in 2000, the Fistula Foundation has broadened its mission to work toward the prevention and treatment of fistula throughout the world and to advocate for fistula repair. Working with the UN Population Fund (UNFPA) in its Campaign to End Fistula, it aims to equip hospitals with surgical equipment and to assist women, once they are healed, in returning to their communities.

Global Fund for Women
San Francisco, CA, USA
Website: http://www.globalfundforwomen.org

The Global Fund for Women, founded in 1987, is a nonprofit grant-making foundation focusing on advancing women's rights worldwide. They provide grants and seed money to female-headed organizations that encourage and promote the economic, health, safety, education, and leadership of girls and women.

Specific focus areas include ending gender-based violence, ensuring economic and environmental justice, ensuring women's access to health, advancing sexual and reproductive rights, expanding civic and political participation, increasing access to education, and encouraging social change philanthropy.

Global Grassroots
Hanover, NH, USA
Website: http://www.globalgrassroots.org

Global Grassroots, founded in 2004, focuses on conscious social change to effect improvement in the lives of vulnerable women in post-conflict societies. The program helps women who have been victimized by civil strife and war to reclaim their lives through education, seed grants, and project development. Many of these women have been raped, widowed, or both, and have contracted HIV/AIDS. Educational programs help them re-adjust to society, help them learn how to take care of themselves and their children on their own, and provide seed grants to launch their own businesses.

Grameen Bank
Dhaka, Bangladesh
Website: http://grameen-info.org

Founded in 1976, the Grameen Bank provides access to credit to the landless poor in rural Bangladesh. One of the best-known banks providing small loans to women entrepreneurs, the bank has distributed $9.19 billion in loans to over 8 million borrowers since it began in 1983. Using peer support and an incremental loan structure as incentives for repayment, Grameen Bank has proven that the poor can be good credit risks and that collateral is not needed to secure loans. The bank has over 2,500 branch offices that serve more than 81,000 villages; 97 percent of its customers are women. The bank also provides scholarships and loans to children of its borrowers.

The Hunger Project
New York, NY, USA
Website: http://www.thp.org

The Hunger Project was founded in 1977 following concerns over world hunger at the first Rome World Food Conference. With a presence in 13 countries in Africa, Asia, and Latin America, THP works with individuals and groups at the grassroots level, as well as local governments, to empower women and men to develop strategies to end hunger in their communities. The project recognizes the importance of women's role in ending hunger and promotes women as key figures in eliminating hunger from their communities.

Institute for Women's Studies in the Arab World
Beirut, Lebanon
Website: http://www.lau.edu.lb/centers-institutes/iwsaw/

Organized in 1973, the Institute for Women's Studies in the Arab World encourages and evaluates research on the history, status, and rights of women in this region. The institute was created the same year as the American Junior College for Women, the first women's college in the Middle East. It conducts research on women in the Arab world; integrates women's studies into the curriculum of the Lebanese American University; develops programs and education to empower women in the Arab world; encourages and facilitates networking among individuals, groups, and institutions; and acts as a catalyst to encourage policy changes that aid in the granting and expansion of women's rights.

Inter-African Committee on Traditional Practices
Addis Ababa, Ethiopia
Website: http://www.iac-ciaf.net

The Inter-African Committee on Traditional Practices Affecting the Health of Women and Children (IAC), a multinational organization, focuses on eliminating female genital mutilation and other harmful traditional practices, including child marriage abduction, widow inheritance, wife-sharing, and skin cutting. IAC offers educational programs and informational seminars, lobbies government agencies to prohibit these practices, conducts research, and makes public service announcements.

International Alliance of Women
(AIF) (Alliance Internationale des Femmes)
Markham, Ontario
Website: http://www.womenalliance.org

Members of the International Alliance of Women include women's organizations and individuals in more than 85 countries. The program advocates for reforms that are necessary to establish real equality between men and women and urges women to use their rights and influence in public life to ensure that the status of every individual is based on respect for human beings and not on sex, race, or creed. Its current focus is on monitoring the fulfillment of the commitments made in the 1995 Beijing Platform for Action, as expanded in 2000 and 2005.

International Center for Research on Women
Washington, D.C., USA
Website: http://www.icrw.org

The International Center for Research on Women (ICRW) is a private, nonprofit organization focused on promoting social and economic development in developing countries with the full participation of women. Working with policymakers, practitioners, and researchers throughout Africa, Asia, and Latin America, ICRW conducts research; helps formulate policy and action concerning the economic, social, and health status of women; and advocates for gender equity based on its research results. It emphasizes women's critical contributions to development, including their dual productive and reproductive roles. The program focuses on economic policies, family and household structure, health and nutrition, agriculture, and the environment.

International Confederation of Midwives
The Hague, the Netherlands
Website: http://www.internationalmidwives.org

The membership of the International Confederation of Midwives consists of national midwives' associations in 87 countries. The program advocates for the availability of midwives before, during, and after childbirth. It works with various agencies, including the United Nations, to reduce the number of women and children who die during childbirth and to improve the standard of care provided to mothers, babies, and the family. Advocacy activities promote midwifery education and the dissemination of information about the art and science of midwifery.

International Planned Parenthood Federation
London, England
Website: http://www.ippf.org

The International Planned Parenthood Federation (IPPF) helps initiate and support family planning services and increase government and public awareness of the population problems of local communities throughout the world. Planned Parenthood promotes effective family planning services and is concerned about the efficacy and safety of various methods of contraception. Program goals include the creation of strong volunteer participation, the promotion of family planning as a basic human right; the improvement of family planning services; addressing the needs of young people; the improvement of the status of women; increased male involvement in family planning; the development of human, financial, and material resources; stimulation of research on subjects related to human fertility and dissemination of the findings of such research; and the development of training programs for the federation's professional workers.

International Women's Development Agency
Melbourne, Australia
Website: http://www.iwda.org.au

The International Women's Development Agency (IWDA) is a multinational organization that focuses on actively involving women in development projects by partnering with local organizations in 11 countries throughout Asia and the Pacific. Believing that many traditional development projects fail because they neglect to seek and consider women's input, the IWDA provides skill training programs, encourages communication among development workers, organizes informational forums, and conducts educational courses. Its current programs focus on women's economic empowerment, safety, and security, as well as their health, well-being, and social inclusion. Programs also address access to education and information, sustainable use and protection of the environment and natural resources, and leadership and meaningful participation in decision making.

International Women's Health Coalition
New York, NY, USA
Website: http://www.iwhc.org

Founded in 1980, the International Women's Health Coalition (IWHC) is a nonprofit organization that works with women and men in Asia, Africa, and Latin America to secure women's reproductive and sexual health and rights. The coalition works to build national and international women's health movements to create conditions necessary for more caring, respectful, and responsible sexual relationships. IWHC also acts directly to influence the work of population and health professionals, national governments, and international agencies. The coalition's goals are to enable women to manage their own fertility safely and effectively; to experience a healthy sexual life that is free of disease, violence, disability, fear, pain, and death; and to bear and raise healthy children as and when they desire to do so. The coalition supports innovative reproductive health programs and services; fosters leadership and alliances among women worldwide; promotes dialogues between women's health advocates and health and population policymakers and researchers; educates decision makers; and advocates policies that will secure sexual and reproductive health and rights for women, girls, and men everywhere.

International Women's Rights Action Watch
Minneapolis, MN, USA
Website: http://www1.umn.edu/humanrts/iwraw

The International Women's Rights Action Watch (IWRAW) consists of an international network of activists, scholars, and organizations that focuses on the advancement of women's human rights. Organized in 1985 at the World Conference on Women in Nairobi, IWRAW monitors implementation of the Convention on the Elimination of All Forms of Discrimination against Women. NGOs are supported by IWRAW, especially in efforts to change law, culture, and society to help women fully participate in their communities. The program provides training programs, conferences, and global events, including the Fourth World Conference of Women, that focus on advancing women's rights. It also publishes a newsletter, various country reports on CEDAW implementation, and a variety of other publications related to women's rights.

International Women's Tribune Centre
New York, NY, USA
Website: http://www.iwtc.org

The International Women's Tribune Centre was established in 1976 as a result of the United Nations' first world conference on women in Mexico City. The organization believes that access to information and the ability to communicate are critical in empowering women. It facilitates the exchange of skills, experiences, and ideas among all groups that promote an active and equitable role for women, especially low-income women in Africa, Asia, the Pacific, Latin America, the Caribbean, and Eastern Europe. Major activities focus on information dissemination, education, communication, and organizing activities. Its four areas of emphasis are human rights, information access and capacity-building, networking and organizational support, and a knowledge-brokering service (Women, Ink).

IPAS
Chapel Hill, NC, USA
Website: http://www.ipas.org

Founded in 1973, IPAS is a nonprofit NGO dedicated to improving women's health through a focus on reproductive health care. Specifically, IPAS concentrates on preventing unsafe abortions, treating complications from abortion, reducing the consequences of abortion, and increasing women's access to a broad range of reproductive health services. Staff members work with governmental officials, health care providers and administrators, and NGO representatives worldwide to develop and implement high-quality, sustainable programs in reproductive health and abortion-related care.

ISIS Women's International Cross-Cultural Exchange
Kampala, Uganda
Website: http://www.isis.or.ug

ISIS Women's International Cross-Cultural Exchange (ISIS–WICCE) is a global women's organization that focuses on promoting justice, equality, and mutually beneficial relationships between women and men. Founded in 1974, its headquarters moved to Uganda in 1993 to incorporate African women's concerns and issues into its program. Over 1,300 female leaders from more than 29 countries have participated in its exchange program, which offers participants the opportunity to learn from one another, exchange ideas, and work on cross-cultural strategies for addressing critical women's issues. The organization has documented human rights violations related to women in armed conflict. It also publishes a variety of research and training reports, professional papers, and audiovisual materials.

Latin American and Caribbean Women's Health Network
Santiago, Chile
Website: http://www.reddesalud.org

The Latin American and Caribbean Women's Health Network is a regional network linking individuals and organizations that work directly or indirectly in fields related to women's health and women's rights. The program works to establish contacts among women and organizations active in women's health issues at the local, regional, and national levels; to encourage the sharing of information, experiences, and ideas through the development of communication networks; to coordinate activities that focus on women's health; and to encourage public awareness campaigns on these subjects.

Latin American Committee for the Defense of the Rights of the Woman
(Comité de América Latina y El Caribe para la Defensa de los Derechos de la Mujer)
Lima, Peru
Website: http://www.cladem.org

The Latin American Committee for the Defense of the Rights of the Woman (CLADEM) is a regional network that works for the protection of gender rights, the promotion of women's political participation, the availability of legal education, and the elimination of discriminatory legislation. Advocacy efforts have produced major legislative reform in Peru and several other countries. CLADEM also works locally with community legal educators and participates in regional and international campaigns concerning issues of importance to women.

Pathfinder International
Watertown, MA, USA
Website: http://www.pathfind.org

Pathfinder International works with organizations and governments in developing countries to improve the accessibility and quality of family planning and related reproductive health services for women and men. The organization focuses on overcoming barriers to the availability of wide-ranging reproductive health care for women and families. Since its inception in 1957, Pathfinder has provided reproductive health care to millions of people in over 120 countries in Latin America, Africa, Asia, the Near East, and Europe. Current areas of involvement include reproductive health and family planning, HIV/AIDS, safe motherhood, adolescents, advocacy, abortion and post-abortion care, community-based work, partner support, and social change.

Population Action International
Washington, D.C., USA
Website: http://www.populationaction.org

Population Action International (PAI) is a private, nonprofit organization that attempts to enhance the long-term well-being of individuals, families, and nations by promoting stabilization of the world's population. PAI advocates for family planning and related health services, for the education of girls, and for economic opportunities for women. The program works with other development, reproductive health, and environmental organizations in support of effective population policies.

Population Communications International
New York, NY, USA
Website: http://www.population.org

Population Communications International's Media Impact program (PCI–Media Impact) focuses on the need for information dissemination and motivation to mobilize individuals and communities to communicate information about and advocate for sexual and reproductive health, prevention and treatment of HIV/AIDS, environmental conservation and sustainable development, and human rights. PCI works with the news media worldwide to promote effective coverage of population and related environmental issues. PCI–Media Impact has expanded the scope of its educational programming to include topics of importance to achieving the UN Millennium Development Goals.

Population Council
New York, NY, USA
Website: http://www.popcouncil.org

The Population Council is a nonprofit NGO devoted to improving the reproductive health and well-being of women and men throughout the world. It studies population issues and trends and conducts research around the world on HIV/AIDS; poverty, gender, and youth; and reproductive health. The Council works with government and private organizations to improve family planning and related health services, helps governments implement effective population policies, reports research results to a wide audience, and helps strengthen professional resources in developing countries. Offices are located in 18 countries and programs exist in over 50 countries around the world.

Population Institute
Washington, D.C., USA
Website: http://www.populationinstitute.org

As a population advocacy organization, the Population Institute provides leadership in creating national and international awareness of the social, economic, and environmental implications of rapid population growth. It provides international support for voluntary family planning programs. Dedicated to bringing about global population stabilization, the Institute educates industrialized countries about the effects of rapid population growth on global resources.

Population Reference Bureau
Washington, D.C., USA
Website: http://www.prb.org

The Population Reference Bureau (PRB) was founded in 1929 and is a nonprofit educational organization providing information on population, health, and the environment. Staff members ensure that policymakers throughout the world have reliable data on which to base population, health, and environmental policies. Its programs focus on four main themes: reproductive health and fertility, children and families, population and the environment, and population futures. PRB hosts several websites that provide valuable information to global audiences. It publishes policy briefs on a variety of topics, including population, health, and environment trends; its bulletins cover issues ranging from immigration to world health to gender. PRB also provides data sheets on world population, women, youth, and the environment; webcasts on family planning, HIV/AIDS, and female genital mutilation; a blog; online discussions; and policy seminars.

Pro Mujer
New York, NY, USA
Website: http://www.promujer.org

An international women's development and microfinance organization, Pro Mujer offers financial services, training, and health care to economically and socially disadvantaged women in Argentina, Bolivia, Mexico, Nicaragua, and Peru. It creates communal banks that serve 18 to 28 women; the women hold regular meetings to repay their loans and deposit money in savings accounts. They also receive training in business skills, good health practices, and business development training, which includes the creation of business plans and use of credit. Pro Mujer believes that good health is key to women's success in their homes, businesses, and communities, and provides its clients with basic health care at neighborhood centers. It also educates them about domestic violence and women's rights.

Program for Appropriate Technology in Health
Seattle, WA, USA
Website: http://www.path.org

The Program for Appropriate Technology in Health (PATH) is a nonprofit NGO focusing on improving health, especially the health of women and children throughout the world. Staff members seek solutions to public health problems, specifically in the areas of reproductive health and widespread communicable diseases. They use advanced technologies to search for solutions for emerging and epidemic diseases, find and employ health technologies designed by local communities, advocate for safer childbirth and health for children, promote health equity for women among the world's most vulnerable populations, and promote the use of vaccines to protect women and children from basic diseases.

Revolutionary Association of the Women of Afghanistan (RAWA)
Quetta, Pakistan
Website: http://www.rawa.org

Started in 1977 as an independent political organization focusing on fighting for human rights in Afghanistan, the Revolutionary Association of the Women of Afghanistan (RAWA) became actively involved in the resistance following the Soviet occupation in 1979. More recently, it has worked to combat the religious fundamentalism advocated by the Taliban and warlords. In Afghanistan, RAWA supports female victims of war, reports human rights violations against women to international human rights organizations, runs home-based schools and literacy courses for women and girls, provides mobile health teams in eight provinces primarily to treat women who are unable to see doctors because of financial constraints, and assists in the development and operation of small businesses. In Pakistan, RAWA runs primary and secondary schools for refugee girls and boys and literacy courses for women, supports mobile health teams, reports the inhumane acts of fundamentalists to international human rights organizations, organizes protests against fundamentalists, assists widows and families of prisoners, and assists in business activities.

Self-Employed Women's Association
Ahmedabad, India
Website: http://www.sewa.org

Founded in 1972, the Self-Employed Women's Association (SEWA) organizes women who are self-employed, increases their access to credit and assets, improves their status, and advocates for working women. Its constituency is composed of women who are poor, self-employed, and without access to the welfare and health benefits offered to salaried employees. It organizes women to help them obtain full employment. SEWA's bank provides credit and other financial services to poor women who want to start their own businesses or expand existing services or products. Services include training courses, technical information, health care, child care, legal aid, maternity benefits, insurance, and communications. SEWA also encourages the development of income-generating opportunities in rural areas. Staff members advocate for women through a variety of campaigns, lobbying efforts, and capacity building.

Shared Hope International
Vancouver, WA, USA
Website: http://www.sharedhope.org

Founded in 1998 by U.S. Congresswoman Linda Smith after she traveled to India and encountered the hopeless faces of women and children forced into prostitution in Bombay, Shared Hope International focuses its attention on the prevention and elimination of sex trafficking and slavery around the world. SHI partners with local organizations to provide shelter, health care, education, and vocational training opportunities to women and children enslaved in the sex trade. Its strategy has three parts: prevent the demand for women and children through public awareness activities, rescue women and children from sex trafficking, and restore women and child victims by building communities to help heal and empower them.

Third World Movement against the Exploitation of Women
Quezon City, Philippines
Website: http://www.tw-mae-w.org/twmaew

Members of the Third World Movement against the Exploitation of Women (TW-MAE-W) include women's groups and individuals in 45 countries who want to combat female sexual abuse and exploitation. The program encourages a transnational approach to women's issues as an effective means for women to liberate themselves. Serving as a networking organization, TW-MAE-W provides a variety of services including education and training in literacy; value formation; basic office, nursing, cosmetology, and other skills; health seminars; alternative health care; advocacy and campaigns; recreational activities; economic assistance; retreats; residential care; educational assistance; counseling; and economic assistance.

Tostan
Dakar-Yoff, Senegal
Website: http://www.tostan.org

Founded in 1991, Tostan (which means "breakthrough" in Wolof, a West African language) encourages African communities to work toward sustainable development through local community efforts. It offers human rights education through its Community Empowerment Program, which provides training in the skills and knowledge communities need to improve their standard of living and become self-sufficient. A video on its website, *Tostan: Empowering Communities to Abandon Female Genital Cutting (FGC)*, describes how its community empowerment program promotes health and human rights and how this unique approach has led to the abandonment of female genital cutting in thousands of African villages.

Vital Voices Global Partnership
Washington, D.C., USA
Website: http://www.vitalvoices.org

Vital Voices Global Partnership was created as a result of the Vital Voices Democracy Initiative started in 1997 by Hillary Rodham Clinton and Madeleine Albright following the UN Fourth World Conference on Women, which focused on promoting the empowerment and advancement of women. Vital Voices works with international coalitions to end human trafficking and other types of violence against women and girls; empowers women as change agents in their local communities and governments; advocates for social justice; and provides women with management, business, marketing, and communications skills so that they can create economic opportunities for themselves and their families.

White Ribbon Alliance for Safe Motherhood
Washington, D.C., USA
Website: http://www.whiteribbonalliance.org

As an international coalition of individuals and groups, the White Ribbon Alliance promotes safe pregnancy and childbirth and campaigns against maternal mortality around the world. The alliance has members in 148 countries who work together to improve women's health and women's rights. It works with members to develop educational materials and seminars adapted to their local environments in order to raise awareness and promote safe pregnancy and childbirth in their communities. It also encourages policy changes to increase funding for efforts to promote safe motherhood.

Womankind Worldwide
London, England
Website: http://www.womankind.org.uk

Womankind Worldwide helps women in developing countries improve their lives by encouraging them to challenge the status quo, become organized, and secure their rights. It works with 37 partner community groups in 15 countries to tackle issues specific to individual communities. It recognizes that the basic causes of gender inequality and discrimination against women cannot be corrected only by providing services to women. Program partners work to change local laws and influence public policy through research and analysis, training and education, lobbying decision-makers, exchanging information with decision makers, and hosting conferences.

Women and Development
(KULU) (Kvindernes U-landsudvalg)
Copenhagen, Denmark
Website: http://www.kulu.dk

Members of Women and Development include regional organizations, women's groups, and individuals. This international organization supports the rights of women in developing countries and attempts to influence national and international policies to this end. The organization monitors legislation dealing with feminist issues, disseminates information, and encourages and helps to fund the creation of women's groups in developing countries.

Women and Men of Zimbabwe Arise
Famona, Bulawayo, Zimbabwe
Website: http://wozazimbabwe.org

Women and Men of Zimbabwe (WOZA) was formed in 2003 to provide a united voice to women throughout the country on issues of importance to them, to empower and encourage women to fight for their rights, to encourage female leadership in local communities, and to advocate on issues important to women. Today, men are included in its membership and participate with women in various nonviolent protests demanding social justice for all Zimbabweans.

Women for Women International
Washington, D.C., USA
Website: http://www.womenforwomen.org

Women for Women International provides support and services to women survivors of war and other conflicts so that they may become self-sufficient. Its one-year program transforms women from victims to survivors to active citizens by giving them basic skills training, rights awareness, leadership education, and vocational and technical skills training. Participants form support groups to discuss the importance of education, voting rights, avoiding domestic violence, and health care. Programs are adapted to the local cultural, economic, political, and religious characteristics of each country. A microcredit lending program provides business development opportunities.

Women in Law and Development in Africa
Accra, Ghana
Website: http://wildaf.org

The Women in Law and Development in Africa (WILDAF) organization is an international program that focuses on empowering women through legal education, law reform, and legal services. WILDAF promotes training and educational programs in legal literacy, conducts research and disseminates information on legal issues affecting women, and coordinates activities with other organizations concerned with women and the law.

Women Living under Muslim Laws
London, England
Website: http://new.wluml.org

Established in 1986 with the goal of ending the isolation that women experience in Muslim countries, the Women Living under Muslim Laws (WLUML) program provides information, solidarity, and support to women in over 70 countries throughout the world. It creates connections among women living in countries where Islam is the state religion, secular states with Muslim majorities, and

Muslim communities. These connections provide a means of sharing information regarding men's control over women's lives and ways of challenging that control. The program currently focuses on fundamentalism, militarization, and sexuality and their effects on women's lives. WLUML provides solidarity and alerts, networking and information services, and capacity building. It also publishes a quarterly newsletter, a biannual newsletter, an occasional journal, and occasional and other papers.

Women Thrive Worldwide
Washington, D.C., USA
Website: http://www.womenthrive.org

Women Thrive Worldwide is an international advocacy coalition consisting of 50 organizations and 40,000 individuals that develops and advocates for economic opportunity policies to help women in developing countries. It believes that women are key change agents in the fight to end global poverty and works to ensure that U.S. foreign policy, international assistance, and trade programs focus on eliminating the social and economic barriers that prevent women from supporting their families and ending poverty.

Women's Environment and Development Organization
New York, NY, USA
Website: http://www.wedo.org

Organized in 1990 by former U.S. Congresswoman Bella Abzug and Mim Kelber with the goal of developing international conferences and actions for women, the Women's Environment and Development Organization (WEDO) continues to advance women's rights through political action, research, and advocacy. WEDO works to encourage the United Nations and other government forums to incorporate women's perspectives into their work. Staff members collaborate with NGOs and individuals in developing countries to advocate for women's economic, social, and gender rights.

Women's Feature Service
Delhi, India
Website: http://www.wfsnews.org

The Women's Feature Service is an international organization that promotes the interests of women on international, national, and local levels. The group disseminates information on women's development and works to eliminate discrimination from the media's portrayal of women. The organization has a network of over 100 female journalists who produce approximately 500 articles each year, written from a women's perspective and with a special focus on developing countries. Stories focus on the political, social, economic, and cultural issues and trends that shape women's lives throughout the world. Topics include the environment, health, politics, economic development, traditional customs, human rights, women's movements, children, and immigration. Regional offices are located in the Philippines, Zimbabwe, Costa Rica, and the United States.

Women's Global Network for Reproductive Rights
Amsterdam, the Netherlands
Website: http://www.wgnrr.org

The Women's Global Network for Reproductive Rights is an international network of women's health groups, reproductive rights campaigns, clinics, health workers, and interested individuals who focus on achieving and supporting reproductive and sexual health rights for women around the world. The network focuses on encouraging grassroots support for a woman's right to control her body, including having a safe and fulfilling sex life, the power to decide when and if to have children, and the right to access safe, legal abortion.

Women's International League for Peace, and Freedom
Geneva, Switzerland
Website: http://www.wilpfinternational.org

Founded in 1915, the Women's International League for Peace and Freedom (WILPF) works through peaceful means to achieve political, economic, social, and psychological conditions throughout the world that will assure peace, freedom, and justice for all people. WILPF works for political solutions to international conflicts, disarmament, the promotion of women to full and equal participation in all of society's activities, economic justice within and among states, the elimination of racism and all forms of discrimination and exploitation, respect for fundamental human rights, and the right to development in a sustainable environment.

Women's Learning Partnership
Bethesda, MD, USA
Website: http://www.learningpartnership.org

Women's Learning Partnership (WLP) focuses on women's leadership and empowerment through partnerships with 18 independent organizations in developing countries, primarily in countries with Muslim majorities. Program goals include increasing the number of women in leadership and decision-making roles in families, communities, and governments and increasing the effectiveness of feminist movements in Muslim countries. It works to accomplish these goals through leadership training curricula, leadership and empowerment programs, organizational capacity building, human rights campaigns, dialogues among developing countries, dialogues with the Global North countries, advocacy, networking, events, and publications.

Women's Refugee Commission
New York, NY, USA
Website: http://www.womensrefugeecommission.org

The Women's Refugee Commission is affiliated with the International Rescue Committee and advocates for the establishment of laws, policies, and programs to protect women and their families who have been displaced from their homes as refugees and asylum-seekers. Its programs focus on reproductive health, fuel and firewood, livelihood, youth, disability, detention and asylum, and gender issues, including gender-based violence. As of 2010, it has chosen a Focus on Five approach to assisting refugees; that is, it has chosen five areas on which to focus—northern Uganda, the Thai–Burma border, south Sudan and Darfur, Liberia, and Jordan—believing that this approach will accelerate change and prove effective in ameliorating the lives of female refugees and their families. The organization will also continue its work in other countries.

Women's World Banking
New York, NY, USA
Website: http://www.swwb.org

Women's World Banking (WWB) is a global nonprofit financial institution that advances and promotes the full participation of women in society. Established in 1979, WWB currently has over 50 affiliates in more than 40 countries. WWB supports, advises, trains, and provides information to its global network of 40 microfinance banks that provide credit to low-income individuals and families in 28 countries around the world. WWB encourages women to play an active economic and social role in their communities to decide the right mix of credit, savings, training, and commercial connections that will provide economic development. As of 2010, WWB and its affiliates have served over 20 million clients, 74 percent of whom are women, and it has an outstanding loan portfolio of $4.3 billion.

Worldwide Fistula Fund
St. Louis, MO, USA
Website: http://www.worldwidefistulafund.org

The Worldwide Fistula Fund in a nonprofit organization that supports international medical education and research on obstetric fistulas. It encourages ethical and comprehensive care for women with obstetric fistulas. It also supports clinical care, training of surgeons, and scientifically valid research in fistula treatment and prevention, as well as advocating for the medical and other needs experienced by women with fistulas.

Zonta International
Oak Brook, IL, USA
Website: http://www.zonta.org

Zonta is a worldwide service organization composed of executives in business and the professions who work together to advance the status of women throughout the world. It has approximately 35,000 members in over 1,100 clubs in more than 65 countries. Members volunteer their time, talents, and energy to local and international service projects designed to advance the status of women. The organization fights gender inequality through supporting global and local efforts to provide women with equal education, health care, legal rights, credit, and employment opportunities. Members advocate for laws that can positively influence women's lives.

Government and Government-Affiliated Organizations

Inter-American Commission of Women
Organization of American States
Washington, D.C., USA
Website: http://www.oas.org/cim

Established in 1928, the Inter-American Commission of Women (CIM) is a specialized agency of the Organization of American States (OAS). CIM was the first official intergovernmental agency created specifically to ensure the civil and political rights of women in the Americas. The commission is composed of 34 delegates from each of its member states. Its mission is the promotion and protection of women's rights and support for member states to ensure the equal participation of women in all aspects of society: political, economic, social, cultural, and legal. It identifies areas to improve women's participation, develops strategies to transform and improve relationships between women and men, encourages governments to take all appropriate measures to remove barriers to women, promotes education of women and girls, and promotes adoption of legal means to eliminate all forms of discrimination against women.

Office of Women in Development
U.S. Department of State, Agency for International Development
Washington, D.C., USA
Website: http://www.usaid.gov/our_work/cross-cutting_programs/wid

The Office of Women in Development, a U.S. government program, focuses on ways to include women in the development activities in their countries. Staff members conduct research, organize conferences and community projects, and offer training programs in development skills. They also provide technical leadership on gender-related issues as well as identifying emerging issues and developing multidisciplinary approaches to deal with them. Major program areas include gender integration, economic growth, education, legal rights, and trafficking in persons.

UN Entities

Commission on the Status of Women
United Nations
New York, NY, USA
Website: http://www.unwomen.org

The Commission on the Status of Women (CSW) has 45 member states and was established by the Economic and Social Council of the United Nations in 1946. Members are representatives from UN member countries. The commission promotes women's rights in political, economic, civil, social, and educational fields; encourages cooperation between organizations seeking to advance the status of women; and advises the United Nations and its member states on situations requiring immediate attention. It also monitors the implementation and progress of measures to advance women's status and reviews critical areas identified during the 1995 Fourth World Conference on Women.

Division for Social Policy and Development
UN Department of Economic and Social Affairs (UNDESA)
New York, NY, USA
Website: http://www.un.org/esa/socdev

The Division for Social Policy and Development monitors and evaluates advances in women's struggles for equality throughout the world. In an effort to eliminate all types of discrimination against women, the center conducts research on women's economic, social, and educational status; prepares reports; and recommends action that groups can take on women's issues. It provides bibliographic search services in French, Spanish, and English. Its publications include *Women 2000* (a magazine in French, Spanish, and English), *World Survey on the Role of Women in Development*, and *National Machinery for the Advancement of Women: United Nations and UN Organizations Focal Points for the Advancement of Women.*

Inter-Agency Network on Women and Gender Equality
United Nations
Website: http://www.un.org/womenwatch/ianwge

The Inter-Agency Network on Women and Gender Equality (IANWGE) is composed of about 60 members who represent

25 UN entities, and it focuses on promoting gender equality throughout the United Nations by monitoring and encouraging the mainstreaming of gender perspectives into the work of the UN entities.

International Research and Training Institute for the Advancement of Women
Santo Domingo, Dominican Republic
Website: http://www.un-instraw.org

The International Research and Training Institute for the Advancement of Women (INSTRAW) is an autonomous institute within the framework of the United Nations. INSTRAW is the leading UN institute focusing on research, training, and knowledge management while working toward gender equality and women's empowerment. As part of its capacity-building activities, the Institute has set up a Gender Training Community of Practice for individuals, NGOs and governments around the world to examine and strengthen approaches to gender training and has also created a Gender Training Wiki to facilitate communication among these groups. INSTRAW also encourages changes based on its research in government policies and programs. It encourages women to become local and government leaders and assists those already in those positions in placing gender issues on the local agenda. Local and distance learning programs provide resources for mainstreaming gender issues.

UN Development Fund for Women
New York, NY, USA
Website: http://www.unwomen.org

The UN Development Fund for Women (UNIFEM) seeks to promote the economic and political empowerment of women in developing countries by providing direct technical and financial support to women's programs. Encouraging the participation of women at all levels of development planning, UNIFEM acts as a catalyst within the UN system to link the needs and concerns of women to all issues on global agendas. Created in 1976 as the Voluntary Fund for the UN Decade for Women, UNIFEM became an autonomous organization in association with the UN Development Programme (UNDP) in 1985. UNIFEM helps women in developing countries by strengthening local, national, and international organizations as well as encouraging connections and partnerships at every level.

The organization's economic empowerment program ensures that women have access to and control over economic resources, assets, and opportunities. The political empowerment program works to strengthen the role of women in government and decision making at all levels, ensuring that women have control over their lives both within and outside the household.

UN Development Programme
New York, NY, USA
Website: http://www.undp.org

One of the purposes of the UN Development Programme (UNDP) is to assist countries in alleviating poverty and reaching the Millennium Development Goals. It accomplishes its mission through implementing programs, providing advocacy, serving as a source of advice on policies and technical support, and building partnerships. One of its major focus areas is gender and poverty, and it works with national partners to promote women's economic rights and opportunities; ensure that essential public services are provided to everyone, regardless of gender; include women in planning and policy development processes; address the gender implications of HIV/AIDS; and strengthen the collection, reliability, and interpretation of gender-disaggregated data.

UN Women
United Nations
Website: http://www.unwomen.org

UN Women was created in July 2010 by the UN General Assembly to address the challenges it has faced in promoting gender equality throughout the world. Chief among the challenges have been inadequate funding and the lack of a single recognized organization to direct and coordinate UN activities concerning gender equality issues. It has three major purposes: (1) to support inter-governmental entities, including the Commission on the Status of Women, as they develop policies and standards; (2) to assist Member States in implementing these policies and standards through the provision of technical and financial support; and (3) to ensure the UN meets its commitments on gender equality, through regular monitoring of progress in meeting these commitments. It offers grants to innovative programs and assists individual governments and NGOs in developing policies, laws, and resources to help women achieve equality.

Several other UN organizations also work with women in developing countries, including:

Food and Agriculture Organization of the United Nations (http://www.fao.org)
UN-HABITAT (Human Settlements) (http://www.unhabitat.org)
UN Human Rights Council (http://www2.ohchr.org/english/bodies/hrcouncil)
UN Population Fund (http://www.unfpa.org)
World Health Organization (http://www.who.int)

8

Selected Print and Nonprint Resources

This chapter contains descriptions of books, agency reports, videos, and websites that focus on all major aspects of women in developing countries. The materials vary from popular accounts and case studies to primary research.

Books

Abirafeh, Lina. 2009. ***Gender and International Aid in Afghanistan: The Politics and Effects of Intervention.*** **Jefferson, NC: McFarland & Co. 232 pages. Bibliography, index.**

Abirafeh's experience on the ground in Afghanistan running an international NGO working with women gives her a unique perspective on women's lives in Afghanistan since the 2001 reconstruction. The book describes and analyzes the process of formulating and implementing social policies, especially as it relates to Afghan women.

Afzal-Khan, Fawzia, ed. 2005. ***Shattering the Stereotypes: Muslim Women Speak Out.*** **Northampton, MA: Olive Branch Press. 338 pages. References.**

Afzal-Khan has gathered an inspiring collection of essays, poems, plays, and short stories that vividly describe the experiences of women who happen to be Muslim. Afzal-Khan herself notes that she never thought of herself as a "Muslim woman" since religion was only "one spoke in the wheel of our lives" growing up in Pakistan (1). Since the events of 9/11, however, people all over the world have become interested in Islam, its basis tenets, what life is like for Muslim women, and other aspects of this religion and culture. Each contributor to this volume provides an illuminating look at her life and experiences as a Muslim woman.

Agrawal, Anuja. 2008. *Chaste Wives and Prostitute Sisters: Patriarchy and Prostitution among the Bedias of India.* New York: Routledge. 251 pages. Bibliography, index.

The Bedia are a small caste found in Madhya Pradesh, Uttar Pradesh, and Rajasthan in northern India. Unmarried women in many of these families earn income through prostitution and their families' survival is dependent upon it. Though wives of Bedia men do not engage in prostitution, they are responsible for all the domestic work in the family. Agrawal examines the social processes and powers that ensure that a Bedia woman will engage in prostitution to support the family and the reaction of male family members and the community at large to this enterprise. He also discusses how the business of prostitution affects and defines family and community structures, stratification, and ideologies, and considers whether these women are primarily viewed as victims or willing agents.

Aikman, Sheila, and Elaine Unterhalter, eds. 2007. *Practising Gender Equality in Education.* Oxford: Oxfam GB. 130 pages. Bibliography, index.

The editors have provided a practical, informative guide for nongovernmental organizations, teachers, researchers, and government officials who are concerned about achieving gender equality in education. The book revolves around five main themes: partnerships among practitioners, policy makers, and researchers; a multipronged approach to reaching gender equality; advocacy actions to encourage changes in policies; government responsibility for basic education; and adequate and ongoing funding.

Antonopoulous, Rania, and Indira Hirway, eds. *Unpaid Work and the Economy: Gender, Time Use and Poverty in Developing Countries.* New York: Palgrave Macmillan, 2010. 336 pages. References, index.

Unpaid work in developing countries includes family work, subsistence production, wood and water collection, sanitation and household maintenance, food production and processing, and family care work. Measurement of unpaid work is difficult and findings are inconsistent and often unreliable. This book explores unpaid work in developing countries through a variety of methodological, theoretical, and policy-oriented discussions. It presents and analyzes empirical data on poverty, gender, and unpaid work from India, Bolivia, and South Africa. Topics include gender inequalities in the distribution of unpaid work; policy issues, including the need for investment in social and physical infrastructure; unemployment; challenges to and achievements in the collection of reliable data; national economic data and the invisibility of unpaid work in these data; and the use of time-use surveys in developing countries.

Bahun-Radunovic, Sanja, and V.G. Julie Rajan, eds. *Violence and Gender in the Globalized World.* Burlington, VT: Ashgate Publishing, 2008. 226 pages. References, index.

The contributors to this volume include academics and activists from around the world who are engaged in examinations of gender and violence. The book focuses on the global variability of expressions of gender violence and the relationship between gender violence and development activities. Individual chapters provide insights into microcredit and violence in India, trafficking in women in South Korea, the impact of the ongoing violence in Palestine on women, and religious rights and feminist activities in Malaysia, among other topics. The intersection of academia and activists makes for a lively presentation of some of the major issues surrounding gender and violence.

Bond, Johanna. 2005. *Voices of African Women: Women's Rights in Ghana, Uganda, and Tanzania.* Durham, NC: Carolina Academic Press. 421 pages. References, index.

Prominent female attorneys from Ghana, Uganda, and Tanzania describe the challenges facing them in their fight for human rights. Chapters explore topics including women's right to participate in public life, violence against women, women's rights within the family, reproductive health, and economic empowerment. The book also examines controversies such as whether female genital cutting is tradition or torture, marital rape as domestic violence, and the benefits of and problems with affirmative action.

Bradley, Tamsin, Emma Tomalin, and Mangala Subramanian, eds. 2009. ***Dowry: Bridging the Gap between Theory and Practice.*** **New York: Zed Books. 245 pages. References.**

The practice of dowry in Southeast Asia continues to make headlines, even though the Indian government banned the practice in 1961. This book provides a comprehensive analysis of dowry practice from its history through the current debates around it, which were a result of the Indian women's movement beginning in the 1960s. It also discusses the role that patriarchy plays in the continuing practice of demanding dowry and ways to limit or extinguish the practice through the inclusion of men's views and experiences. It analyzes changing patterns and practices of dowry through detailed case studies from Bangladesh and India and considers the relationship between dowry and the preference for male children. The amount of dowry demanded has increased over the years at a greater rate than inflation and continues to do so; the book explores theories explaining this increase, including the role of microcredit availability. The role of expanded public advocacy campaigns by NGOs against the practice is examined.

Britton, Hannah, Jennifer Fish, and Sheila Meintjes, eds. 2009. ***Women's Activism in South Africa: Working across Divides.*** **Scottsville, South Africa: University of KwaZulu-Natal Press. 294 pages. References, index.**

The 1994 transition to democracy in South Africa provided women with many opportunities for gain in social and political arenas. This book explores ways in which women have been able to reconstitute South African society through social change and democratization. The contributors—scholars, academics, and activists—explore women's participation in competitive sports, domestic violence programs and services, national unions, rights-based activism, and political organizations, and consider the challenges and successes of the struggle for gender rights in South Africa.

Cabezas, Amalia L., Ellen Reese, and Marguerite Waller, eds. 2007. ***The Wages of Empire: Neoliberal Policies, Repression and***

Women's Poverty. **Boulder: Paradigm Publishers. 248 pages. Bibliography, index.**

Contributors to this volume examine the negative consequences of neoliberal economic policies and the repressive policies that support them on low-income women in developing countries. Many of these macroeconomic and structural adjustment programs have increased the burdens on poor women. Part one analyzes the basic ideologies of neoliberalism and its effects on women. Part two discusses recent shifts in government policies, including trade liberalization and structural adjustment, and the negative impact of these shifts on women's lives. Part three examines the negative effects of these policies through case studies from Mexico, Colombia, and El Salvador. Part four looks at war and military repression and the ways that neoliberal policies affect poor women in ways similar to military occupation.

Chamberlin, Ann. 2006. ***A History of Women's Seclusion in the Middle East: The Veil in the Looking Glass.*** **New York: Haworth Press. 298 pages. Bibliography, index.**

This book offers an interdisciplinary approach to understanding the practice of the seclusion of women in the Middle East. Chamberlin draws on her extensive knowledge of Middle Eastern culture to challenge the common Western assumption that seclusion is an oppressive practice that harms women. She demonstrates that seclusion may in fact be an empowering force for women. Topics examined include ancient veiling, domestic architecture, sacred architecture, evolution, biology, the clan, environment for seclusion, trade, capital and land, individual liberation, slavery, and honor.

Cloutier, Luce. 2006. ***Income Differentials and Gender Inequality: Wives Earning More than Husbands in Dar es Salaam, Tanzania.*** **Dar es Salaam: Mkuki na Nyota Publishers. 300 pages. References.**

Following the imposition of structural adjustment programs in Tanzania in the 1980s, women's roles changed to focus on domestic work and community activities in order to replace the loss of government-provided services under these programs. This book examines ways in which urbanization has shaped gender relations and how women are creating opportunities for equality within patriarchal and capitalist systems. Like many other countries, Tanzania has seen a growing gap between rich and poor, especially in urban areas, which has led to growing conflicts between social classes as well as between men and women. This book provides a fascinating look at how some families have coped with these issues.

Cornwall, Andrea, Sonia Correa, and Susie Jolly, eds. 2008. ***Development with a Body: Sexuality, Human Rights and Development.*** **New York: Zed Books. 257 pages. References, index.**

Even though three of the Millennium Development Goals are related to sexual and reproductive health, none of them specifically refer to sexual and reproductive rights. The editors of this book believe that the critical role sexual and reproductive health plays in development should be explicitly recognized. The international community is beginning to understand the relationship between human rights, development, and sexuality. Contributors to this volume explore this relationship, encouraging readers to understand that promoting the health and well-being of individuals is fundamental to successful development and that sexuality is an important aspect of development. Individual chapters examine sexual rights as human rights; sex trafficking and HIV; children's sexual rights; discrimination against lesbians in the workplace; ruling masculinities in South Africa; gender, identity, and *travesti* in Peru; reproductive and sexual rights in Bangladesh; sexuality education as a human right; and the integration of sexuality into gender and human rights frameworks.

Cuklanz, Lisa M., and Sujata Moorti, eds. 2009. ***Local Violence, Global Media: Feminist Analyses of Gendered Representations.*** **New York: Peter Lang. 276 pages. References, index.**

This collection of essays offers a global perspective on the various ways that gender and sexual violence are understood around the world, examining how these acts of violence are treated and described by the media. With advances in technology, the media have become one of the primary means of distributing information and news concerning gender-based violence. This book examines how the media have depicted a variety of news reports concerning women and violence, including serial prostitute homicide in the Chinese media, battered women in Peru, and the 1995 rape of a 12-year old girl in Okinawa, among other cases. It defines gender-based violence, outlines the legal and policy changes regarding how that violence can be depicted, and explores the variety of activities that communities have undertaken to combat it.

Ebadi, Shirin. 2007. ***Iran Awakening: One Woman's Journey to Reclaim Her Life and Country.*** **New York: Random House. 236 pages. Index.**

Shirin Ebadi is a lawyer, former judge in Iran's Ministry of Justice, and winner of the Nobel Peace Prize in 2003. In this biography, she describes growing up in Tehran and attending law school; she also discusses her experiences as the most distinguished female judge in the Tehran court until she was demoted in the 1979 Islamic Revolution. Ebadi details the impact of the Revolution on her life and the lives of other women in Iran, the harassment she faced, her imprisonment, and the attempts on her life. She describes her return to law as an attorney in the 1990s handling many human rights cases pro bono, and the compromises she has been forced to make in order to prevent the most egregious human rights abuses.

Elliott, Carolyn M., ed. 2008. ***Global Empowerment of Women: Responses to Globalization and Politicized Religions.*** **New York: Routledge. 399 pages. References, index.**

This volume grew out of the meetings of the Fulbright New Century Scholars Program on Global Empowerment of Women, which included 31 researchers and experts from 22 countries. These meetings examined a wide variety of issues concerning women, including sexual autonomy, the effects of the changing global order on women's empowerment, the use of gender in constructing national and ethnic identities, and gender violence. Part one of this volume considers globalization and neoliberal governance, including the experiences of women in Nepal; female migrant workers in China and Saudi Arabia; and women and microcredit. Part two discusses politicized religions and citizenship, including the marriage acts in Trinidad and Tobago; law as it relates to female Muslims; and Shari'a activism in Nigeria. Part three analyzes gender violence and the use of truth commissions in many countries. Part four examines sexual autonomy and global politics, looking at women and HIV/AIDS in sub-Saharan Africa, youth sexual relationships in Uganda, and family planning in Peru.

Farmer, Paul. 2005. ***Pathologies of Power: Health, Human Rights, and the New War on the Poor.*** **Berkeley: University of California Press. 402 pages. Bibliography, index.**

Farmer, a physician who has spent a great deal of time providing medical care to the poor under some of the worst circumstances around the world, has seen the devastation that the lack of social and economic rights can wreak on poor families. This book describes the struggles women and men face in gaining the right to health care, housing, clean water, and education, especially in developing countries. Farmer examines the differences among varying approaches to development, including charity and social justice approaches. He believes that medicine and allied health sciences have not been sufficiently involved in human rights work and need to become more involved in the fight for social and economic rights for all.

Gebremedhin, Tesfa G. 2002. ***Women, Tradition and Development: A Case Study of Eritrea.*** **Lawrenceville, NJ: The Red Sea Press, Inc. 261 pages. Bibliography, index.**

Although it focuses on women and development in Eritrea, Dr. Gebremedhin's analysis can be applied to women in other developing countries as well. He discusses institutional barriers to gender equality, the importance of men and women being equal under the law, the importance of equal access to resources and opportunities, and common beliefs and cultural practices surrounding gender roles. Individual chapters examine women and tradition, education, health, politics, employment, agriculture, poverty as well as contemporary structural changes and prospects for change and development.

Grown, Caren, Geeta Rao Gupta, and Aslinhan Kes. 2005. ***Taking Action: Achieving Gender Equality and Empowering Women.*** **Sterling, VA: Earthscan. 257 pages. Bibliography.**

Sponsored by the UN Development Programme, this book describes the priorities set by the UN Millennium Project Task Force on Education and Gender Equality to achieve equal access to education. The authors discuss the important role education for girls and women plays in promoting health for women and their families, increasing women's income earning potential, preventing domestic violence, and increasing the age of women at marriage. They also discuss strategies for achieving gender equality.

Halperin, Helena. 2005. ***I Laugh So I Won't Cry: Kenya's Women Tell the Stories of Their Lives.*** **Trenton, NJ: Africa World Press. 350 pages. Index.**

Using illustrations from the lives of Kenyan women, Halperin examines the struggles facing these women in their everyday lives. An American, she spent 14 months teaching at Shamoni Secondary School in Western Kabras, Kenya. She was enthralled by the stories of women she met and traveled back to Kenya several times, interviewing over 250 women of all ages, ethnic groups, and lifestyles in an attempt to capture the essence of their lives. Halperin covers a variety of topics that influence these women's lives. Chapters examine arranged marriage, multiple wives, raising children, education, women's work, genital cutting, ethnic tensions, and women's self-help groups. Numerous details from individual women's lives enhance the discussion of these serious challenges that Kenyan women face on a daily basis.

Handy, Femida, Meenaz Kassam, Suzanne Feeney, and Bhagyashree Ranade. 2006. ***Grassroots NGOs by Women for Women: The Driving Force of Development in India.*** **Thousand Oaks: SAGE Publications, 236 pages. References, index.**

Based on five years of research into small NGOs in Pune, India, the authors analyze the organizational structure and social impact of twenty successful NGOs. Part one profiles the founding members of the NGOs. Part two describes the progression of the organizational structures from the beginning of the programs to their current incarnations. Part three analyzes the social impact of these NGOs and the growth of some as they have modified their programs to meet changing needs.

Husseini, Rana. 2009. ***Murder in the Name of Honor: The True Story of One Woman's Heroic Fight against an Unbelievable Crime.*** **Oxford: Oneworld Publications. 250 pages. Bibliography, index.**

Husseini was a journalist in Jordan when she came face to face with the existence of honor killings. Kifaya, a young woman in Jordan, was killed by her family because she was raped by her brother and thereby dishonored the family. Husseini was appalled by the murder of Kifaya and began researching the depth and breadth of honor killings. In this book, she discusses the varied reasons that families murder one of their own, including rape, adultery, engaging in sex before marriage, or adopting Western ways. She also considers the growing number of honor killings in Europe and the United States. Husseini describes her efforts to change Jordanian attitudes toward and laws addressing these murders.

Inglehart, Ronald, and Pippa Norris. 2003. *Rising Tide: Gender Equality and Cultural Change Around the World.* New York: Cambridge University Press. 226 pages. Bibliography, index.

Traditional sex roles have evolved over the course of the twentieth century, with major variations between rich and poor countries and between younger and older generations. This "rising tide" of change is explored in this book, which analyzes the causes of change in cultural attitudes toward gender equality. Generational attitudes vary between industrial and agrarian societies and these attitudes are explored, as well as variations in support for gender equality in the political arena, at home, and at work. It also looks at the important role religion plays in influencing attitudes toward gender equality. Finally, it discusses the political consequences of these changing attitudes.

Iwanaga, Kazuki, ed. 2008. *Women's Political Participation and Representation in Asia: Obstacles and Challenges.* Copenhagen: Nordic Institute of Asian Studies. 315 pages. References, index.

In many Asian countries, as in other countries around the world, women are often marginalized from the political process for a variety of reasons. Religious and cultural expectations and limitations on women's public roles, which vary from country to country, are a primary reason for the limited participation of women in politics. This book examines women's opportunities for participation in China, Taiwan, Japan, South Korea, Cambodia, Thailand, the Philippines, Sri Lanka, and Bangladesh.

Jaquette, Jane S., ed. 2009. *Feminist Agendas and Democracy in Latin America.* Durham: Duke University Press. 258 pages. Bibliography, index.

Following a trip to Chile, Brazil, Argentina, and Peru in 2006, Jaquette realized that the nature of women's movements in Latin

America was changing. This book examines the major shifts in strategy now taking place in women's movements in Latin America. In Part one, contributors reflect on feminism and the state, including feminist politics in Chile, gender quotas for legislative candidates in Argentina and Brazil, and feminist activism in Venezuela. Part two focuses on legal strategies and democratic institutions and discusses legal strategies in Argentina, violence against women in Brazil, and gender and human rights in Peru. Part three analyzes international and cross-border activism, the progress (or lack thereof) of Latin American governments toward gender equity, and the daily obstacles faced by female migrant workers in Mexico.

Jaquette, Jane S., and Gale Summerfield, eds. 2006. *Women and Gender Equity in Development Theory and Practice: Institutions, Resources, and Mobilization.* Durham: Duke University. 364 pages. Bibliography, index.

The shift in policies and actions as a result of the September 11, 2001, attack on the United States has changed development work around the world. Amid growing concerns that the movement concerning women and gender in development was losing its momentum as a result of the growing complexities in the field, the editors brought together a wide range of experts—among them academics, activists, policy makers, and researchers—to provide thoughtful examinations of the major issues related to this topic. The book is divided into three major sections, which examine institutional opportunities and barriers to gender equity, control of resources and livelihood, and women's mobilization and power.

Kabeer, Naila. 2008. *Mainstreaming Gender in Social Protection for the Informal Economy.* London: Commonwealth Secretariat. 411 pages. Bibliography, index.

The risks faced by women from low-income households around the world are the focus of this book. The term "social protection" as it is used here is defined as "particular policy approaches and instruments that deal with the problems of risk and vulnerability" (4–5). Kabeer examines approaches to social protection advocated by the World Bank and the International Labour Organization, the global labor force, institutional protection, employment, financial services, protection as women age, and development policy.

Kara, Siddharth. 2009. ***Sex Trafficking: Inside the Business of Modern Slavery.*** **New York: Columbia University Press. 298 pages. References, index.**

Pursuing an interest in sex trafficking that had started in college, Kara traveled to refugee camps in Slovenia and brothels, shelters, and villages in India, Nepal, Burma, Thailand, Vietnam, Italy, Moldova, Albania, the Netherlands, the United Kingdom, Mexico, and the United States. This book is based on the knowledge and experience Kara gained during these trips and focuses on an analysis of the sex trafficking industry and its operations throughout the world. The book also suggests means of eradicating this practice, including increasing the penalties for getting caught as a trafficker or intermediary.

Leckie, Jacqueline, ed. 2009. ***Development in an Insecure and Gendered World: The Relevance of the Millennium Goals.*** **Burlington, VT: Ashgate. 246 pages. Bibliography, index.**

The UN General Assembly adopted the Millennium Declaration and the eight Millennium Development Goals in 2000 as part of an ambitious program to cut the world poverty rate in half by the year 2015. This book examines those goals and the major criticisms of them, specifically in the areas of development, security, and gender. Topics include the absence of a human rights framework in the MDGs, the MDG's limitations relative to the global economy, the failure to identify gender equality as a condition of fulfillment of the MDGs, the omission of universal access to quality sexual and reproductive health care, and the absence of a call for a reduction in human conflicts and wars.

Lichter, Ida. 2009. ***Muslim Women Reformers: Inspiring Voices against Oppression.*** **Amherst, NY: Prometheus Books. 513 pages. References.**

Lichter profiles Muslim women who have fought or are working to eliminate gender discrimination by challenging discriminatory laws and ideology. Included are veteran reformers such as Nawal El-Saadawi, Fatima Mernissi, and Shirin Ebadi as well as others who have recently joined the crusade. Lichter also includes several men who have supported the fight. The book takes an in-depth look at reforms taking place in Afghanistan, Iran, and Saudi Arabia, but also reviews reforms in other countries including Canada, France, and the United States. It also provides a list of websites that advocate for reform of discriminatory laws and ideology.

Lindio-McGovern, Ligaya, and Isidor Walliman, eds. 2009. ***Globalization and Third World Women: Exploitation, Coping and Resistance.*** **Burlington, VT: Ashgate Publishing. 214 pages. References, index.**

The contributors to this volume describe the ways in which marginalized women are coping in a world where distances between and across cultures have shrunk and political and economic policies promote private ownership of the means of production, free markets, and free trade. They examine migrant domestic workers in Johannesburg, Filipino migrant workers, the impact on women of the Mau Mau resurgence in Kenya, and Mexican women who have been left behind following the passage of NAFTA, as well as structural adjustment programs in Africa, and the experiences of women in Nigeria, Costa Rica, and Ecuador who are fighting corporations that want to extract oil from the ground.

Masquelier, Adeline. 2009. ***Women and Islamic Revival in a West African Town.*** **Bloomington: Indiana University Press. 343 pages. Bibliography, index.**

Masquelier met Malam Awal on a trip to Niger; Awal was a Sufi "preacher" who had been asked by the local orthodox elite in Dogondoutchi, Niger, to encourage the local residents to return to the "true" form of Islam. The book explores this Islamist reform movement and its effects on the women in Dogondoutchi. It examines women's reactions to this reform from an anthropological perspective. It also considers the history of Islamic religious practices. Using the lens of individual experiences, Masquelier looks at Malam Awal's effects on the community's religious beliefs and behavior, on shifting dynamics in relationships, on marriage practices, and on public dress.

Moghadam, Valentine M., ed. 2007. ***From Patriarchy to Empowerment: Women's Participation, Movements, and Rights in the Middle East, North Africa, and South Asia.*****Syracuse: Syracuse University Press. 414 pages. Bibliography, index.**

Women in the Middle East, North Africa, and South Asia, as well as in other regions around the world, have historically been subjected to patriarchal striuctures that have prohibited them from fully participating in society. Today, many patriarchal practices have been overcome, at least to some degree, as development agencies work to bring women into the mainstream of development. Contributors to this book examine patriarchy and gender relations in light of globalization, describing and analyzing a variety of economic, political, and cultural processes that have been impacted by the incorporation of women into these processes. Individual chapters offer historical and contemporary perspectives on women's participation in nationalist movements and political processes; their recasting of cultural practices through filmmaking, literature, and use of current computer technologies; their fight for basic human rights; and their responses to war and other human conflicts.

Mukhopadhyay, Maitrayee, and Shamim Meer, eds. 2008. ***Gender, Rights and Development: A Global Sourcebook.*** **Amsterdam: Royal Tropical Institute. 160 pages. Annotated bibliography, index.**

The editors of this volume believe that promoting women's empowerment as a means to alleviate poverty is more acceptable to individuals, communities, and governments than promoting empowerment as a human right. Contributors examine the ability of development programs and activities to view women as entities in and of themselves rather than solely in a gender role as subservient and secondary to men. Chapters address the marginalization of women's reproductive rights in the case of health care for HIV-positive pregnant women in South Africa; sexual, reproductive, and abortion rights in Nicaragua; women's struggle for their rights after the Bhopal gas disaster in India; rights of women in the Arab world; and feminism and development.

Murray, Ann Firth. 2008. ***From Outrage to Courage: Women Taking Action for Health and Justice.*** **Monroe, ME: Common Courage Press. 311 pages. Bibliography, index.**

Murray, the founder of the Global Fund for Women (see Chapter 7), sees women's health as an issue of social justice, rather than primarily in medical terms. Through facts and personal stories of courageous women around the world, this book illustrates the struggles that women face in gaining access to health care. Murray examines women and poverty; the preference for male children that results in sex-selective abortion of female fetuses or female infanticide; unequal access to education, nutrition, and health care; female genital mutilation; early marriage of girls; and lack of access to reproductive health care. She also looks at various forms of violence against women, including domestic violence, honor killing, and dowry death, and examines the devastating effects of war and conflicts on women, including women's experiences as refugees. The book discusses sex trafficking, aging, and women's unrecognized contributions to the labor force. It also explores the global women's movement and feminist activism. Resources are provided, including journals on international health and lists relevant international governmental organizations and NGOs.

Murthy, Padmini, and Clyde Lanford Smith, eds. 2010. *Women's Global Health and Human Rights*. Sudbury, MA: Jones and Bartlett Publishers. 556 pages. References, index.

In many areas of the world, women's health and human rights have not improved over the last several years. Murthy and Smith have brought together a wide range of contributors to explore women's health as a human right through comparisons of the challenges women experience around the world regarding their health. Section one discusses women's health as a human right. Section two examines the impact of gender-based violence on women and girls, including violence, war, terrorism, trafficking, and the Global Gag Rule. The relationship among women, economics, and human rights is reviewed in Section three. The fourth section analyzes the problems and challenges faced by women regarding their health. Section five reviews the effects of migration, the environment, and cultural practices such as FGM on women and girls. Section six examines challenges to women's well-being and the progress currently being made to meet these challenges. The final section offers recommendations regarding the promotion of a human rights-based approach to improving women's health.

Nazir, Sameena, and Leigh Tomppert, eds. 2005. *Women's Rights in the Middle East and North Africa: Citizenship and Justice*. New York: Freedom House. 367 pages. References.

In an effort to examine the status of women's rights in several countries, Nazir and Tomppert have put together a collection of essays that provides information and analysis on the legal status and experiences of women in 16 countries and one territory. Countries examined include Algeria, Bahrain, Egypt, Iraq, Jordan, Kuwait, Lebanon, Libya, Morocco, Oman, Palestine, Qatar, Saudi Arabia, Syria, Tunisia, United Arab Emirates, and Yemen. Contributors describe the contrast between legislation granting women equal rights and the actual day-to-day discrimination they face in an effort to assist local and global efforts to expand women's legal rights.

Ng, Cecilia, and Swasti Mitter, eds. 2005. ***Gender and the Digital Economy: Perspectives from the Developing World.*** **Thousand Oaks, CA: SAGE Publications. 262 pages. Bibliography, index.**

Rapid development and the spread of new information and communication technologies (ICT) have marked societies around the world since the 1970s. This book explores the growth of ICTs; relationships among gender, development, and ICTs; gender positions within the digital economy; and the politics and policies of gender and ICTs. It examines the ability of ICTs to empower women and how the gains women make can be sustained. It discusses the importance of examining the benefits of e-commerce in different cultures and of designing ICT initiatives that include issues of importance to women in developing countries. In addition, it describes the advantages to women of building virtual communities for networking purposes.

Onubogu, Elsie, Linda Etchart, Rawwida Baksh, and Tina Johnson. 2005. ***Gender Mainstreaming in Conflict Transformation: Building Sustainable Peace.*** **London: Commonwealth Secretariat. 232 pages. Bibliography.**

This book examines the importance of incorporating women into processes of peace and conflict-resolution, from peace-building activities to post-conflict reconstruction. A UN Security Resolution (UNSCR 1235) emphasizes this need by calling for women's "equal participation and full involvement" in maintaining and promoting peace and security. In support of their points, the authors provide examples from women's experiences in Bangladesh, Cyprus, India, Jamaica, Papua New Guinea, Sierra Leone, and Sri Lanka.

Oyewumi, Oyeronke, ed. 2003. ***African Women and Feminism: Reflecting on the Politics of Sisterhood.*** **Trenton, NJ: Africa World Press, Inc. 273 pages. Bibliography, index.**

The contributors to this book focus on the often-contentious relationship that African women have with feminism. Although a variety of views on feminism exist, including those that have emerged from white, black, Western, and African contexts, most of the emphasis in development is on Western feminism. The contributors to this volume, all born and raised in Africa and, at the time of writing, teaching in the United States, examine the effect of Western feminism on development and human rights issues in Africa, including the choice of sisterhood as the basis of feminist alliances and approaches to female genital cutting or mutilation.

Parker, Lyn, ed. 2005. ***The Agency of Women in Asia.*** **New York: Marshall Cavendish Academic. 235 pages. References, index.**

In this collection of essays, Parker attempts to provide an alternative to images of Asian women as sex slaves, mail-order brides, and child prostitutes—in other words, as oppressed victims. Chapters examine female healers in Lombok, an island in Indonesia; rural women giving birth in Bali (hospital vs. in-home deliveries); female performers in Indonesian theater; unmarried women in Japan; South Korean and Filipino women who have married Japanese men; and Indonesian women working in Singapore as domestic workers. Contributors illustrate women's everyday self-expression and resistance to oppression.

Petchesky, Rosalind Pollack. 2003. ***Global Prescriptions: Gendering Health and Human Rights.*** **New York: Zed Books. 306 pages. Bibliography, index.**

Petchesky provides a comprehensive review of women's participation in a variety of international venues, including UN conferences, international and regional networks, and national advocacy campaigns, with an emphasis on sexual and reproductive health. She explores the growth of transnational women's health movements as well as their characteristics; their successes and failures; and their contributions to the development of gender, health, and human rights. She also provides an assessment of the global impact of UN conferences on women, and analyzes the relationship of HIV/AIDS and the human right to health to global capitalism. Petchesky examines the evolution of health issues under global capitalist policies, including the increased burden on women to cope with health care as governments cut budgets for social services and health care. She also analyzes the roles of NGOs in the women's health arena as advocates, providers, monitors, and implementers of programs and policies.

Peterson, V. Spike, and Anne Sisson Runyan. 2010. *Global Gender Issues in the New Millennium.* Third edition. Boulder: Westview Press. 300 pages. Bibliography, index.

Peterson and Runyan provide an overview of gender in international relations and policymaking through an examination of the re-positioning of men and women in global governance, security, and politics. Individual chapters offer discussions of gender and global issues, gendered lenses on world politics, gender and global government, gender and global security, gender and global political economy, and gendered resistances.

Rai, Shirin M. 2008. *The Gender Politics of Development: Essays in Hope and Despair.* New York: Zed Books. 216 pages. Bibliography, index.

Rai examines the emergence and development of gender politics in postcolonial states, addressing the role of women's movements in the development of state policies with regard to key issues of concern to women. Chapters describe the struggles of female street vendors in New Delhi for recognition and protection; the use of quotas in local governments; and the development of a research network of gender, law, and governance. They explore the relationships among gender, knowledge, innovation, and property rights. They discuss the costs versus the benefits of empowering women; when individuals and organizations develop programs that empower women, they must examine the dangers the women may face by participating.

Robinson-Pant, Anna, ed. 2004. *Women, Literacy and Development: Alternative Perspectives.* New York: Routledge. 259 pages. Bibliography, index.

A great deal of the recent literature on women and development emphasizes the major role that education plays in the success of development programs involving women. The popular theory is that an educated woman will understand the importance of education for all her children and will be more aware of the role that nutrition and hygiene play in ensuring a healthy family, thus becoming better capable of providing for her family. Robinson-Pant has brought together researchers, policy makers, and practitioners who offer a different approach to women's literacy. Part one looks at new research approaches to women and literacy, Part two identifies the major issues on literacy policy and programming, and Part three describes and analyzes attempts to provide literacy programs for women in developing countries.

Saliba, Therese, Carolyn Allen, and Judith A. Howard, eds. 2005. *Gender, Politics, and Islam.* New Delhi: Orient Longman Private Ltd. 354 pages. Index.

This collection of essays by Muslim women illustrates the wide variety and range of their experiences. Not all women who are Muslim are similar, nor are they passive victims of their religion and environment. The book explores the experiences of women from Bangladesh, Canada, Egypt, Iran, Israel and Palestine, Pakistan, and Yemen as they fight for their political, economic, and legal rights.

Samarasinghe, Vidyamali. 2008. *Female Sex Trafficking in Asia: The Resilience of Patriarchy in a Changing World.* New York: Routledge. 234 pages. Bibliography, index.

Samarasinghe examines attempts to define sex trafficking and considers the major issues of smuggling and migration as well as the issue of women's willing participation versus coercion and force. The book also explores issues of female vulnerability and subordination, patriarchy, militarism, and globalization, and considers their influence on the practice of sex trafficking. It describes and analyzes major female sex trafficking issues in Nepal, Cambodia, and the Philippines. It also examines the male-dominant demand side of the equation, including the clients, the intermediaries, and the institutions that support or at the very least ignore the problems of sex trafficking.

Segrave, Marie, Sanja Milivojevic, and Sharon Pickering. 2009. *Sex Trafficking: International Context and Response.* Portland, OR: Willan Publishers. 226 pages. References, index.

National and international attention on sex trafficking, especially the trafficking of women into sex slavery or servitude, has grown in recent years. This book examines this issue and the policies developed to respond to it based on the experiences of policy-makers, NGOs, and trafficked women themselves. Case studies from Australia, Serbia, and Thailand provide rich details of the perspectives of police, immigration authorities, social workers, lawyers, and activists. The authors are concerned that assumptions are made based on gender regarding anti-trafficking efforts, that opinions and experiences of the women being trafficked are often ignored in policy development, and that the relationship between criminal justice efforts and the growth of human trafficking and vulnerability of individuals is being ignored.

Skaine, Rosemarie. 2005. *Female Genital Mutilation: Legal, Cultural and Medical Issues*. Jefferson, NC: McFarland & Co. 321 pages. References, index.

Female genital mutilation (FGM) or female genital cutting (FGC) is practiced in many parts of the world, but primarily in Africa. Efforts to eliminate it probably started as early as the 17th century, and today emotions surrounding the issue still run high. Skaine begins by describing the definitions and types of FGM, the justification for its existence, and reasons for its prevalence. She discusses legal attempts to ban it, not only in Africa but in countries around the world. She examines the ethical, political, and legal aspects of this practice. Skaine conducted research on FGM as practiced among the Maasai in Tanzania, and she presents information drawn from her interviews on the subject of both male and female circumcision. Cultural norms play an important role in any discussion of FGM and Skaine offers an analysis of culture as it relates to this practice. Appendices provide information on legislation and outreach attempts to curb or ban the practice in countries where it has traditionally been practiced as well as information about the practice in industrialized countries.

Skaine, Rosemarie. 2008. *Women Political Leaders in Africa*. Jefferson, NC: McFarland & Co. 206 pages. Bibliography, index.

Women hold leadership positions throughout Africa, although some countries are more progressive than others. Skaine discusses the history and current status of female African leaders, their changing roles, and regional and international laws regarding human rights of women, as well as providing profiles of female leaders including Ellen Johnson-Sirleaf, Wangari Maathai, and Luisa Diogo. In Part two of the book she summarizes each country's economic program, its government policies and practices, and the status and progress of its women.

Tembon, Mercy, and Lucia Fort, eds. 2008, ***Girls' Education in the 21st Century: Gender Equality, Empowerment, and Economic Growth.*** **Washington, D.C.: The World Bank. 313 pages. References, index.**

Based on the background papers presented at an international, multidisciplinary symposium on gender, education, and development, this book explores the challenges facing educational development and the struggle for gender equality as well as the need to continue the progress being made in many countries in providing education for girls. Part one examines the relationships among education quality, skills development, and economic growth, with the understanding that the quality of education must be improved in many areas. Part two discusses gender equity in education and the issues and factors that prevent countries from achieving it. Part three offers examples of approaches to improve the rate of enrollment of girls in schools, examining the ways that individual countries have addressed the varying sociocultural and economic issues that keep girls out of school.

Terry, Geraldine, ed. 2007. ***Gender-Based Violence.*** **Oxford: Oxfam. 195 pages. References and index.**

This collection provides a broad understanding of the many manifestations of gender-based violence, including femicide; domestic and sexual violence; female genital mutilation; sexual abuse of girls in schools; and sex trafficking in locations around the world, including South and East Asia, sub-Saharan Africa, and Central America. It discusses various approaches to reducing violence against women and girls. An extensive section on resources lists relevant publications, websites, and programs. This book is intended for development and humanitarian practitioners, policy makers, and academics.

Thiara, Ravi K., and Aisha K. Gill, eds. 2010. ***Violence against Women in South Asian Communities.*** **Philadelphia: Jessica Kingsley Publishers. 255 pages. References, index.**

Thiara and Gill have gathered together researchers and practitioners to explore current research, policy, and practice on the topic of violence against women in South Asian communities throughout the United Kingdom (as of 2010, there were approximately 2.5 million South Asians living in Britain). Chapters address these women's struggles against gendered violence, the impact of governmental multicultural policies on the rights of minorities, the dichotomy of tradition and modern practices, forced marriage, the extent to which the law should accommodate religious and cultural diversity, domestic violence occurring after divorce, and suggested approaches to eliminating gender-based violence.

Welchman, Lynn, and Sara Hossain, eds. 2005. ***Honour: Crimes, Paradigms and Violence against Women.*** **New York: Zed Books. 384 pages. References, index.**

Contributors from diverse backgrounds offer a wide variety of experiences and insights into the problem of honor killings. They offer strategies to respond to these crimes, whether they occur in Europe, the Middle East, Asia, or elsewhere. The book offers an international perspective focusing on violence against women as well as on the human rights aspects of honor killings. Chapters include discussions of UN approaches to honor crimes; Western experience with and influences in honor crimes; and how nations such as Italy, Latin America, the United Kingdom, and the Nordic countries have dealt with the issue of honor killings.

Agency Reports

International Labour Organization. 2009. ***Global Employment Trends for Women.*** **Geneva: ILO. 78 pages.**

The impact of the world financial crisis and the effects of the resulting slowdown in economic growth on women are explored in this report. It analyzes recent market developments and examines the relationship among economic growth, the labor market, and gender inequality. It also explores the effects of gender inequality in sectoral employment and vulnerable employment, in African agriculture, in wages, and in poverty. It discusses the outlook for the labor market and policy recommendations regarding women's roles in economic recovery, investment in physical and social infrastructure, social security issues, legal frameworks and gender equality, the Millennium Development Goals, and globalization and the gender gap. Annexes contain tables displaying a wide range of statistical information regarding women and work.

PATH, Intercambios, MRC, and WHO. 2008. *Strengthening Understanding of Femicide: Using Research to Galvanize Action and Accountability*. Washington, D.C.: PATH, Intercambios, MRC, and WHO.

Four organizations, the Program for Appropriate Technology in Health (PATH), the Inter-American Alliance for the Prevention of Gender-based Violence (InterCambios), the Medical Research Council of South Africa (MRC), and the World Health Organization (WHO), convened a conference on femicide, meaning the act of murdering a female based solely on the fact that she is female. This report presents an overview of the conference, covering current research findings on the prevalence of femicide, the risk factors of victimization, and tactics to close gaps and hold those involved in femicide accountable for their actions.

Social Watch. 2008. *Social Watch Report 2008: Rights Is the Answer*. Montevideo, Uruguay: Third World Institute. 225 pages.

Created in 1995, the Social Watch network has members in more than 60 countries who focus on social development and gender discrimination around the world. This annual report provides an analysis of progress made toward eliminating gender discrimination and problems that continue to slow the progress of the struggle to achieve gender equality and reduce poverty. Topics include food security, education, information science and technology, public expenditure, development assistance, water and sanitation, health, reproductive health, and gender equity.

UN Department of Economic and Social Affairs (ECOSOC). 2009. *2009 World Survey on the Role of Women in Development: Women's Control over Economic Resources and Access to Financial Resources, including Microfinance*. New York: United Nations. 114 pages.

Women's access to economic and financial resources is critical to alleviating poverty and supporting the well-being of families and communities; access empowers women and enhances opportunities for sustainable economic development. Even though progress has been made in providing women with greater opportunities, discriminatory practices and cultural norms have made progress difficult in many countries. This report explores global policies and legal frameworks that hinder women's empowerment, including the financial crisis that has impacted much of the world since its beginnings in 2008. Individual chapters and sections focus on access to full employment and decent work; to land, housing, and other productive resources; to financial services; and to social protection. The final section offers recommendations on how to expand women's access to these valuable resources.

UNESCO. 2010. *Reaching the Marginalized.* Paris: UNESCO.

While some progress has been made in reaching the Millennium Development Goals and the Education for All (EFA) goals, the world financial crisis has impacted that progress. This report assesses how far UN nations have come to date in achieving universal primary education and increased secondary school enrollment. The first chapter examines the impact that the financial crisis has had on development projects and describes international action that is needed to avert further slowing in goal attainment. The second chapter reviews the progress that has been made in reaching the EFA goals. The third chapter looks at marginalization in education and the social inequalities that lead to groups of people becoming marginalized, and suggests ways to reach the marginalized. The fourth chapter examines how the international donor community can assist in meeting the MDGs and EFA goals.

UN High Commissioner for Refugees. 2008. *UNHCR Handbook for the Protection of Women and Girls.* Geneva: UNHCR. 394 pages.

This handbook is designed to provide guidelines for protecting women and girls who are under the purview of the UNHCR, including asylum seekers and refugees, the internally displaced, returnees, the stateless, and those who have integrated into new communities. It sets standards for working with women and girls and suggests strategies for cooperating with local partners to protect their interests. Chapters provide information on the ways women and girls are affected by displacement, ways to employ to achieve gender equality, and ways to identify and respond to risks. The book also explains the importance of partnerships, examines women's primary rights and how they are violated, and discusses the international legal framework in place to protect women and girls.

UNICEF. 2008. *The State of the World's Children 2009.* New York: UNICEF. 160 pages.

Each year UNICEF publishes a report on the state of the world's children, focusing on a specific topic. This report examines maternal and newborn health, reviewing the reasons so many women are still dying during pregnancy and childbirth and suggesting steps to be taken to save the lives of more women and newborns. Some of the interventions discussed are adequate nutrition, better hygiene, prenatal and postnatal care, skilled birth attendants, and available emergency care.

World Health Organization. 2008. *Eliminating Female Genital Mutilation: An Interagency Statement, OHCHR, UNAIDS, UNDP, UNECA, UNESCO, UNFPA, UNHCR, UNICEF, UNIFEM, WHO.* Geneva: WHO. 41 pages.

According to this collaborative report, approximately three million girls are at risk of undergoing FGM every year. This statement calls on all governments, international and national NGOs, and local communities to protect women and girls and uphold their rights by eliminating this practice. It encourages all UN agencies and others to support activities and programs that persuade local communities to cease female genital mutilation or cutting. The authors describe the legal and human rights aspects of this problem, offer statistics on the prevalence of FGM, and present findings that explain the reasons for its persistence. They also describe the steps that are needed to put a stop to this practice as well as those necessary to support women and girls who have endured it.

World Health Organization. 2009. *Women and Health: Today's Evidence, Tomorrow's Agenda.* Geneva: WHO. 91 pages.

Understanding that gathering reliable data on the status of women and health throughout the world is difficult, this report provides an analysis of what is currently available and identifies those areas in which additional research must be conducted to fill the many gaps in our knowledge of the health of women around the world. The report covers the health of girls and women from childhood through old age. It found that there are widespread disparities between the accessibility of health services to men and women; that reproductive health is central to women's overall health; that other health challenges to women include chronic diseases, injury, and mental health issues; that many of the health problems women face have their origin in childhood; and that, overall, health systems around the world are failing women.

Journals and Journal Articles

The journals listed below often contain articles that focus on subjects of concern to women in developing countries and may lead the reader to additional resources on this topic.

African Population Studies (http://www.uaps-uepa.org or http://www.bioline.org.br/ep). Journal articles are available in English and French; many are available for free download.

Asia-Pacific Population Journal (http://www.unescap.org/esid/psis/population/journal/index.asp). Published by the UNESCAP secretariat and distributed at no charge to policymakers, NGOs, and other qualified groups. Online subscriptions are also available at no cost.

Comparative Education Review (http://www.journals.uchicago.edu/toc/cer/current).

Demography (http://muse.jhu.edu/journals/dem/). Abstracts available online.

Development (http://www.palgrave-journals.com/development/index.html). Some articles available for free download.

Development and Change (http://onlinelibrary.wiley.com/journal/10.1111/%28ISSN%291467-7660).

Economic Development and Cultural Change (http://www.journals.uchicago.edu/EDCC/home.html). Abstracts available online.

Feminist Studies (http://www.feministstudies.org/home.html).

Food and Nutrition Bulletin (http://www.foodandnutrition bulletin.org/fnbhome.php).

Global Public Health (http://www.tandf.co.uk/journals/titles/17441692.asp).

Health Policy and Planning (http://www.heapol.oxfordjournals.org).

Human Organization (http://www.sfaa.net/ho).

Human Rights Quarterly (http://muse.jhu.edu/journals/hrq/). Abstracts available online.

International Journal of Health Services (http://www.baywood.com/journals/previewjournals.asp?id=0020-7314). Abstracts available online.

International Journal of Middle East Studies (http://journals.cambridge.org/action/displayJournal?jid=MES). Abstracts available online.

International Perspectives on Sexual and Reproductive Health (http://www.guttmacher.org/journals/aboutper.html).

Jenda: A Journal of Culture and African Women Studies (www.jendajournal.com). Copies of 2006 and earlier journals are available free online.

Journal of Biosocial Science (http://journals.cambridge.org/action/displayJournal?jid=JBS). Abstracts available online.

Journal of Comparative Family Studies (http://soci.ucalgary.ca/jcfs/).

Journal of Developing Areas (http://muse.jhu.edu/journals/jda/). Abstracts available online.

Journal of Population and Social Studies (http://www.ipsr.mahidol.ac.th/IPSR/Journal/Content.htm). Abstracts and articles available for free download.

The Lancet (http://www.thelancet.com). Selected articles available for free download with registration.

Medical Anthropology Quarterly (http://medanthro.net/maq/index.html).

Population and Development Review (http://www.wiley.com/bw/journal.asp?ref=0098-7921&site=1).

Population Studies (http://www.tandf.co.uk/journals/titles/00324728.html).

Signs: Journal of Women in Culture and Society (http://www.journals.uchicago.edu/toc/signs/current). Abstracts available online.

Social Science and Medicine (http://www.elsevier.com/wps/find/journaldescription.cws_home/315/description#description).

Studies in Family Planning (http://www.wiley.com/bw/journal.asp?ref=0039-3665).

Women's Studies International Forum (http://www.elsevier.com/wps/find/journaldescription.cws_home/361/description#description). Abstracts available online.

World Development (http://www.elsevier.com/wps/find/journaldescription.cws_home/386/description#description). Abstracts available online.

World Health Forum (http://www.ajtmh.org/cgi/content/abstract/30/6/1344-a).

World Views: Global Religions, Culture, and Ecology (http://www.brill.nl/m_catalogue_sub6_id9007.htm).

Videos and Electronic Resources

This section provides annotated descriptions of videos and films that focus on women in developing countries.

Africa Rising: The Grassroots Movement to End Female Genital Mutilation.

Paula Heredia, color, 62 minutes, DVD, 2009. $295, institutions; $89, K-12 and public libraries.

Available from Women Make Movies, 462 Broadway, Suite 500WS, New York, NY 10013, http://www.wmm.com.

Produced by Equality Now, this film provides a poignant examination of female genital mutilation in several African countries including Burkina Faso, Kenya, Mali, Somalia, and Tanzania. It tells the stories of girls who have experienced FGM and describes the actions that African women and men are undertaking to end this violation of human rights. The activists portrayed in the film work with circumcisers, encouraging them to stop FGM, and urge the police to implement current laws outlawing FGM in many jurisdictions; they also provide leadership, encouragement, and training for girls and young women.

After the Rape: The Muktar Mai Story.

Catherine Ulmer, color, 58 minutes, DVD, 2008. $295, institutions; $89, K-12 and public libraries.

Available from Women Make Movies, 462 Broadway, Suite 500WS, New York, NY 10013, http://www.wmm.com.

In 2002 in a small remote village in rural Pakistan, a young woman, Muktar Mai, came to the defense of her brother Shakur after he was gang-raped by men from a local clan. In an attempt to deflect the accusations, these men accused Shakur of raping a girl in their clan. To compensate for the alleged rage of the young girl, the tribal council decreed that they would punish Shakur by having Muktar gang-raped. Following the rape, most locals expected Muktar to commit suicide as a result of the humiliation. Instead she fought back, reported the rape, and received $8,300 in compensation. She used the money to build two schools for girls in her village and establish a crisis center for abused women. This film documents her inspiring story and demonstrates the resilience and strength of Pakistani women.

The Al-Hadji and His Wives.

Jie Li, color, 50 minutes, 2006. $39.95, individuals; $195, institutions.

Available from Documentary Educational Resources, 101 Morse St., Watertown, MA 02472.

This documentary offers a brief glimpse into the lives of an Mbororo Fulani patriarch and his wives and his daughters, including his 16-year-old daughter Amina. It examines challenges faced by Al-Hadji Isa and his wives as they try to raise their daughters according to local tradition; it also explores their religious and political beliefs. A marriage is arranged for Amina and the video describes the process and reasoning behind her parents' decision to force her into this marriage.

Anna from Benin.

Monique Mbeka Phoba, color, 45 minutes, VHS, 2000. $295, institutions; $89, K-12 and public libraries.

Available from Women Make Movies, 462 Broadway, Suite 500WS, New York, NY 10013, http://www.wmm.com.

One of 31 children from her father's five wives, Anna received an extraordinary opportunity to study in France. This film documents her experiences living with her domineering father in Benin and later as a 17-year-old alone in France without the protection of her many family members. Viewers are provided with a unique look at the struggles of a young woman from a country in which girls are not expected or encouraged to receive an education.

Enemies of Happiness (Vores Lykkes Fjender).

Color, 59 minutes, VHS/DVD, 2006. $295, institutions; $89, K-12 and public libraries.

Available from Women Make Movies, 462 Broadway, Suite 500WS, New York, NY 10013, http://www.wmm.com.

This film, in Farsi and Pasthu with subtitles, portrays the life of Malalai Joya, a 27-year-old Afghan woman who decried the activities of corrupt warlords at the Grand Council of tribal elders in 2003. In 2005, she was a candidate for an assembly seat when Afghanistan held its first parliamentary elections in 35 years. The film examines the final weeks of her campaign, including the death threats she received and the resulting restrictions on her campaigning. It demonstrates the obstacles faced by women in Afghanistan today as well as the strength and power of women fighting for change.

Mammy Water: In Search of the Water Spirits of Nigeria.

Sabine Jell-Bahlsen, color, 60 minutes, 1989. $49.95.

Available from Documentary Educational Resources, 101 Morse St., Watertown, MA 02472.

Many members of the Ibibio, Ijaw, and Igbo groups of southeastern Nigeria worship Mammy Water, a goddess believed to provide wealth and children and comfort in difficult times. This video offers an inside look into the worship of Mammy Water through an examination of the rituals and ceremonies performed by priestesses; it demonstrates the power of traditional religion in the lives of its female followers.

New Dimensions.

Joanne Burke, color, 30 minutes each. $295 for all four videos in the set.

Available from Women Make Movies, 462 Broadway, Suite 500WS, New York, NY 10013, http://www.wmm.com.

Burke has created a series of four 30-minute videos describing the lives of women in four developing countries. The video entitled *Women of Zimbabwe* (1997) examines five women who changed their circumstances for the better by becoming carpenters. *Women of Thailand* (1997) profiles a woman who created a foundation to work with women in Bangkok's largest slum. *Women of Guatemala* (2000) profiles two Mayan women who lead a group of 75 women providing health education and education about other social problems that Mayan women face in Guatemala. *Speaking Out: Women, AIDS and Hope in Mali* (2002) profiles an HIV/AIDS support project in Bamako and three women who have devoted their lives to helping those infected in HIV/AIDS.

Poto Mitan: Haitian Women, Pillars of the Global Economy.

Renee Bergan and Mark Schuller, color, 50 minutes, 2009. $29.95, retail; $79.95, organizations; $195, public performance or educational use.

Available from Documentary Educational Resources, 101 Morse St., Watertown, MA 02472.

This documentary depicts the experiences of five Haitian women and the effects of neoliberal globalization on their lives. Marie-Jeanne describes the horrific working conditions she endures to provide education for her children; Solange details the violence that has resulted from the economic crisis; Frisline examines Haiti's current situation; many issues, including public health issues, facing women in Haiti are illustrated by Therese's experience and analysis; and Helene organizes a grassroots effort against violence after being forced off her land. Interviews with individuals from various NGOs, government representatives, and educators provide additional analysis of Haitian women's daily experiences and potential solutions to their problems.

Through the Negev.

Ya-Hsuan Huang, color, 18 minutes, 2007. $39.95, individuals; $145, institutions.

Available from Documentary Educational Resources, 101 Morse St., Watertown, MA 02472.

This short documentary tells the stories of several female refugees who have escaped from Sudan and traveled through Egypt to Israel. Naka, a 10-year-old girl, and her mother escaped religious persecution. An Arab Muslim student was tortured for attempting to organize a student union and fled Sudan following this horrifying experience. A woman from Darfur describes her life without her husband. Ida explains simply and powerfully how having a home is a basic human right.

(Un)veiled: Muslim Women Talk about Hijab.

Ines Hofmann Kanna, color, 36 minutes, 2008. $39.95, individuals; $145, institutions.

Available from Documentary Educational Resources, 101 Morse St., Watertown, MA 02472.

Ten Muslim women, now living in Dubai but from a variety of backgrounds, engage in a lively discussion of their views on the hijab, the headscarf, and the incorrect assumptions that many outsiders make about their lives. They talk about their thoughts on feminism, freedom, human rights, and modern beliefs.

Unveiled Views: Muslim Women Artists Speak Out.

Alba Sotorra, color, DVD, 52 minutes, 2009. $295, institutions; $89, K-12 and public libraries.

Available from Women Make Movies, 462 Broadway, Suite 500WS, New York, NY 10013, http://www.wmm.com.

This film presents the stories of five Muslim women, describing their work and aspirations as well as discussing the overall status of women and human rights in their countries. Alma Suljevic, from Bosnia, clears landmines near Sarajevo and then sells the earth from the minefield in European art galleries. In Turkey Eren Keskin, a human rights lawyer and activist, works to change laws that perpetuate domestic violence. Iranian Rashan Bani-Ehmad, a filmmaker, often pushes her country's censorship policies to the limit. Moshagan Saadat is an Afghani poet. Nahid Siddiqui, a Pakistani dancer, continues to teach others even after her work was banned by her government.

Yindabad.

Mariano Agudo and Rol Guitian, color, 55 minutes, 2007. $49.95, individuals; $195, institutions.

Available from Documentary Educational Resources, 101 Morse St., Watertown, MA 02472.

The Narmada Valley Development Project in India was begun in the 1960s to construct over 3,000 dams of varying sizes along the Narmada River. In the process over 2.5 million people, primarily Adivasis or indigenous people, have been forced to relocate. They have fought for over 20 years for fair compensation for their losses, and Adivasi women have been particularly vocal in the struggle. This documentary describes these events from the women's point of view, in the process examining the problems associated with focusing on global rather than local development and self-management.

Websites and Blogs

African Women on the Internet

http://www-sul.stanford.edu/depts/ssrg/africa/women.html

This site offers links to sub-Saharan websites that focus on women in Africa.

Amnesty International

http://www.amnesty.org

This site provides information on Amnesty International and its human rights activities throughout the world.

Arab Women's Home Page

http://www.arabinfo.org/arabwomen/main.html

This site provides Arab women worldwide with an open forum in which to share their experiences. It creates connections among

Arab women as well as women from other cultures. Links are provided to related pages.

Choike

http://blog.choike.org

This portal provides a forum for NGOs working on women's issues as well as other important issues in the Global South. It provides a searchable directory of NGOs as well as in-depth reports on a variety of women's issues. It also disseminates information about various campaigns run by associated NGOs. It is operated by the Instituto del Tercer Mundo, an NGO in Montevideo, Uruguay.

Eldis Gender Violence Resources

http://www.eldis.org/gender/gender_based_violence.htm

Eldis provides access to a wide variety of resources concerning development policies, practices, and research. This website offers free downloads of a wide variety of full-text documents, resource guides, country profiles, email newsletters, and newsfeeds, as well as breaking news, upcoming events, and job openings.

Honor Killings

http://www.stophonourkillings.com

This website posts information on recent honor killings and provides forums on various topics regarding honor killings and related blogs. Individuals and organizations can also post information concerning this issue.

Human Rights Country Reports

http://state.gov/g/drl/rls/hrrpt

Country reports on human rights conditions in many countries can be found at this site hosted by the U.S. Department of State.

One World

http://oneworldgroup.org

A community of over 120 leading global justice organizations is contained at this site, which provides news services and links to related sources of information. It provides current news, organized by country and by theme, on issues ranging from agriculture, civil rights, and freedom of expression to human rights, women's rights, poverty.

Population Reference Bureau

http://www.prb.org

The Population Reference Bureau offers a wealth of information on this website to assist in research activities, from articles and reports, data and analysis, and webcasts to blogs, online discussions, and other materials.

Siyanda

http://www.siyanda.org

Siyanda is an online database containing resources on a variety of development and gender-related topics, from education and employment to gender-based violence and femicide. It provides short summaries of online resources; many resources are available for free download. The site also offers an interactive component so that those interested in gender issues can communicate with each other.

Special Rapporteur on Violence against Women

http://www2.ohchr.org/English/issues/women/rapporteur/

This website includes descriptions of the Special Rapporteur's mandate as well as annual reports, publications, links to international standards, and complaint forms for reporting alleged cases of violence against women.

UN Department of Public Information

http://www.un.org

This site provides information on the United Nations and its programs, activities, and publications.

UN Development Fund for Women

http://www.unwomen.org

This site offers information about the UN Development Fund for Women (UNIFEM) and its programs and publications; it also provides links to other sites related to women in development.

UN Millennium Project

http://www.unmillenniumproject.org/index.htm

This site contains extensive information on the Millennium Development Goals, including progress reports and related documents.

UN Research Institute for Social Development

http://www.unrisd.org

This agency within the United Nations conducts research on the social aspects of development. The website provides information regarding its areas of research and publications as well as up-to-date news, relevant events, and links to related sites.

UNICEF

http://www.unicef.org/

The UN Children's Fund (UNICEF) advocates for the rights of children. This site contains a wide variety of information concerning the rights of children and families and the struggles facing many women, children, and families in developing countries.

U.S. Department of State

http://www.state.gov/g/drl/rls/hrrpt/

This website provides reports on every country regarding the status of its human rights, including women's rights in education, medical care, employment, trafficking, and other areas.

Women Watch

http://www.un.org/womenwatch/

This website provides a directory of UN resources on gender and women's issues; it is the main gateway to all UN information and materials on gender equality and the empowerment of women.

World Health Organization

http://www.who.int

The World Health Organization (WHO) focuses on global health matters. Resources addressing the progress that nations have made on many health issues of interest to women can be found at this site.

Glossary

Bride Price The payment to the bride's family from the groom's family, generally in the form of livestock, goods, or money.

Burqa An outer garment worn by many Islamic women that almost completely covers their bodies when they are in public. Their eyes and hands remain uncovered. Also *burka, burkha,* or *burqua.*

Dowry The money and/or goods that a bride's family brings to her husband and his family upon their marriage. Dowry demands can continue throughout the marriage. Occasionally referred to as "groom price."

Fatwa An Islamic religious ruling including an opinion on a matter of law issued by an Islamic scholar or other religious authority.

Female Genital Mutilation All procedures involving partial or complete removal of female genitalia for non-therapeutic reasons. Also referred to as *female genital cutting, female cutting,* or *female circumcision.*

Femicide The murder of a female simply because she is female.

Hijab The traditional head covering for Muslim women. Also refers to the modest dress style of Muslim women.

Infanticide The intentional killing of infants, most often female infants.

Microenterprise A small business created using a small amount of capital and generally employing fewer than 10 people. A popular business model in developing countries.

Midwife A person who is trained to assist a woman in childbirth. A midwife also may provide prenatal care for the mother and postnatal care for the mother and newborn.

Obstetric Fistula A serious medical condition in which a hole develops between the rectum and vagina or the bladder and vagina. Caused by severe problems during childbirth and lack of adequate medical care. Often easily repaired when medical care and personnel are available. Most frequently occurs in rural areas of developing countries. Can also result for rape or other sexual abuses of women during war.

Polygamy The practice of taking more than one spouse in marriage at the same time. Polygyny refers to a man taking more than one wife at a time; polyandry refers to a woman taking more than one husband at a time.

Purdah The seclusion of women from the public practiced by Muslims and some Hindus. It can include exclusion from public observation through the wearing of clothing that reaches from head to toe or segregation from the public through the use of enclosures, screens, or curtains.

Sati Also known as *suttee,* the practice of Hindu widows (in India) throwing themselves on the funeral pyres of their husbands. The women were believed to have failed in using their traditional female powers to ensure the long life of their husbands.

Shari'a Law The code of law based on the Koran. The Koran does not distinguish between religion and other aspects of life; therefore, Shari'a law governs all of these. Also *sharia.*

Trafficking, human The illegal trade of persons for commercial sexual exploitation or forced labor.

Index

About the Author

Karen L. Kinnear holds an M.A. in Sociology from Case Western Reserve University and is a professional researcher, editor, and writer with more than 25 years of experience in sociological, economic, statistical, and financial analysis. She is also a paralegal and frequent traveler to developing nations. Among her previous publications are *Violent Children: A Reference Handbook*, *Childhood Sexual Abuse: A Reference Handbook*, *Gangs: A Reference Handbook*, *Women in the Third World: A Reference Handbook*, and *Single Parents: A Reference Handbook*, all part of ABC-CLIO's Contemporary World Issues series.